D0856795

PALM OIL AND PROTEST

AFRICAN STUDIES SERIES 59

GENERAL EDITOR
J. M. Lonsdale, *Lecturer in History and Fellow of Trinity College, Cambridge.*

ADVISORY EDITORS
J. D. Y. Peel, *Charles Booth Professor of Sociology, University of Liverpool.*
John Sender, *Faculty of Economics and Fellow of Wolfson College, Cambridge.*

Published in collaboration with
THE AFRICAN STUDIES CENTRE, CAMBRIDGE

OTHER BOOKS IN THE SERIES

PALM OIL AND PROTEST

An Economic History of the Ngwa Region,
South-Eastern Nigeria,
1800–1980

SUSAN M. MARTIN

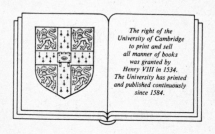

The right of the
University of Cambridge
to print and sell
all manner of books
was granted by
Henry VIII in 1534.
The University has printed
and published continuously
since 1584.

CAMBRIDGE UNIVERSITY PRESS

CAMBRIDGE

NEW YORK   NEW ROCHELLE   MELBOURNE   SYDNEY

Published by the Press Syndicate of the University of Cambridge
The Pitt Building, Trumpington Street, Cambridge CB2 1RP
32 East 57th Street, New York, NY 10022, USA
10 Stamford Road, Oakleigh, Melbourne 3166, Australia

First published 1988

Printed in Great Britain at the University Press, Cambridge

British Library cataloguing in publication data

Martin, Susan M.
Palm oil and protest: an economic history of the Ngwa region,
south-eastern Nigeria, 1800–1980. – (African studies series; 59).
1. Nigeria – Economic conditions
I. Title. II. Series
330.9669'4   HC1055

Library of Congress cataloguing in publication data

Martin, Susan M.
Palm oil and protest: an economic history of the Ngwa region,
south-eastern Nigeria, 1800–1980 / Susan M. Martin.
        p.   cm. – (African studies series: 59).
Bibliography.
Includes index.
1. Palm-oil industry – Nigeria – history – 20th century.
2. Igbo (African people).
I. Title. II. Series.
HD9490.5.P343N66 1988   87-17373   CIP
338.4'76643–dc19.

ISBN 0 521 34376 3

Contents

Contents

Maps

Figure

Acknowledgements

Among the many people who have helped in the preparation of this study, I would especially like to thank my supervisor, Professor A. G. Hopkins; and, in Nigeria, Dr E. J. Usoro, Drs Paul and Rina Okonkwo, and Mr G. G. Onyia, without whose help my fieldwork would have been impossible. Financial support for my first two years of research was provided by the S.S.R.C., and academic support during my stay in Nigeria was provided by the Institute of African Studies, University of Ibadan. My colleagues and students at the School of Oriental and African Studies in London have, over the past six years, provided me with rather more food for thought than can be reflected in this study; I would like to thank them, and my teachers and friends at Birmingham, especially Gareth Austin, Sue Hargreaves and . Marion Johnson. I have also received many stimulating ideas, and some material support, from Professor A. E. Afigbo, Dr and Mrs I. O. Akobundu, Mrs Ify Anagbo, Dr S. Babayemi, Professor S. O. Biobaku, Mr A. F. B. Bridges, Mr K. H. Dickenson, Miss Ada Eneli, Dr A. Epelle, Dr J. I. Guyer, Dr C. Ifeka, Dr G. I. Jones, Dr A. J. H. Latham, Martin Lockett, Dr C. W. Newbury, Colleen and Dutch Newfield, Dr D. Northrup, Dr and Mrs A. Nwachuku, Mrs A. Nwokoye, Mrs C. Purisch, Dr and Mrs T. U. Torti and Dr B. N. Ukegbu.

I would like to thank the librarians and archivists of all the collections on which I have worked, but especially Mr E. O. Unuigbe of the Nigerian National Archives, Ibadan, and Mr J. E. N. Nwaguru, Mr B. O. Nwaigwe, Cecilia Nwokoye and Innocent Udeh of the Nigerian National Archives, Enugu. Many members of the staff of the World Bank Smallholder Oil Palm Project expressed an interest in my research, and gave me a great deal of help during my stay in the Ngwa region: I would especially like to thank Mr Prince Cajetan Egbuka, and Mr Mba, Mr Ndukwu, Mr Lawrence Anya Njoku, Mr Dyke Ogbonnaya and Mr I. E. Umezie. I would like to thank all the friends who made my stay in Ahiaba-Okpuala such a pleasure, especially Miss Catherine Obioma Chigbundu, Mr Chris U. Emelogu, and

Mr Monday Nwosu. I owe a special debt to Mr and Mrs Johnson Nwosu, Mr and Mrs Sylvester Nwogu and Mrs Regina N. Osuji, who provided me with hospitality and companionship throughout my stay in the Ngwa region. Many of these Ngwa friends helped me both as translators and as tutors in their language; I hope they will enjoy reading the results, and will forgive the simple, unaccented form of the few Igbo words transcribed in the text which follows. My final debt, but by no means the least, is to Mrs Ruth Cranmer for her invaluable aid in producing a legible manuscript!

Abbreviations

A.E.T.C.	African and Eastern Trade Corporation
A.R.	Annual Report
A.R.A.D.	*Annual Report on the Agricultural Department, Nigeria*
A.R.C.D.	*Annual Report on the Customs Department, Nigeria*
A.R.E.P.	*Annual Report on the Eastern Province, Southern Nigeria*
A.R.F.D.	*Annual Report on the Forestry Department* (or *F.A.*, *Forest Administration*), *Nigeria*
A.R.M.D.	*Annual Report on the Marine Department, Nigeria*
A.R.S.P.	*Annual Report on the Southern Provinces, Nigeria*
Ass. Rep.	Assessment Report
Bull.Imp.Inst.	*Bulletin of the Imperial Institute*
C.R.A.	Colonial Reports (Annual)
Cal. Prov.	Calabar Province
D.C.	District Commissioner
D.O.	District Officer
Dist.	District
Div.	Division
E.M.B.	Empire Marketing Board
F.F.A.	Free fatty acid content of palm oil
Int. Rep.	Intelligence Report
J.A.H.	*Journal of African History*
J.H.S.N.	*Journal of the Historical Society of Nigeria*
N.D.P.	Niger Delta Pastorate
N.R.	*Nigeria: Annual General Report*
N.R.A.R.	*Nigerian Railway: Administrative Report*
Ow. Prov.	Owerri Province
P.C.O.P.	Provincial Commissioner, Owerri Province
P.P.	Parliamentary Papers
R.C.P.	Resident, Calabar Province
R.H.	Rhodes House Library, Oxford

R.O.P.	Resident, Owerri Province
S.N.R.	*Southern Nigeria: Report*
S.S.P.	Secretary, Southern Provinces (Nigeria)
T.R.	*Trade Report, Southern Nigeria*
U.A.C.	United Africa Company

The terms 'eastern' and 'south-eastern' Nigeria refer to the geographical region shown in Map 1. Capitalised terms like 'Southern Nigeria', 'Western Nigeria', etc., refer to administrative units existing at the time referred to in the text.

1

Introduction

The dominant themes in rural West African economic history during the past two hundred years are usually held to be the impact of capitalism and colonialism.[1] This study began as an attempt to follow convention, in exploring the colonial-period history of a region which was heavily involved in cash cropping. But during the research and writing, the region itself, and the Ngwa people, took hold of the author's loyalties and imagination. The result is a history of the Ngwa people which shows how the economic opportunities open to them were influenced by the local environment and by the social structures which they created, as well as by the economic and political changes wrought by outsiders. The interaction between local and external causes of change is explored in detail for the period between the First and Second World Wars, and shown to have continued up to the present day.

Over the past decade, scholars have increasingly turned to history for help in understanding recent African economic difficulties. They seek to uncover the roots of 'underdevelopment' and of the current 'food crisis'.[2] In eastern Nigeria, problems of 'underdevelopment' and of 'food crisis' have been relatively muted. In the 1970s the collapse of the oil palm export industry, which during the colonial period provided most of the region's import-purchasing power, caused no drop of incomes overall because it occurred simultaneously with the rise of profitable urban industries and of state employment, fuelled by the mineral oil boom. Meanwhile the region's farmers developed a profitable industry supplying *gari* (cassava meal) to the local towns. The signs of strain lay below the surface of the regional economy: in the disparity between urban men and rural women, especially in the generation which had reached adulthood during the 1960s; and in the growing pressure of population on the land. Eastern Nigeria had survived the Atlantic slave trade with one of the highest population densities in sub-Saharan Africa, but by 1980 this advantage had become a liability.

How could one begin charting the history of this regional economy, and how could one explain its special problems in the 1970s and 1980s? I began with the assumption that the expansion of the oil palm industry from 1800, and the imposition of colonial rule from 1891, must have had a strong impact upon the domestic economy. This assumption was rooted in the very different approaches of vent-for-surplus and dependency theorists.[3] Yet I was also interested in the work of the geographers and anthropologists who tried to describe the domestic economy itself in village studies made during the colonial period.[4] Finally, I wanted to develop the theoretical insights of contemporary anthropologists, who may differ from their predecessors in philosophy but who usually share their desire to understand the internal structures of village societies, as well as their interaction with the outside world.[5]

On arrival in Nigeria I rapidly discovered that none of these approaches, taken alone, could reflect the views of the farmers I lived with or of the local authors whose studies were kindly lent to me and drawn to my attention. I had chosen to study the Ngwa region because it was heavily involved in the oil palm export industry and yet little studied by economic historians, most of whom had focused on the Delta region and the Ibibio area near Calabar (see Map 1).[6] Source material had been a secondary consideration; yet it turned out that the Ngwa region was surprisingly rich in local sources, at least for twentieth-century history.[7] The Ngwa are a relatively large and coherent Southern Igbo ethnic group: in 1931, when they were first recognised as such and surveyed by colonial officials, they inhabited an area of 474 square miles and numbered at least 123,000 people. By 1953, their population had grown to nearly 200,000.[8] In recent years, they have produced many scholars and there have been several important local contributions to their history and geography.[9] During my stay in the village of Ahiaba-Okpuala, in 1980–1, many people were eager to help with this fresh study (see Map 2).[10] Finally, the Ngwa had been heavily involved in the Igbo Women's War of 1929, after which many local women had spoken before the Aba Commission of Enquiry. The 'Notes of Evidence' printed by the Commission provide a rare insight into contemporary village-level views of colonial history.[11]

The view which emerged from these local sources often stood at variance with that recorded in the archives. In the memories of the old people who spoke to me, local imperatives of food production, local traders and African missionaries stole the limelight from the transport innovations, currency changes, administrative structures and export sector fluctuations which filled the official mind. While officials debated whether to allow European firms to take land for plantations, eventually deciding to leave the local economy in the hands of African smallholders, the smallholders themselves were transforming their economy and society in unexpected and often unseen ways.[12]

Both the official and the local perspective clearly encompassed vital aspects of the region's history. It was necessary to make a synthesis of the two, just as it was necessary to balance the theoretical approaches of the economists and the anthropologists. The two tasks of synthesis overlapped,

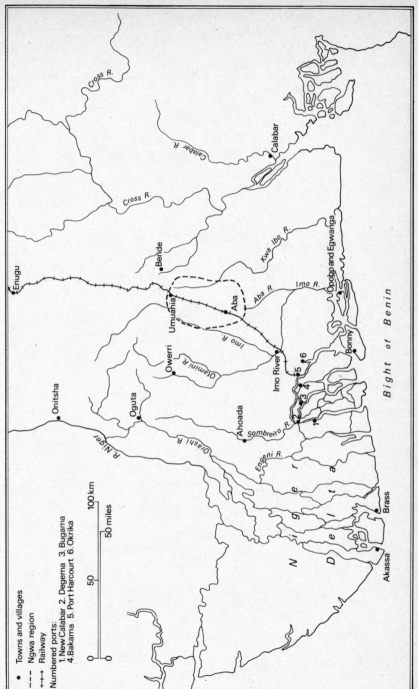

Map 1. Ports, river and rail trade routes, south-eastern Nigeria

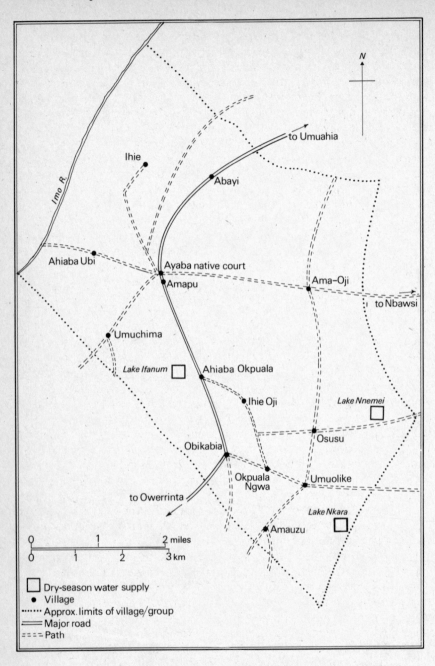

Map 2. Ngwa-Ukwu (Ofo-Asato) village group

in that the official view had much in common with the dependency and vent-for-surplus theories, and even with some of the work of neo-Marxist economic anthropologists, while the local view was reflected and supported by the work of other anthropologists and geographers. This Introduction will provide a survey of these two broad types of theoretical approach, which will be set in the context of classical economic theory and of the more recent 'farming systems' approach to agricultural economics. In comparing these approaches, we will focus on two main points: firstly, on the theorists' 'ideal-types' of economic progress and secondly, on their view of the main causes of economic change within rural African societies. Theorists adhering to the classical 'ideal-type', as outlined below, usually emphasise external causes of change; those who are moving towards the definition of alternative forms of agrarian change more often emphasise local or internal causes of change.

The classical 'ideal-type' model of economic development has clearly been modified and refined by economic theorists over the two hundred years since it was first set out in the work of Adam Smith. However, its basic assumptions about the nature and root causes of economic progress still provide the framework for most contemporary debates over African economic policy, and also provide the setting for the debate between dependency and vent-for-surplus theorists. Thus the starting-point for our discussion will be the vision of Smith himself, as set out in the *Wealth of Nations* in 1776. The essence of this vision was innovation through the use of capital and the division of labour, stimulated by market demand through international and town–country trade, and protected by the state through the maintenance of law and order.[13] In the agricultural sector, Smith held that there was relatively little scope for increasing the productivity of labour through refinements of the division of tasks. However, he held that capital could usefully be employed in extending and improving the cultivated land. 'Stock' was needed to purchase seed, tools, cattle and labour; and further capital could be used to finance improvements like 'buildings, drains, enclosures and other ameliorations'. Such improvement held forth the prospect of solid prosperity and full employment for the nation, while more rapid growth of labour productivity could be achieved by the development of complementary urban industries.[14]

In Smith's view, the development of complementary relations of trade and investment between town and countryside was essential to a nation's prosperity, but economic growth could also be furthered by the extension of such complementary relations to other nations. Both farmers and manufacturers benefited from international trade by exchanging the range of goods which their natural resource base tied them to producing, for others which were not locally available. Trade made it worthwhile for them to produce a surplus above national needs, and so achieve full employment and go beyond it, investing capital and energy in the 'improvement' of their 'productive powers'.[15]

Smith's theory has stimulated and provoked economists for the past two centuries. The vent-for-surplus theory of international trade has caused especially heated debate, both in the nineteenth century when John Stuart Mill gave it this label, and since the 1950s when elements of it were rediscovered and developed by Hla Myint.[16] Less attention has been paid to Smith's view of agriculture's role in economic development, yet it will be argued below that this view has profoundly influenced both neo-classical and Marxian writers: it has become an unexamined bedrock of Western thought on Third World problems.

Unfortunately, Smith himself did not elaborate his view that progress in agriculture was to be achieved by investing capital in the improvement of land. He appeared to take British agricultural technology and land/labour combinations for granted; his main chapter on agricultural economics was significantly entitled 'Of the Rent of Land'.[17] This in itself should warn us against applying his assumptions without examination in an African context. As a number of recent studies have emphasised, sub-Saharan African farmers dispensed for centuries with such hallmarks of Eurasian technology as the plough and the wheel. Goody's stimulating works explore the consequences of this regional divergence; while Boserup has searched for explanations, emphasising that the Eurasian concern with improving the land need not be shared in the many African regions with sparse population.[18] These studies cannot provide complete answers to the questions of whether and why African farmers innovated or improved their productivity in ways which do not fit Smith's European model; but they indicate that the questions need to be asked.[19]

There is a great divide between those who think that the Smithian model provides the basic blueprint for progressive innovation, and those who ask whether there are alternatives. The nature of the division is complex; for example, current forms of political radicalism may conflict with the search for alternative definitions of economic and technological progress. To explore the divergence between African and Western views of innovation can be seen as a distraction from the study of the political oppression and social divisions which have often handicapped all potential innovators, whatever their aims.[20] Implicitly the new radical standpoint may well be grounded not only in Smith's faith in the virtues of capital and the improvement of land, but also in Marx's belief that capitalism and the Industrial Revolution had brought unparalleled advances in technology, which ought to be applicable to nations other than those which had invented them.[21] In this view, the plough might be useless in regions without oxen, but the tractor is truly international. Yet both inventions form part of a continuum in Western development by which capital is used to clear and improve land, in the tradition praised by Smith.

The congruence between radical and neoclassical views of technical progress may be seen in the long-running debate between dependency and vent-for-surplus theorists. Hla Myint began the debate with an exposition of

Smith's ideas in 1958. He argued that agriculture in the Third World had failed to develop before the rise of trade with Europe, largely because of poor communications and a lack of town–country symbiosis. The imposition of colonial rule was followed by a rush towards development through transport innovations, foreign investment in mills and plantations, and a vent-for-surplus export boom in peasant farming communities. However, the innovations in agriculture which Smith had expected to result from trade did not follow in the peasant communities, because land remained in abundant supply and few communities even reached the stage of diverting labour from other uses to export production. In recent years, heavy taxes have given farmers fewer opportunities to accumulate capital, and even fewer incentives to invest it in the improvement of land.[22]

In this view, foreign investments in mills, plantations and infrastructure are added to Smith's criteria of commercialisation, specialisation and capital investment in land, to provide a theoretical model of economic growth applicable to Third World nations. But just as this view was being formulated, the idea that a creative role could be played by foreigners was beginning to draw keen opposition from radical writers of the dependency school. The Marxian economist Baran produced a theory that foreign investment and colonial economic policies had progressively impoverished the economies subjected to them. This theory became famous when it was applied to Latin America by André Gunder Frank.[23]

For those economies whose colonial economic links had been forged more through trade than direct investment, the most relevant development of dependency theory was Emmanuel's controversial notion of 'unequal exchange'.[24] This concept was originally intended to describe a universal feature of colonial trading patterns, but it was weakened by disputes over its grounding in the labour theory of value.[25] Nevertheless, it continued to be cited in discussions of deteriorating terms of trade for Third World exports. Rodney argued that in the African case, impoverishment had occurred during the 1930s when the terms of trade facing African producers fell, but colonial pressure forced them to continue selling on the international market. The creation of monopolies among foreign trading firms also allowed them to reduce the real prices they paid to producers.[26]

This discussion of why African farmers gained so little from trade led naturally to the question of why they entered it in the first place, and did not withdraw when prices fell. There is an interesting divergence between dependency theorists on this issue. Frank argues that Africans were initially commercially minded, and sacrificed other industries to specialise in the export trade before the terms of trade began to decline, thus becoming 'dependent' in the classic way. In this, he echoes Smith's thoughts on the dangers of international trade.[27] However, Amin argues that African communities were incapable of self-transformation into capitalist societies, and that force was needed to break down rural resistance to the spread of commodity exchange.[28]

Both Frank and Amin attempt to explain the failure of African economies to achieve capitalist development, including industrialisation; and in
this they share an aim with Myint. However, in contrast to Myint's model of
capitalist development thwarted by over-abundant natural resources and
taxation, they produce the models of capitalist development thwarted by
colonialism on the one hand, and local lack of interest on the other. Several
conflicting and testable propositions about the history of village economies
have been produced in the course of the debate. Did land and labour remain
abundant as agricultural exports expanded, or did specialisation occur? Had
African farmers developed a trade in food or raw materials with local craft
producers before the colonial period? Did they have to be forced into the
export economy, and forced to remain there from the 1930s, or did they
enter voluntarily in search of profits? Did low incomes or limited ambitions
hold them back from capital investment before the 1930s?

All these questions are stimulating and will be taken up in this study of
Ngwa history, but it is notable that at the height of the dependency debate
they were thrown out as conflicting statements, rather than questions.
Dependency theorists devoted most energy to elaborating their views on
the role of foreign firms and colonial officials; and so, as the debate
developed, the nature of the stimulus which the theorists provided to
historians changed. While some early studies of vent-for-surplus export
expansion in West Africa emphasised African initiatives, the most detailed
work inspired by the debate over dependency focused on world market
forces, foreign firms and colonial policy decisions.[29] In this way, the debate
encouraged researchers to reflect the view of documentary rather than oral
sources. Ironically, the importance attached by both sides to their conflicting views of the role of foreigners reflects the views of the foreigners
themselves, for whom their own actions were naturally of prime interest and
who shared the theorists' belief in the universality of Western ideals of
progress.

As the debate progressed, only one group of writers sympathetic to the
dependency view turned their attention to the study of village economies.
These were the neo-Marxist economic anthropologists, who shared Amin's
view that African economies did not operate according to capitalist principles. Marx himself had hinted, in his *Grundrisse*, that there might be
several different sets of principles on which pre-capitalist societies might
operate. For example, in the Germanic mode of production, farming
households lived independently, linked to one another by loose alliances
and maintaining a complex relationship with their urban counterparts;
whereas in the Ancient mode, the farmers themselves lived in towns and
held property as individuals.[30] However, Marx had not developed this line
of thought in any detail, and the French neo-Marxist economic anthropologists who sought to describe African village economies in the 1960s were
forced to construct their own theoretical models.

One of the models constructed by the French writers will be outlined in

8

some detail here, because it clarifies the social divisions within agricultural communities in a way which is highly relevant to early colonial Ngwa history. The model itself has undergone several mutations: its outlines were established by Claude Meillassoux but it has been substantially modified by its creator, and by Terray and Rey. Rey's term, the 'lineage mode of production' will be used to refer to it, since its essence is the analysis of power structures within lineages. The model identifies a hierarchy of age and sex, which governs the distribution of tasks, power and income not only within households but also within descent groups and village communities.[31]

Meillassoux's initial model focused on the relationships between men of different generations within village communities which were assumed to be self-sufficient. He emphasised the reciprocal benefits of these relationships, while noting the authority held by older men and the importance of their control over access to women. In his later work, he developed his ideas on the importance of women to elder or senior men. He argued that senior men sought to ensure the community's biological reproduction, rather than to make material gains from production, and that women's value lay in their fertility rather than their productive powers.[32]

Meillassoux's emphasis on biological reproduction was first challenged by Terray, who argued that within the overall hierarchy of age and sex, it was possible to identify various sets of social relations governing each of the many economic activities performed within a self-sustaining community. He drew attention to the extremely complex division of tasks and income relating to each activity, reworking Meillassoux's own field data on the Gouro.[33] This approach has been used in the present study to clarify the impact of palm produce export expansion upon different groups within Ngwa society. However, Terray himself did not take it this far, and indeed was criticised by Rey for side-stepping the issues of power and income distribution within the village economy as a whole. Rey emphasised the existence of slavery as a sign of the exploitation latent within senior–junior relations.[34]

The neo-Marxist anthropologists as a group were also criticised by feminists for neglecting the role of women in agricultural production. Boserup had already shown how much work women did within many systems of hoe agriculture. This point, combined with the neo-Marxist emphasis on the strength of male control over women within lineage societies, raised possibilities of exploitation which had been overlooked by Terray and Meillassoux in their stress on harmonious elder–junior relations.[35]

In developing these ideas Rey made a significant advance, which has been built upon in this study of Ngwa history. He began to explore the differences between senior men and the junior men, women and children whose labour they partly controlled, not only in terms of power and wealth, but also in terms of their attitudes towards new economic opportunities and innovations. He argued that new crops were most likely to be adopted by junior men and women, with the aim of establishing their right to farm them without the direct supervision and control of the elders.[36] This argument implies a distinction between areas of relative autonomy for women and junior men, and areas under the elders' control. Such a distinction provides an interesting new perspective on different economic sectors, which are more usually classified by terms like rural and urban, export and domestic, or cash and subsistence.

One major difficulty remains in applying neo-Marxist theory to the experience of a region heavily involved in cash crop production. Rey, like Meillassoux and Terray, held that lineage societies were essentially self-sufficient, being brought into 'articulation' with the capitalist mode of production by force, and in a position of subordination. In this respect, the neo-Marxist writers belong within the well-established tradition of 'peasant studies'.[37] Within this tradition, the state, the bourgeoisie or the landlords, rather than the peasants, are assumed to be the main initiators of economic change. Yet the Ngwa entered into the palm oil trade in the nineteenth century without European coercion; and they will be shown in this study to have played an active role in the many changes which occurred in the colonial period.

Within the peasant studies field, Chayanov and Kula have come closest to the analysis of peasant actions within a wider economy. They have demonstrated that the market decisions of non-capitalist producers can be heavily influenced by their consumption needs and by their systems of property rights. Kula also discussed the uses of wealth in pre-capitalist societies. He provided a detailed exposition of the view that in pre-capitalist societies, wealth acquired by trade could not be used to reproduce and extend itself (as in the capitalist model), because productive resources could not be bought. Nevertheless, wealth could be used for consumption and display.[38] His approach suggested that one could go beyond the simple assumption that pre-capitalist societies were not dominated by the profit motive, to ask whether wealth was desired, even if only for display; how wealth could be acquired, and how the rise of different occupations changed the possibilities for using it. Looking at the Ngwa evidence with these questions in mind, it became possible to come to terms with the high value which all sources hold that local people placed upon wealth; and to begin analysing the informal and fluid local hierarchy based on wealth. This ran alongside the lineage hierarchy of seniority, at times being closely identified with it, and at times taking on a life of its own.[39]

All these theories helped to clarify the probable cleavages within village society, between senior and junior men, poor and wealthy, men and women, slave and free; they helped to identify the different social groups which may have initiated change for different reasons. However, they gave little insight into the kind of changes that Ngwa or neighbouring villagers might have wished to initiate or into the possible causes of change other than coercion or market stimuli. The Smithian view of economic and technological progress was allowed to stand by default. Yet the empirical work of anthropologists, geographers and historians on West African societies provides evidence of a number of changes which are difficult to fit within the Smithian model of commercialisation, specialisation and capital investment in land or machinery. Meanwhile, relatively little evidence has been found of changes which do conform to this model.[40]

Eastern Nigeria provides an unusually strong example of this disjunction between the Smithian 'ideal-type' and African realities. In other parts of West Africa, the expansion of the cocoa and groundnut industries placed heavy demands on local supplies of land and labour. Initially, capital was needed to cover the costs of extending the cultivated area – in one of the main forms of agricultural investment praised by Smith.[41] Migrant labour became important as the plantations of cocoa and groundnuts grew beyond the extent which could be managed by local populations.[42] Finally, there is some evidence of a growing trade in staple foodstuffs; and Jane Guyer has shown that in Cameroon, the land and labour resources available for food production were gradually restricted.[43]

In eastern Nigeria the main exports were palm oil and kernels, which were produced from the fruit of a semi-wild tree. The industry placed great demands on local labour supplies, but did not absorb large areas of freshly cleared land. The dense population of the region limited the need for long-distance migrant labour to harness its natural resources. To the outside eye, little change appeared to be occurring: no use of capital to finance new production methods, no diversion of land or labour to fresh uses and no sudden increases in the area under cultivation. The oil palm industry has been seen as a classic case of vent-for-surplus expansion, in which no innovation occurred because no resource pressures made it necessary.[44] The main debates among the region's historians have focused on the fortunes of various groups of traders, and on the failure of colonial officials to encourage expatriate mill-and-plantation schemes.[45]

Within the classical Western economic framework, and taking the oil palm industry as an *agricultural* export industry, the passive role assigned to the farmers in these histories of their region appeared inevitable. Yet the evidence available from local sources and from the works of geographers and anthropologists who had known the region in the 1940s and 1950s suggested that significant economic and social changes had been taking place, on the initiative of farmers. These included changes in religion, in property rights, in cropping patterns, in palm processing methods and in systems of labour use. Two shifts in perspective were necessary in order to begin understanding these changes.

Firstly, it was necessary to appreciate that although production in the oil palm industry was carried out by farmers, it was not essentially agricultural work: within Smith's analytical framework, it had more in common with manufacturing. As production expanded, changes could be expected to

11

occur in the division of labour and in processing methods, but these were by nature less visible than changes in land use or in the extent of cultivation. Furthermore, the more such changes were successful in reducing strains on local labour supplies, the fewer long-distance migrants would be needed to swell the local work-force. In this way, evidence of change at the local level could be reconciled with its invisibility in histories based on central government sources.

Changes in property rights, in labour use and in processing methods could be understood following this shift of perspective, but the questions of why changes in cropping patterns occurred, and why the oil palm industry continued to be the main source of Ngwa farmers' export earnings in the twentieth century, remained intractable. Farmers in Cameroon, in western Nigeria and in the Gold Coast switched from palm produce to rubber and then cocoa during the late nineteenth and early twentieth centuries, and changes in food cropping patterns thereafter could be explained by the pressures placed by cocoa on land supplies. The Ngwa continued to export palm produce, and when they adopted cassava they were not motivated by population pressure on land.[46] In considering these issues, it was necessary to shift perspective again and to accept the possibility of an alternative logic of agricultural development which lay outside the classical Western model.

This shift of perspective had already been made by some scholars, notably by the farming systems school of agricultural economists, by the *Annales* school of historians in France, and by a few Africanists working in other disciplines. As yet, the new perspective has not been reflected in a distinctive theory of African agricultural development. Instead, those who share it have produced a set of suggestive ideas which help to clarify the picture of Ngwa history provided by local sources, and by the more detailed descriptions of colonial observers.

Farming systems analysis became popular among Western development planners in the 1970s. At this time, the balance in aid donors' preferences between smallholder-oriented 'modernisation' schemes and large-scale, state-managed projects was beginning to tip in favour of the former.[47] Clearly, smallholder schemes were most likely to be successful if they were founded on an accurate knowledge of local economies and of the potential usefulness of the proposed technical innovations.[48] Farming systems analysts began the task of evaluation by finding out as much as possible about all aspects of economic life within each village. They described the complete range of crops grown, mapped the field system, recorded the range of fallow periods and explored the other sources of food and income available to farmers. They noted recent changes in cropping patterns, fallow periods or labour use, and tended to ascribe these less to the impact of market forces than to environmental changes and population pressure. Their approach had much in common with that of the late colonial anthropologists and geographers, who sought to understand village economic life 'in the round'.[49] The main problem with this approach is that it tends to produce findings of great local interest, rather than fresh concepts with wider applicability.

A stronger theoretical approach has been taken by Ester Boserup and by the *Annales* historians, who explore the effects of population pressure and climate, the two main internal causes of agricultural change identified by the farming systems school. These two forces cause quite different patterns of change. In Boserup's view, the first response of African farmers to increasing population pressure was to reduce fallow periods and to employ more labour-intensive methods of cultivation. As population continued to increase, farmers would begin to innovate in the Smithian sense, investing in ploughs and engaging in land-intensive farming methods. Beyond a certain point, growing population density could thus substitute for market incentives as a cause of agricultural intensification.[50]

By contrast, environmental constraints or changes have rarely been viewed by theorists as a cause of this kind of innovation. Emmanuel le Roy Ladurie, of the *Annales* school, has stressed the unpredictability of the challenges posed by climate.[51] It then follows that unless farmers have the technology required to master and control nature, they may have more success in meeting its challenges through flexibility and mobility than through the rooted process of specialisation and intensification outlined in the Smithian model. In short, in the absence of population pressure and exogenous technical change, the challenges of climate could inspire farmers to make economic changes of a kind quite different from those expected by mainstream Western economists.

John Sutton has shown that in sub-Saharan Africa before 1900, the availability of small areas of exceptionally well-watered or fertile land sometimes created a situation of localised land scarcity and so stimulated the development of irrigation and other land-intensive farming techniques.[52] However, in general the variability and fragility of African micro-environments stimulated other patterns of innovation: the breeding of many different varieties of a staple food crop like the yam, the construction of complex sequences of 'phased planting' of different crops on the same piece of land, the use of plots of land with different types of soil or varying access to dry-season water supplies, and the development of alternative strategies for coping with wet years and dry years in savanna regions.[53] Entry into long-distance trade could also be seen as an important means of transcending the limitations of local natural resources.[54]

In eastern Nigeria, and within it the Ngwa region, rainfall was high and it was not necessary for farmers to develop complex field systems to maintain access to water under conditions of intermittent drought. However, the Ngwa shared problems of low soil fertility and seasonal aridity with most other West African agriculturalists.[55] Furthermore, the population density of the Ngwa region, though high by West African standards, did not attain levels which threatened their long-fallow farming system until the 1950s.[56] Thus, while the Ngwa were by no means typical as forest cash crop producers, their history as food farmers may well shed light on a pattern of innovation common to many forest regions of West Africa.

It will be argued in this book that this pattern was essentially one of diversification, by which farmers not only spread their labour burdens and food supplies more evenly over the agricultural year, but also created a system of intercropping which helped to conserve soil fertility.[57] A strong element of hunting and gathering was retained within the economy. Although primarily agriculturalists, the Ngwa maintained a varied range of occupations within which new activities like export production, retail trade or school-teaching could be included at will. They continually extended the range of crops cultivated by adopting exotic plants like maize, cocoyam, tomatoes, pineapples and cassava.[58] The adoption of new crops or economic activities is not always dignified by the term 'innovation' in Western scholarly works, especially where the change involves the adoption of a crop or technique originating elsewhere. However, when the adoption of a new crop or the acquisition of a skill first developed elsewhere is undertaken on local initiative, and leads both to memorable changes in a people's way of life and to an increase in their standard of living, then the use of the term 'innovation' is surely appropriate.[59]

Having thus arrived at a set of working definitions of which different groups of people might have initiated economic changes within Ngwa society, and which different types of innovation might have appealed to them for different reasons, I then set out to write a narrative of Ngwa history in which both the Ngwa and the Europeans who lived in their country might appear as actors. Wherever possible, this involved the comparison of oral accounts and village-level views of a given event or process, with the view provided by more polished official reports. This technique proved easiest with notable political events, such as a court boycott or the Women's War, which lingered in people's memories and which were also well recorded in the documents left by contemporary officials. It was far less easy in the case of slow processes of change like the evolution of property rights, the coming of cassava or the conversion of the Ngwa to Christianity. The methods used to reconstruct these changes will be outlined briefly below, as a preliminary to the narrative chapters which follow.

The chronological background to the narrative has been provided by statistics collected from official records at all levels – District, Province, Colony and Colonial Office. These indicate the main periods of boom and slump in the oil palm industry and make it possible to compare population densities and changing levels of export production in the Ngwa region with those in neighbouring parts of eastern Nigeria and in the Yoruba region to the west. Palm oil and kernel price statistics for Liverpool, Lagos, Opobo, Aba and Umuahia have also been compiled, to give an impression of the relationship between the port price statistics (the basis for the long-term indices) and buying prices inland. Like the weather, palm produce prices were highly variable, and the tables of relatively raw data demonstrate this.

A more human perspective on the economic and social history of the region was provided by the writings of contemporary missionaries and anthropologists. Official sources also provided unexpected insights through remarks made by district officers, either in passing or in reply to questionnaires. Small details gleaned in this way often proved surprisingly valuable when set within the wider narrative. Further insights were provided by the personal papers of former officials, collected at Rhodes House; and by two former officials, G. I. Jones and A. F. B. Bridges, in personal correspondence. In this way, enough material was gained from written sources to permit a detailed reconstruction of Ngwa economic history before the 1920s.

From the 1920s, it was possible to draw upon eyewitness reports from Ngwa farmers and so to reinforce the picture of village-level change which was beginning to emerge from the writings of anthropologists, missionaries and district officers. This picture provided a sharp contrast to that of 'Western impact – local response' which emerged inexorably from the higher-level official sources. The contrast was two-fold: firstly, in the differing causes and types of economic change which appeared in the two pictures; and secondly, in the fragmentary and diffuse character of the information from which the second, village-level picture was built up. The village-level picture does not emerge as a clear statement of opinion or theory in any one of the sources; however, mutually reinforcing fragments of it, and views on specific issues, appear in them all.

Oral tradition, as opposed to oral testimony, has been used sparingly in this study; the traditions which have been used were collected largely by others.[60] Much work has been done on the oral traditions both of the Ngwa and of other African peoples, and the merits and flaws of the collective memory are well known.[61] This book is, in part, an experiment in the uses of individual life-stories and eyewitness accounts. Ngwa people who agreed to be interviewed were asked to give information only on those aspects of village economic activity in which they had been personally involved. They were not asked to make general statements about the nature of the village economy, though such statements were sometimes made in passing.

This approach has its limitations, both in the kind of information it yielded and in the time-span which this information covered. Inevitably, the focus of the interviews was on the limited experience of each person, rather than the collective experience of the community. Because I was dividing my time between oral and archival work I was able to conduct only a limited number of formal interviews, mainly within the village where I was living and among the older relatives of people in the compound where I stayed. Also, I was able to find very few Ngwa women over the age of sixty-five, and very few men over the age of eighty, so that the earliest period for which substantial information was available was the 1920s. The 'memory' of the official custodians of village history clearly stretches further, as Oriji has demonstrated.[62]

However, these limitations of the approach did not prejudice its main aim, which was to provide a sense of how the changes chronicled in the documentary evidence affected the lives of ordinary people. Through living in the village I learnt a great deal about farmers' lives as they are lived today, and was able to tell which of my informants had led especially distinctive lives in the past. Many valuable insights were gained through informal conversations with friends and neighbours, especially through the occasional spontaneous comment about important economic changes within their lifetimes. Such comments drew my attention to aspects of village history which were mentioned only in passing, if at all, in official documents. Informants' recollections of changes in cooking methods, for example, also suggested that aspects of village life which anthropologists and geographers regarded as immutable, might well have changed during the time between one anthropologist's visit and the next. On a renewed scrutiny of the written sources, this proved to be the case.

In this way, oral information provided the impetus for the re-examination of existing theories of rural African economic history which has been conducted in this chapter. While the strictly chronological and analytical account of Ngwa history which follows is inevitably different in style from the histories which were related to me, one of its main aims is to reflect the central preoccupations and events of those informal, individual histories. At the same time, the history of the Ngwa region itself will be explored, with the aim of shedding light on the questions raised in this chapter about the nature of locally initiated rural development and the long-term impact of Western capitalism and colonial rule upon a West African forest economy.

2

Ecology, society and economic change to 1891

The Ngwa have been settled yam farmers for as long as they can remember. Yet their traditional food producing economy was by no means static. Before the nineteenth century, migrations and the adoption of new crops helped to produce a distinctive social and economic system within which diversification was a continuing process, and youthful mobility an outstanding motif. During the nineteenth century the expansion of the oil palm export industry brought changes in production methods, further additions to the local diet, and changes in the balance of labour demands, power and responsibilities between men and women. Differences of wealth and seniority which had already arisen within the food producing economy came to take on a new meaning as the Ngwa became involved in cash crop production. Yet past patterns of production and social relations continued to have a vigour and an inner logic of development which influenced export sector developments, not only during the earlier nineteenth century, but also from 1891 under colonial rule.

These broad generalisations may seem at first sight to rest upon fragile foundations, for very little is known directly about the Ngwa economy in the pre-colonial period. The first written description of the region was made only in 1896, by a hostile observer who had passed through the region hastily on his way to a major market further north.[1] However, two extensive sets of local oral traditions have been collected, by Jackson and Allen in the 1930s and by Oriji in the 1970s.[2] The evidence which these provide on the standard Ngwa self-image and on the history of migration and settlement can be supplemented by archaeological findings and more recent observations of rural Igbo economies, which combine to indicate the major changes which have occurred in Ngwa food production over the centuries.[3] Finally, the role of trade in this process of change can be explored through the more specialised studies of Latham, Northrup and Ukegbu.[4]

The Ngwa belong to the southern or Owerri branch of Igbo culture, which the archaeologist and linguist Onwuejeogwu describes as a distinctive rain-forest culture lacking in some of the typical features of the Northern Igbo culture which centres on Nri. In particular, the Owerri culture lacks the institution of the Ozo title, which had encouraged a relatively high degree of individual eminence to develop within pre-colonial Northern Igbo societies.[5] Within an ethnic group renowned for liberal sharing of power among men, the Ngwa and other Southern Igbo peoples thus had an exceptionally egalitarian social structure.

In the Ngwa case this egalitarianism was accompanied by marked trends of mobility, which in themselves gave plenty of scope for ambitious junior men to achieve autonomy. Oral traditions indicate that the Ngwa see themselves as a fast-moving people. Three brothers, Ngwa-Ukwu, Nwoha and Avosi, are said to have set off from Umu Noha (Umunneoha) near Owerri. They and their companions were seeking uncleared land. They had halted beside a small stream for a meal of yams, which Ngwa-Ukwu and his brothers ate boiled rather than roasted, thus finishing long before their friends. Suddenly the brothers saw the stream beginning to grow, and crossed rapidly – just in time. The stream swelled to become the Imo River, and the Ngwa brothers' slower friends were stranded permanently on the other side.[6]

The region into which the early Ngwa settlers travelled was not exceptionally hospitable to farmers. It was thinly populated and densely forested, presenting yam cultivators with a back-breaking initial task of land clearance. Like neighbouring regions, the Ngwa area today has a long rainy season lasting from March to November, and an annual rainfall of between 80 and 100 inches. Again typically, local temperatures are high, reaching 34°C at the height of the dry season and 28°C during the heavy rains of July. However, one unusual feature of the Ngwa area is that it is very flat, with few rivers or streams apart from the Imo River itself. The dry-season water supply is provided from lakes, which form in the rare pockets of impermeable clay in a region of generally sandy, porous soils. Dense vegetation, infertile lateritic soils, poor dry-season water supplies and the prevalence of mosquitoes and tsetse flies combined to make life difficult for early farmers (see Maps 2 and 3).[7]

One of the main ways in which the earliest Ngwa settlers coped with this problem was by continued migration in search of fresh forest soils or more congenial locations. Possibly from as early as the thirteenth century, or as late as the seventeenth, the Ngwa began spreading out from their initial settlement at Okpuala-Ngwa. Their movements are shown on Map 4; in the corresponding traditions it is stressed that the regions entered were all relatively thinly populated, and that migration proceeded peacefully until the settlers reached the south and east (see Map 4).[8] It is likely that the traditions here reflect the truth, not least because most ethnic groups within the region have retained very similar, but separate cultural identities and traditions of settlement. Any writer seeking to construct a theory of cultural assimilation as an alternative to the Ngwa view would have great difficulty in explaining the unique appeal of the Ngwa culture, the most distinctive feature of which is that villages claim a common origin in migration from Okpuala-Ngwa.

18

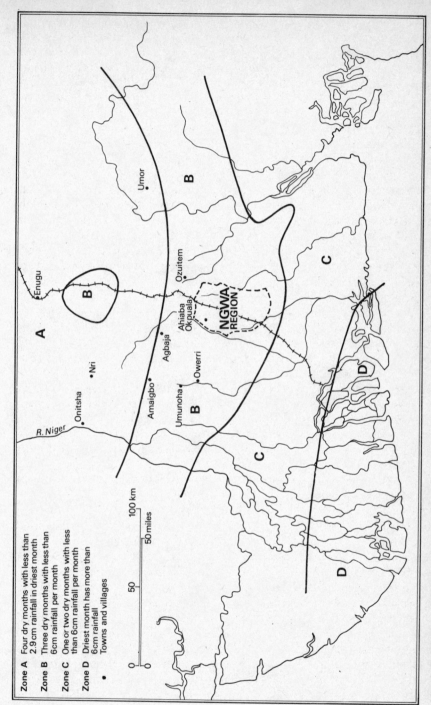

Map 3. Rainfall zones, south-eastern Nigeria

Zone A Four dry months with less than
        2.9 cm rainfall in driest month
Zone B Three dry months with less than
        6cm rainfall per month
Zone C One or two dry months with less
        than 6cm rainfall per month
Zone D Driest month has more than
        6cm rainfall
    •   Towns and villages

100 km
50 miles

0   50

R. Niger
•Onitsha
•Nri
•Enugu
B
A
•Umor
B
•Amaigbo
•Agbaja
Umunoha•
B
•Owerri
Ozuitem•
Ahiaba
Okpuala•
NGWA
REGION
B
C
C
D
D

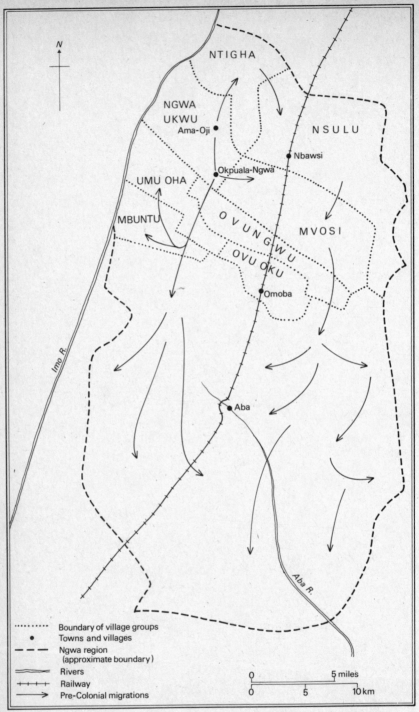

Map 4. The Ngwa: northern village groups and main routes of pre-colonial migrations

20

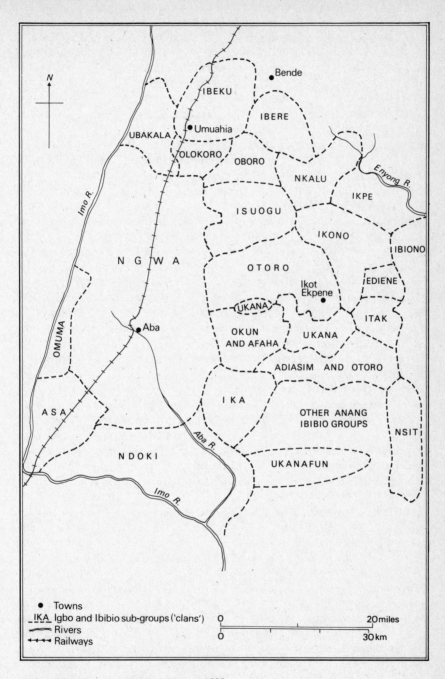

Map 5. The Ngwa and their neighbours, 1930s

The Ngwa account of speedy movement through thinly populated country is again supported by the fact that the migrants covered relatively large distances by local standards. By 1930 the Ngwa occupied a far larger area than any of their eastern neighbours (see Map 5).[9] These more densely packed peoples all occupied land with better access to river transport and dry-season water supplies, and had used trade rather than migration as an outlet for population pressure on local food supplies – a tactic which the Ngwa too were to adopt in the nineteenth century, as will be shown below. Meanwhile, southern and eastern peoples like the Asa and Ibibio guarded their land rights with great vigour, as Ngwa migrants found to their cost when they entered this region in the late nineteenth century. Early colonial records of border disputes indicate that the encounters between migrants and established Asa and Ibibio farmers were by no means peaceful.[10]

The Ngwa thus placed a great emphasis on migration, but in their traditions they linked the act of moving with the foundation of fresh settlements. Within each settlement many families stayed put and concentrated on improving their range of crops and skills in land use, while younger and more ambitious members banded together periodically to move on.[11] Among settled households, a major means of improving material life was the development or adoption of new crops, combined with the continued use of a wide range of forest resources. Indigenous plants like okra, garden egg and melons were domesticated, and the yam itself was widely experimented upon.[12] By the 1930s, when the anthropologist Jack Harris conducted a survey in the Ozuitem region (just to the north-west of the Ngwa area), local farmers knew of at least twelve main varieties and fifteen sub-varieties of yam. Each had its own seasonal cycle of cultivation, and was suited to a certain type of soil.[13]

Many of the foods upon which Southern Igbo farmers relied were not strictly agricultural products, but semi-wild plants which grew in symbiosis with their long-fallow farming system. Harris found in the 1930s that these included camwood, oil beans, okazie and other leafy plants, mushrooms and melons.[14] Perhaps the most useful of these semi-wild plants was the oil palm, which does not thrive under shade and so is rare in primary forest. The Southern Igbo region, with its heavy rainfall and sandy soils, provided an ideal environment for the growth of the palm once the initial task of land clearance had been accomplished; and palm oil came to be a staple ingredient in the local diet.[15]

The Atlantic trade began to impinge upon this farming system from the sixteenth century, with especially strong effects during the eighteenth and nineteenth centuries as the slave trade grew and was then accompanied, and finally succeeded by palm oil exports. Ironically the period of overseas trade coincided with the movements of migration and settlement described earlier and, although the Ngwa and neighbouring areas were major sources of slaves, by 1900 the region was one of the most densely populated in sub-Saharan Africa.[16] Northrup explains this paradox by stressing that slaves were drawn from a very wide area, by kidnapping or by judicial means rather than by warfare, thus minimising the demographic impact of the trade on any one community.[17] However, it is also possible to argue that the trade had economic side-effects which both aided migrant farmers to conquer virgin forest, as in the Ngwa region, and improved the diet of their settled neighbours.[18] These side-effects were the importation of iron and guns, for use in farming and hunting; and the introduction of new food crops to vary the local diet.

The most important of these two main effects was the introduction of new food crops. Iron was already available within eastern Nigeria to the north of the Ngwa region, and itinerant smiths from Nkwerre and Abiriba were able to supply farmers with hoes and matchets; imported iron gave these smiths more abundant and possibly finer raw material.[19] Guns clearly had a dual importance as weapons for hunting and for warfare. But the new food crops had an unequivocal value in enabling farmers to vary their diet and reduce the length of the local hungry season. A large number of New World crops proved suitable for growth in eastern Nigeria, ranging from maize, cocoyams and plantains to tomatoes, peppers and pineapples.[20] Cassava was also introduced to coastal areas, but seems to have moved no further north than the Ndoki region by the late nineteenth century.[21]

The most useful of the pre-nineteenth-century additions to Southern Igbo agriculture was probably the cocoyam. Together with the development of different varieties of yam which could be harvested at different times, the adoption of this exotic crop helped to reduce the hungry season to just a month or so within each year. It also meant that labour burdens were spread out relatively evenly within the entire farming year, as anthropologists found when compiling 'Farmers' Calendars' for southern Igbo and Cross River communities in the late 1930s (see Figure 1).[22]

The last point was more true for women than for men: newer crops like cocoyam tended to be labelled 'female crops', meaning that women harvested them as well as carrying out the 'normally' female tasks of planting, weeding and carrying the crops home from the farm.[23] Women were also responsible for collecting leaves, firewood and water, for cooking and childcare, and for petty trade. All of these were time-consuming tasks carried out on a daily basis throughout the farming year.[24] Men's work was more seasonally specific. Men concentrated on the dry-season farm tasks of land clearance and harvesting, house-building and path clearance, all of which were carried out between September and March. At other seasons, they were relatively free to engage in craftwork and village politics, and to travel (weather permitting).[25]

This clear-cut sexual division of labour is and has been one of the most striking features of Ngwa society. Many other African societies practising hoe-based agriculture have a similar system, though the definitions of 'male' and 'female' tasks vary from society to society and will be shown in this book to vary over time.[26] Historians have barely begun to explore the causes of

23

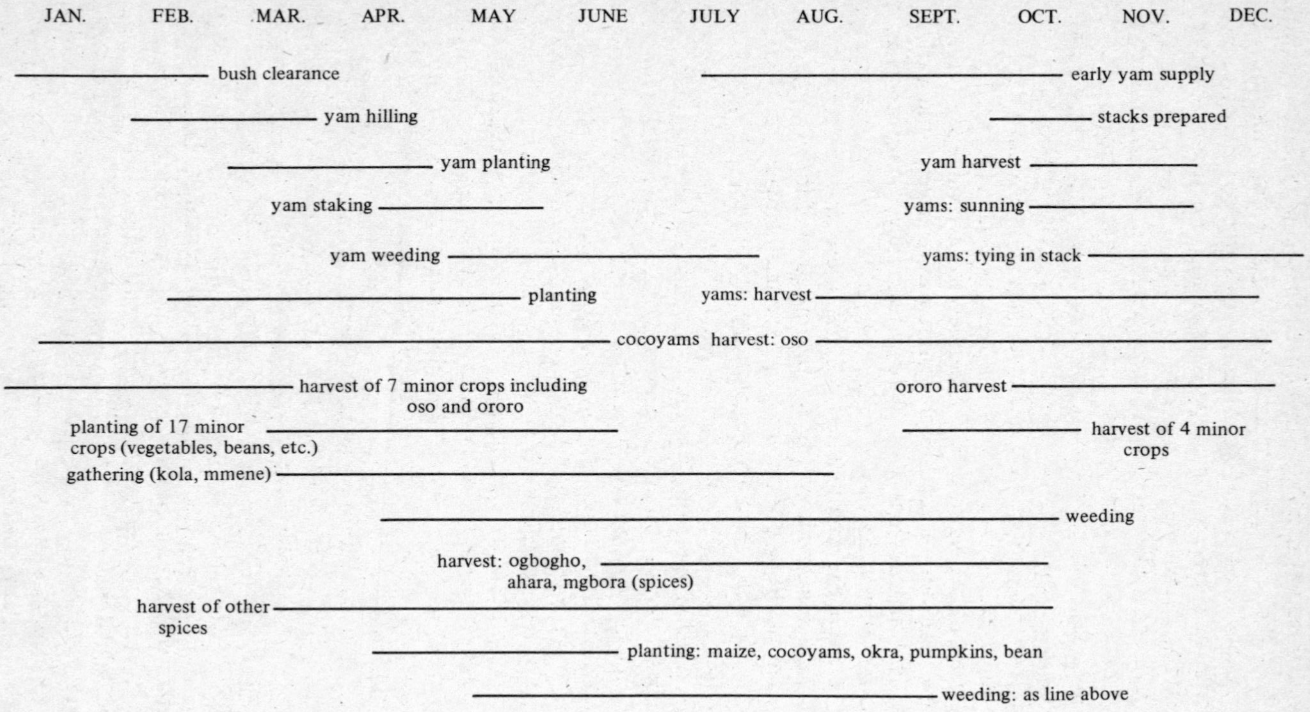

JAN.	FEB.	MAR.	APR.	MAY	JUNE	JULY	AUG.	SEPT.	OCT.	NOV.	DEC.

bush clearance

yam hilling

early yam supply

stacks prepared

yam planting

yam staking

yam harvest

yams: sunning

yam weeding

planting

yams: tying in stack

yams: harvest

cocoyams harvest: oso

ororo harvest

harvest of 7 minor crops including oso and ororo

harvest of 4 minor crops

planting of 17 minor crops (vegetables, beans, etc.)

gathering (kola, mmene)

weeding

harvest: ogbogho, ahara, mgbora (spices)

harvest of other spices

planting: maize, cocoyams, okra, pumpkins, bean

weeding: as line above

N.B. Weeding is performed at least twice on all farms.
This calendar excludes hunting, gathering, palm production, path clearance, housework and trade.

Figure 1. Farmer's Calendar, south-eastern Nigeria, 1930s

such variations, though Klein and Robertson have recently published an interesting collection of case studies which suggests ways in which regional variations of this kind may have influenced the demand for slaves within Africa.[27] For Africa in general, the authors argue that more men than women were exported across the Atlantic. This was certainly true of the Igbo region.[28] However, in some regions as many women as men may have been enslaved, the women being retained within Africa by their new owners' preference. This preference was strongest in societies which were matrilineal, and so in which kinless wives gave fathers power over their children; in societies where the status of women was high, and so in which free women could own slaves and use them to release themselves from work; and in societies which were highly militarised, and so in which female docility was valued by slave-owners who were nervous of revolt.

By all these criteria, Ngwa society is unlikely to have valued female slaves highly. Ngwa traditions emphasise that there was relatively little warfare in the region and that descent was traced patrilineally.[29] Furthermore, the general status of women was not high. Detailed evidence on this topic comes only from the colonial period, but there are no traditions or theoretical arguments which challenge the antiquity of the system.

Women's inequality was most obvious in the sexual division of labour and of income. Male tasks were defined as being dangerous, yet critical to the success of the whole farming enterprise. Women were not allowed to climb palm trees, harvest yams or clear the bush prior to farming; men's work here was considered sufficiently important to justify their ownership of the land itself, of the yams and of the palm fruit they had harvested, despite women's contribution through weeding, planting and other tasks.[30] Women owned the crops they had harvested and the minor foodstuffs they had gathered, but they could expect to make relatively little from their sale. Observers during the colonial period commented that women spent an enormous amount of energy on petty trade, but that the value of the goods exchanged was very low.[31] This financial weakness reinforced a basic male authority over women which may originally have been grounded in physical strength and force.[32]

Southern Igbo and Ibibio women also spent a great deal of time looking after their children. Motherhood was central to a woman's sense of identity.[33] Yet women had very few rights in their children. Igbo daughters helped their mothers in their work before marriage, but on marriage had to move away to a different compound, or even village. Bridewealth was paid to both parents by the husband, but the father received the largest share of this, together with help in farming given by the fiancé during the period of betrothal.[34] Sons remained in the village, but could not help with 'female' tasks. They could give valued help to widowed mothers in land clearance and palm cutting, but had no obligation to provide gifts.[35] When a husband provided bridewealth for a wife, as Meek noted with approval, 'it guarantees that the husband shall have custody of any children born . . . And it

25

guarantees also that a husband shall have the continuous services of a wife for himself and of a mother for his children.'[36] Women were main producers of food and of children; but men held the ultimate power over both.

Alongside the sexual division of labour, income and responsibilities, there were divisions of authority within households and within villages, following a number of cross-cutting definitions of seniority. The oldest of these was probably the distinction between senior and junior men according to their position within the lineage. In order to understand this distinction, it will be necessary to provide a brief outline of the Ngwa settlement pattern and lineage system, as it appeared to early twentieth-century observers.

As with Southern Igbo society in general, Ngwa society was highly decentralised. The Ngwa settlement pattern was characteristically dispersed even in the mid twentieth century, by which time the region was densely populated.[37] The household, a unit consisting of one senior man, his wives, children, slaves and clients, formed the basic unit of agricultural production.[38] The basic residential unit was the compound (*Onu Ovu*), consisting of a small number of closely related men (for example, a father and his sons) and their respective households. This group of household heads was often coterminous with the *Ezi*, or minimal patrilineage, the members of whom all worshipped at the same shrine. The senior member of the *Ezi*, the father or senior brother of the other men, held its sacred staff or *ofo*, and officiated in all sacrifices to the family deities.[39]

The *ofo*-holder was extremely powerful within Ngwa society, as is reflected in the traditional accounts of Ngwa settlement. The establishment of a new shrine was a key stage in the founding of each new settlement; and the desire to escape the authority of a father or senior brother was a key motive for such a move.[40] In the early twentieth century, each *ofo*-holder was responsible for allocating the family farmland among adult males at the start of each farming season, although he could not alienate this land without the permission of all the male *Ezi* members. He received a gift of gin, palm wine and a few yams from each person to whom he allocated land, together with a share of any wild animal killed or any sacrifices made by his people. *Ezi* members had to work on their *ofo*-holder's personal farm on every *Orie* day (that is, on one day in every four).[41]

This high degree of patriarchal authority and agricultural co-operation was rarely found in units larger than the *Ezi*. Ngwa men still owe allegiance to two larger patrilineal units. One is the *Umunna*, or exogamous village-section: for example, Umuigwe where I lived while in the village of Ahiaba-Okpuala. The second is the *Onumara*, a group of men who trace their descent from one of their village's founders. The village or *Mba* consists of one or more *Onumara*, together with the members' households.[42] Ngwa traditions record that the village head or *Eze-Mo* (also known as *Ezeala*, or *Onye-Nwe-Ala*) was the custodian of the village shrine to *Ala*, the earth deity. He had the duty to keep the village calendar, to settle disputes between members of different lineages and to enforce the necessary sacrifices to *Ala* for serious crimes. He also convened periodic meetings of the village council or *Amala* to discuss laws relating to the village as a whole. All men in the village could attend and speak at such meetings; women and children could also attend providing they sat quietly on the fringes.[43]

Within the sphere of agriculture, the economic power of the *Eze-Mo* was limited by the low degree of village-level co-operation. Young men were formed into village-wide age-grade associations, but these were used mainly to co-ordinate their efforts in warfare and path clearance.[44] Among women, the main form of co-operation appears to have been among co-wives in farm work, for example in weeding. Even co-wives co-operated very little in off-farm work. Each wife had her own kitchen, and cooked for herself, her children and (in turn) her husband. Only a very young wife, without children, might be called upon to share the kitchen of her senior wife or mother-in-law.[45]

During the period of the Atlantic slave trade, probably the main way in which village-level authority could be used for economic gain was through control of the process of law enforcement. The custom of selling persistent debtors or adulterers into slavery, which was recorded in the early twentieth century, may well have begun during the Atlantic slave trade period.[46] Certainly, the Ngwa region lay on the major routes to the coast from the fairs of Bende and Uburu, and local traditions record a history of participation in the trade.[47] However, it is likely that the trade had more radical effects than simply strengthening the power of men who were already senior in lineage terms. Oriji has argued that the gains to be made from the trade by kidnappers and clandestine traders – rather than judges – led to the development of a new form of social organisation, linking the wealthy rather than the senior and crossing village boundaries. He holds that the powerful *Okonko* secret society, which colonial observers thought to be of very recent origin, was actually founded by the Aro slave traders. The society's members were able to trade in slaves under the cloak of ritual secrecy. Any man could join the society by paying fees, so that it provided a means of gaining power without having attained seniority within the lineage.[48]

Another means by which junior men could attain power or at least independence in the Atlantic slave trade period was through the process of migration, as has already been suggested. Title to land was rooted ultimately in the act of clearing the land.[49] Hence, although areas already under long-fallow cultivation were owned communally by the *Ezi*, the act of clearing virgin forest entitled a man to the status of the founder of a new *Ezi* which would work the new land. This logic underlies all the Ngwa traditions of migration cited earlier, and it helps to explain why migration was one of the major responses to increasing population during the pre-colonial period.

As the process of migration continued and the forest was gradually cleared by the Ngwa and neighbouring Southern Igbo and Ibibio farmers, a new landscape appeared within which farmers were able to cultivate an ever-widening variety of crops, and gather still more from the secondary forest which surrounded them. Yet they were still faced with problems – a scarcity of salt, except for that derived from vegetable ash; a scarcity of raw materials for textile manufacture; and, growing as the forest was cleared, a shortage of animal protein.

Domestic animals, especially cattle, are notoriously hard to rear in the West African forest environment. Early farmers had been able to make up for this by hunting; but as they cleared the primary forest, the sanctuary of the larger animals and, as their own numbers grew, wild game began to disappear from the local landscape. Ivory and leopard-skins had been among the earliest items of trade within eastern Nigeria, but by the 1920s elephants and leopards were no longer to be seen.[50] Colonial officials reported that in the Ibibio area the killing of a leopard was in theory the occasion for a gathering of the whole 'clan' at its founder village – an occasion which rarely arose. For ceremonial feasts, sacrifices, legal fines and fees, the animals used were domesticated cows, goats, sheep and fowls.[51] In the Ngwa area, these problems were exacerbated by the scarcity of lakes and streams, which meant that fish could not be obtained.

This scarcity of salt, cloth, meat and fish did not prejudice the survival of Ngwa farmers, but it did provide them with a strong incentive to engage in regional trade. In the mid twentieth century Ngwa farmers spent a large part of their incomes on fish from the coast, imported stockfish from Europe and meat from northern Nigeria.[52] A trade in yams, palm oil, fish and cattle along the Cross River is attested in nineteenth-century European records.[53]

Northrup has argued that the Atlantic slave trade provided a strong impetus to the growth of such regional links, firstly through the growth of trading networks and their co-ordination by the Aro, and secondly through the demand for provisions for slave caravans.[54] However, this is more likely to have been true for areas which were relatively close to the coast and through which large slave caravans passed publicly, in contrast to the Ngwa region where the emphasis lay on individual enslavement and on trade which was either secretive or seen as part of the process of justice. In the Ngwa region, the greatest growth in regional trade involving agricultural produce is likely to have been that which accompanied the rise of an export market for palm oil in the nineteenth century.

The European demand for palm oil arose in the early nineteenth century, when it began being used on a large scale in the manufacture of candles, and as a lubricant for the machinery of the Industrial Revolution.[55] Exports of palm oil to Britain rose rapidly from 112 tons per annum in 1807 to 23,467 tons per annum in 1847; and eastern Nigeria rapidly became a major supplier. Here, exports were drawn initially from the Ibibio region, which supplied Old Calabar. Shipments of oil from this port rose from 1,200 tons per annum in 1812–17 to 4,500 tons in 1864. Meanwhile, exports from neighbouring Bonny rose from 200 tons per annum in 1812–17 to 8,227 tons in 1849.[56]

One of the principal sources of the oil shipped from Bonny was the Ngwa region. Bonny, and later Opobo traders bought much of their oil in the Ndoki region, which at that time bordered the highest navigable stretch of the Imo River. Both Ngwa and Ndoki traditions record that the Ngwa brought their oil overland to Ndoki markets like Obegu and Ohambele: the porters in this trade being Ngwa women, escorted by men.[57] Clearly the palm oil trade involved new groups of hinterland traders, to some extent bypassing the old networks created by the Aro.[58]

It remains unclear how far the palm oil trade became integrated with the everyday trade carried on in Ngwa markets. By the mid-twentieth century, a complex network of markets existed in the region, and it was possible to visit a different local market on each day of the Igbo week. The week had four days, running in sequence *Afo, Nkwo, Eke* and *Orie*. Most markets were held on *Orie* or *Nkwo* day, usually once every two weeks in each place, though the large market at Aba was held daily (see Map 6).[59] However, informants say that the palm oil trade largely bypassed the smaller local markets, as producers preferred to carry their own oil to the bulking points along the Imo River.[60] Imports probably reached the smaller markets, as Birtwistle reported for the Ibibio area in 1905, in a rather disparaging manner: 'I seldom saw anything but gin, salt, tobacco, and a very poor assortment of cotton goods.'[61] Although Birtwistle despised these items, they were highly prized locally not only as consumer goods but also as forms of currency. Gin, manillas, cowries and tobacco were all key currencies by the early twentieth century in the Igbo area. The latter three, having low unit values, were particularly useful for small-scale village trade.[62]

The prevalence of such items in early twentieth-century village markets was the result of a century of change in the character of the import trade, through which a new stress was placed on 'currency' items like gin and tobacco and on a range of cheap consumer goods. During the period of the Atlantic slave trade, the main goods imported had been expensive textiles, guns and hardware, together with iron bars.[63] Many of these items would have been beyond the reach of most farmers, with the exception of the hoes and matchets which local smiths made from imported iron. The nineteenth century saw both an increase in imports of iron bars, and a new wave of cheap consumer imports: Lancashire salt and textiles, American tobacco and Dutch gin. Salt, in particular, was closely associated with the early palm oil export trade; while imports of cotton calicoes and prints rose fifty-fold between 1820 and 1850; and tobacco and gin rose to become staples after 1850.[64] Indeed, the availability of new imports and a fall in their price may have been the main incentive to export production before 1850. As Newbury has shown, the prices of salt, textiles and gunpowder fell sharply between 1817 and 1850. Meanwhile, Liverpool palm oil prices fluctuated around a slowly falling trend.[65]

29

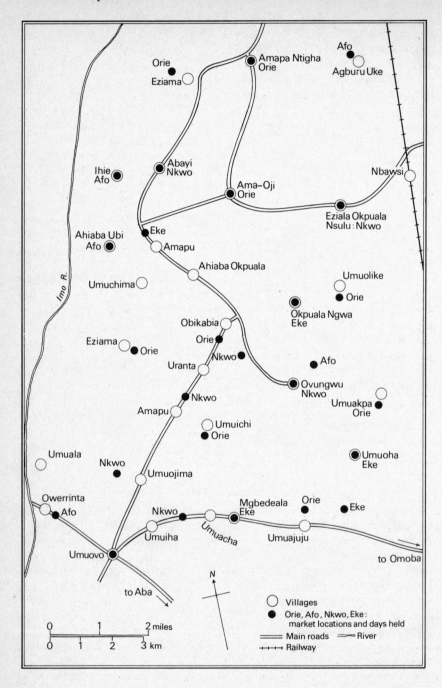

Map 6. Markets and market-days, north-western Ngwa region, 1933

The rise of the palm oil trade and the new range of imports which accompanied it may have ushered in a new period of prosperity and economic growth for Ngwa farmers, but the transition from slave to palm oil exports was by no means painless for the *Okonko* members who had grown wealthy beforehand. Hopkins has drawn a famous contrast between the large-scale capture and sale of slaves, which was open only to the very wealthy and powerful, and the production of palm oil for sale, which could be carried out by small farmers.[66] This contrast needs some modification in the Ngwa case, for *Okonko* members can hardly be described as merchant princes with great wealth and power. Much of the debate over Hopkins' view of the nineteenth century has centred on the very wealthy traders, and on the question of whether they were able to use large slave-based palm plantations to profit from the new era of 'legitimate commerce'.[67] In the Ngwa case, the contrast between *ofo*-holders and *Okonko* members was one of source of power, rather than scale of operations. However, the problems faced by *Okonko* members in making use of old forms of power in a new era may well have parallels elsewhere.

One major problem that *Okonko* members faced was that of gaining access to land on which to plant palm trees, or acquiring ownership of palms already growing on farms and on abandoned compound land. Ukegbu has argued from oral evidence collected in the Ngwa and neighbouring regions that there were no special rules governing the ownership of oil palms before the rise of the nineteenth-century export trade. During the nineteenth century, it was the *ofo*-holders who successfully laid claim to palms growing on the land they were currently cultivating, on compound land and on the sites of previous lineage settlements. They also began to regulate the harvesting of wild or 'bush' palms, which by the mid twentieth century took place on four 'open' days in every three months.[68]

As we have seen, it was also the *ofo*-holders who allocated land for fresh planting. Meanwhile, the supply of virgin forest for clearance by those who lacked seniority within existing lineages was beginning to run out. As the Ngwa spread southwards they began to enter inhabited territory and to encounter fierce resistance from the Asa, to the south-west, and the Ibibio, to the south-east.[69] The Ngwa were still able to maintain a long-fallow system of yam farming, with a gap of about seven years between crops on each patch of land; and there is no evidence of commercialisation of land tenure.[70] Yet there was sufficient pressure on supplies of land to have made it difficult for *Okonko* members who were not already *ofo*-holders to start slave plantations; and to make it difficult for *ofo*-holders to extend their operations beyond the level made possible by harvesting all the existing palms. In the early twentieth century, after a century of export expansion, officials observed that the Ngwa preserved oil palms while clearing land for farming, but did not plant them.[71]

In the event, the existing supply of palms was more than sufficient to allow for a rapid expansion of the export industry. Oil palms grow in a rare symbiosis with food farming in eastern Nigeria, which has been called 'the greatest grove area of Africa'.[72] In 1907, there were about 3.5 million palms in Aba District (the southern Ngwa region) alone, of which perhaps 40 per cent were being regularly harvested.[73] The main problem which the *ofo*-holders might have been expected to face was obtaining a sufficient supply of labour. Indeed, Oriji suggests that *Okonko* members were able to profit from the new trading conditions by selling slaves to other farmers or retaining them within their own households. Allen also mentions that local wealthy men had often purchased those enslaved judicially in the late nineteenth century.[74]

However, slavery did not develop as a large-scale or plantation-style institution in the Ngwa region during the nineteenth century. Early twentieth-century sources record that there was a large-scale trade in slaves within eastern Nigeria, but that this trade largely bypassed the Ngwa region. Slaves went mainly to regions which produced yams on a commercial scale, or which were heavily involved in large-scale, usually canoe-based palm oil transportation.[75] The modest extent of domestic slavery in the Ngwa region is related to three main features of the local economy and society. Firstly, within the local sexual division of labour women assumed most of the labour burdens involved in palm production. Secondly, these labour burdens did not pose major conflicts with their work in domestic production and petty trade. Finally, the weak position of women and junior men within the lineage system combined with the modest scale of production indicated by land constraints to minimise the need for senior men to seek outside sources of labour. Given that *ofo*-holders could profit from exploiting their own reserves of palms using family labour, there was little incentive either for them to sell land to wealthier men, or for them to buy many slaves from *Okonko* members.

Before the nineteenth century palm production had been viewed by most southern Nigerian farmers as part of the cooking process, and so as an exclusively female affair. Women collected windfall fruit and prepared oil from it by boiling and pounding, then removing the kernels, washing and squeezing the fibrous pulp. The oil-and-water mixture could then be poured directly into the cooking pot.[76] The boiling and pounding technique is typical of Ngwa cooking methods, both for yam and for soup ingredients like okra, tomato and crayfish.

When commercial production of palm oil began in the nineteenth century, new large-scale techniques were adopted. In Lagos and in the Niger Delta, men took over virtually all stages of the process, moving it to stream-side locations and, in the Niger Delta, eliminating the boiling stage to produce a cheaper but lower-grade 'hard' oil.[77] In the Igbo and Ibibio areas, this did not happen until the mid twentieth century; during the nineteenth century, men intervened in the production process only at the stages of harvesting and processing the fruit. This intervention served to establish their ownership rights over the oil and to relieve production bottlenecks; yet it did not challenge the principles of the local sexual division of labour, by which women dealt with fire and water and did the bulk of routine work.

The harvesting of palm fruit was exclusively masculine work, and usually the work of agile young men, for it was extremely dangerous. The palm-climber was supported only by a pair of ropes, one being looped round his left thigh, the other round his right foot, each rope being tied round the trunk of the tree. He moved rapidly up the tree in a series of jerking movements, and once at the crown would walk round it, removing excess palm fronds and chopping down the ripe bunches of fruit with his matchet. Since the palms could grow to a height of between 14 and 60 feet, a fall could be fatal.[78]

Once cut down, the fruit bunches were carried home by women and children and left in a cool place for several days, after which it became possible to pick individual fruits from the spiky bunch. The fruit was then boiled for about two hours until it softened. At this point the men returned to pound the fruit in a large mortar or a hollowed-out tree stump for about half an hour, until it was reduced to a mass of fibres and nuts within which the dark-red oil had begun to appear. Women would then remove the mass to a wooden trough, extract a small portion which they would wash and squeeze to obtain oil, boil this oil and return it to the trough, after which they would begin squeezing the whole mass of fibre in earnest. Earth was often added during pounding, which made it easier to get a grip on the coarse fibre.

The tasks of removing the nuts from the fibre, repeated squeezing and finally thorough washing of the fibre in order to extract the last traces of oil, were all extremely time-consuming and repetitive. Women were still extracting palm oil in this way in 1980–1; then, it took two women about an hour of washing and squeezing to extract one gallon of oil from the pounded fruit. However, the oil obtained was of high quality, with a low percentage of free fatty acid. Oil with a high percentage of free fatty acid easily turns rancid and becomes solid in cool temperatures; hence the distinction between high quality 'soft' oil and low quality 'hard' oil. The boiling of the palm fruit and the oil itself after processing by the 'soft' method destroys the enzyme which creates the free fatty acid.[79]

Early colonial officials took a keen interest in the quality of oil exported from different regions of eastern Nigeria, and found that the 'soft' oil production method described above was typical of the Imo River and Ibibio areas. In the Niger Delta and in some regions north and east of Bende 'hard' oil production was more common.[80] The latter regions were relatively thinly populated, and there were heavy demands on local labour for canoe transportation in the Delta, and commercial yam farming along the upper Cross River.[81] In the Ngwa and Ibibio areas, on the other hand, palm production was the main commercialised activity. The adoption of 'soft' oil production methods here indicates that providing palm production was the only major commercial activity, it did not impose such major strains on local labour supplies as to provoke the invention of new production methods or the redefinition of male and female tasks.

This is a classic vent-for-surplus picture, and it can be explained partly with reference to the Ngwa agricultural calendar. Just as the cultivation and harvesting of the full range of crops cultivated spread over ten months of the calendar year, so also palm fruit could be harvested at any time of year, although the peak yielding season for palm trees was between January and May.[82] Palm oil extraction excluded women from work on other household and farm duties for one or two days at a time, but in this it was similar to marketing when a journey to a major local market was involved.[83] This kind of work could easily be fitted in on odd days taken off from farming, though it was more disruptive of domestic work which needed to be carried out daily.

Unfortunately, the sphere of domestic labour is the area of village life which is least accessible to outsiders, and we have no evidence of the kind of changes which could indicate strain in this area: for example a wider spacing of children, an increasing import trade in staple 'female' crops, innovation in cooking techniques or even a higher mortality rate or other signs of increasing exhaustion in women. Thus, we are left with the plain vent-for-surplus view of no visible strain on palms or on labour resources, though this may not be the full story.

Essentially, it has been argued above that within this visible vent-for-surplus pattern of export expansion, those with 'customary' or lineage-based access to resources, for whom commercial production was only one aspect of their activities, were well able to profit from the new export trade. There was no switch from planting yams to planting palms, and the work involved in palm processing was carried out in the interstices of farming activities. The income earned was spent on new luxuries and on foodstuffs additional to the range produced locally.

In the early twentieth century, palm oil production was usually carried out within the household, by a brother and sisters or by co-wives and a husband. Women received a small amount of oil for use in cooking, and retained the dry fibre for use as kindling, together with the nuts which could be cracked and fried to obtain a soothing medicinal oil. But the bulk of the palm oil produced belonged either to the owner of the tree or to the man who had harvested the fruit, if a wild palm had been used. Some oil would be given to the harvester and to the man who pounded the fruit, if the tree was owned by a senior man who had not joined in the work.[84]

Palm oil production at this time bore a close resemblance to yam farming, both in the distribution of the product and in the social organisation of production. In both cases, *ofo*-holders claimed ownership of the essential natural resources (land and palm trees). Junior men were involved in the process of production at certain key stages (land clearance, harvest, and palm fruit pounding). Women did much of the time-consuming, routine

34

work (weeding, wood and water collection, fruit and yam cooking, oil-squeezing and yam-pounding). However, women were allowed to keep only as much of the oil and yams as was needed for feeding the family. Junior men could gain more only if they could gain access to unclaimed land and palms and persuade women within their household to co-operate. Such cash gains would often be absorbed in bridewealth payments to senior men. Meanwhile, *ofo*-holders were able to accumulate cash through the sale of yams and, especially, palm oil.

Within this setting *Okonko* members, if they had wealth but not senior lineage status, were in a weak position. Oriji has suggested one way in which they might have been able to compensate: by levying tolls on trade routes. However, his sole source for this is a set of speculative comments made by Leonard on the possible uses of the *Okonko* houses which he saw along his route to Bende in 1896. In the absence of supporting evidence, it should not be assumed that Leonard's guess was correct. His account of the hurried and defensive journey is coloured with fear and suspicion; for example, he assumed that an African visitor who failed to remove his hat had intended to insult him.[85]

Another way in which *Okonko* members may have tried to strengthen their position was by turning the society itself into a respectable bastion of village-level government. Both Oriji and Allen record that just before the colonial period the *Okonko* society had become increasingly involved in village politics, taking over some of the law-enforcing powers of the village council in secular matters like debt recovery. Its membership widened and it gained a reputation as a form of investment: in the mid twentieth century new members paid fees of 5,000–10,000 manillas each, to be shared out among existing members. Each new member also provided a feast for the rest.[86] While the early nineteenth-century *Okonko* members may not have been able to use their cash and their access to slaves to become specialist palm planters, they were able to use their institution and their experience of commercial disputes to attract cash from newly rich *ofo*-holders and their sons. In this way they both experienced and survived a 'crisis of transition' – one of a rather unorthodox kind.

For Ngwa farmers in general the centuries before 1900 saw the establishment and successful diversification of a yam-farming economy in which hunting, gathering and finally overseas trade were useful ancillary elements. By 1900 their region had been fully settled and the main social divisions between men and women, senior and junior men, wealthy *Okonko* members and lineage heads, had been clearly established. These divisions were not rigid, and the following years were to see further profound changes both in the balance between various economic activities and in the relationships between different social groups.

3

The Ngwa and colonial rule, 1891–1914

British rule was gradually extended over the hinterland of eastern Nigeria from 1891, but the Ngwa had remarkably little direct experience of colonial rule before 1914. The small white community which was established at Aba in 1902 intervened sparingly in the lives of its African neighbours and made rare forays into the surrounding region. It is difficult to discover much about the relationship between local officials and those subjects with whom they did establish contact, since record-keeping was poor and few documents have survived. However, it is possible to piece together a general picture of British colonial rule in eastern Nigeria from higher-level sources. In this chapter we will use this material, and the few available local records, to explain why the early colonial presence was so remote and to trace the origins of attitudes and policies that were later to affect Ngwa life more directly.

British colonial rule was established slowly and piecemeal in eastern Nigeria, over a period of thirty years. In 1884 Consul Hewett began the process by making a series of treaties of protection with coastal rulers, and in 1891 the Niger Coast Protectorate was established with the ultimate aim of securing British authority in the hinterland.[1] However, the conquest of the hinterland began in earnest only with the launching of the Aro Expedition in 1901; and it was concluded only with the suppression of a wave of wartime revolts in 1914–16.[2]

Financial constraints underlay this slow pace of action and continued to influence the development of economic and administrative policy in newly conquered regions. Colonial officials both in Britain and in Nigeria often had grand ideas about the transformation of the local economy, but lacked the funds needed to implement them. Furthermore, many officials working in Nigeria lacked the detailed local knowledge and the sense of security needed to develop viable institutions of government and realistic economic policies. Over the period 1891–1914 these difficulties of funding, security and knowledge were gradually alleviated, but one final difficulty remained. The Ngwa and neighbouring ethnic groups were extremely well-established entities with their own methods of justice and local government. The authority of district officers and their allies was superimposed upon that of senior local men, but the newcomers were barely able to restrain, let alone take over, their rivals' power. In the absence of a firm local power base, white officials were unable to implement their more cherished interventionist policies, such as the abolition of domestic slavery. The Ngwa and their neighbours were left in control of their own economic affairs.

The financial constraints faced by early colonial officials in eastern Nigeria had their ultimate origin in the world trade depression of the late nineteenth century which, as Cain and Hopkins have recently emphasised, coincided with the partition of Africa.[3] While the depression may have provided metropolitan interest groups with fresh reasons for seeking control over tropical markets, it also reinforced the parsimony of the British Treasury. During the 1880s very little cash was available even for the conquest of newly partitioned territories.[4] In the 1890s the process of conquest gathered pace in West Africa, but Joseph Chamberlain's pleas for the development of 'tropical estates' fell on deaf ears. Treasury funds between 1890 and 1914 were absorbed mainly in expeditions of conquest, railway building and the relief of regions which had suffered earthquakes or similar disasters. This pattern persisted through the First World War and the 1930s depression.[5]

Given the scarcity of metropolitan funds it was essential for the Niger Coast Protectorate administration to find local sources of revenue. Given the Protectorate's limited geographical power base in the main ports and the European river-trading stations, import duties were the most obvious source, especially when the Brussels Conference of 1889–90 had sanctioned their use in combating the gun and liquor trades.[6] In 1891 Sir Claude MacDonald introduced duties on spirits, gunpowder, guns, tobacco and salt. He used the income to finance the establishment of the Niger Coast Protectorate Force, which spearheaded the conquest of the hinterland from 1901.[7]

The revenue thus raised took a heavy toll on the incomes of the Ngwa and neighbouring farmers. In 1896–7 the administration collected £109,101 in import duties, representing 14 per cent of the region's foreign exchange earnings (as measured by the value of its exports).[8] By 1900 this figure had risen to £238,881 per annum, or 26 per cent of the total value of exports.[9] By 1910, with the addition of Lagos to the Protectorate, customs revenues had risen to £1,440,284 or 29 per cent of export earnings. Court fees and railway revenues from the Western Nigerian line added a further £397,227 to the administration's income, but import duties remained by far the most important source of revenue. Of all customs duties 69 per cent was raised on imports of trade spirits, 9 per cent on those of cotton goods and 7 per cent on those of tobacco.[10]

Having established themselves financially, British administrators in eastern Nigeria began to make ventures into the hinterland. In 1894 Roger Casement made several brief journeys through the southern Ibibio region, and in 1896 A. G. Leonard travelled through the Ngwa region to Bende. Leonard reported that the people of Aba were armed to the teeth with swords, rifles, bows and arrows, though he was allowed to pass unharmed.[11] Meanwhile, the first 'punitive expeditions' were being launched in retaliation for trade stoppages and attacks on visiting district commissioners or court messengers in the better-known riverside regions.[12]

In 1901 the expansion of British control entered a new phase with the launching of a major offensive against the Aro. The Aro Expedition has been described in detail by many historians as a turning point in the history of eastern Nigeria.[13] It inaugurated a series of dry-season expeditions of conquest which concluded with the Niger–Cross River Operations of 1908–9.[14] The expeditions were violent and destructive, often involving the burning and shelling of villages, with summary trials and the wholesale confiscation of guns following in the wake of colonial victory. These experiences put an end to most villagers' military resistance to British rule: in 1905 Governor Egerton was able to travel by bicycle from Owerrinta to Aba, through country known to be peaceful.[15]

The Ngwa are hard to identify in the reports relating to the Aro Expedition and its aftermath, and indeed the process of conquest had left little impression on the older people whom I interviewed in 1980–1. The military imposition of colonial rule appears to have been most dramatic in the Anang and Kwa regions, where villagers fought bitterly during the Aro Expedition and continued to experience show-of-force patrols for the rest of the decade.[16]

If the process of conquest may be said to have passed relatively lightly over the Ngwa, so too may the early years of colonial administration. Martin Chanock has recently shown how the British in Central Africa concentrated initially on destroying the more 'public' aspects of African judicial systems – the larger-scale local judicial authorities and the more spectacular practices, in particular the ordeal trial – while putting very rudimentary white-run court structures in their place. This left a void in some areas of justice, but allowed many village-level African institutions to continue operating and developing in their own way.[17] Similarly, in eastern Nigeria the early officials concentrated on destroying the 'Jujus' or oracles of the Aro and other regionally influential cult leaders, but allowed village *dibias* (diviners) to continue their work unimpeded. The authority of the *dibias* was still widely recognised by Igbo and Ibibio farmers in the 1930s.[18] On a more secular level, the local power of *Okonko* members and *ofo*-holders also remained unrecognised and so unchecked by colonial officials.[19]

In highly decentralised societies like those of the Ngwa and their neighbours, this tendency of colonial officials to eradicate only larger-scale and spectacularly public judicial institutions, and to mount campaigns of conquest targeted on 'leaders' or on 'dominant' groups like the Aro meant that many indigenous power structures were left alone. Nineteenth-century rivalries and patterns of authority survived and continued developing according to their own internal logic during the early colonial period. Officials faced a difficult task in trying to superimpose their authority upon these groupings, all the more because local ethnic identities were diverse and strongly rooted. The small size and strong loyalties of most ethnic groups in eastern Nigeria meant that it was difficult for officials to organise them into large and tractable administrative units. This situation stands in contrast to that in British Central African colonies, where new ethnic alliances had been forged in the turbulent late nineteenth century and where a further remoulding of peoples into 'tribes' of convenient size was possible for early colonial officials.[20] As Iliffe has commented, 'stateless societies were easy to defeat but difficult to rule'.[21]

Before the Second World War, white officials were very thin on the ground in Nigeria and their administrative centres were widely spaced. The early district commissioners travelled widely and did their best to get to know the region; they spent much time organising path clearance so as to make this task easier.[22] However, they were slow to appreciate the intricacy of the local ethnic groupings, and divided the Ngwa for example arbitrarily between the Districts of Bende and Aba.[23] Furthermore, they very rapidly came to rely upon local agents to carry out most of their administrative and judicial work and, as Afigbo has eloquently shown, they usually chose collaborators who had little or no indigenous claim to authority.[24] One major result of this was that the native councils and minor courts which operated within each district commanded little local respect. The warrant chiefs who were appointed to head them became a byword for corruption, along with their clerks and court messengers.[25] Meanwhile, the system distanced the D.C. further from the mass of the local people, who usually came to him via the chiefs, either as labourers or as petitioners and disputants. In these circumstances white officials were unable to gain detailed information about local economic affairs; still less were they able to exert a direct influence over the conduct of everyday life.

These general observations are powerfully reinforced by the story of a dispute which broke out at the Ngwa-Ukwu village of Obikabia in 1914. By this time, minor courts had been established at Omo Ohia (Umuahia) and Owerrinta, in Bende and Aba Districts, and Ngwa-Ukwu village group straddled the boundary between their zones of jurisdiction. The people of Osusa (Osusu) attended Omo Ohia Native Court, but their neighbours at Obikabia came under the sway of Owerrinta. In January 1914 this authority was put to the test when a court messenger was sent to arrest one Wogu of Obikabia for trial at Owerrinta. Wogu and his neighbours attacked and beat up the messenger, and successfully repulsed two further attempts at arrest – one by a squad of police, and the other by the district officer in person (accompanied by an escort). Finally, in early February troops were sent to the area. They found Obikabia deserted, save for the local warrrant chief, Aforole (Afurele). Wogu had fled to Osusu, where he was given up on 4

February by Chief Wakama. Not content, the troops remained in the area until the other leaders of the 'insurrection' had been surrendered, on 12 February. These men were then tried and punished for their insubordination.[26]

The official record is silent on the aftermath of this incident; but one local man who remembers the affair, Mr S. O. Nwaogwugwu, says that the men were sent to Egwanga and imprisoned. Wogu (whose name is recalled by Mr Nwaogwugwu as Nwatu) was also tortured by being forced to eat boiling hot yam. After their release, the men returned to Obikabia. Some years later, the British came to the village again and everyone fled into the bush, as before – except for Nwatu who, feeling that after his experience of boiling yam he had nothing left to fear, stood his ground. The British were so impressed by his bravery that they made him a warrant chief, in succession to Chief Aforole. Nwatu had power to judge at Umuahia, as well as Owerrinta. He became very rich and married eight wives.[27]

This conclusion to the story of Wogu (Nwatu) may well be apocryphal, and the documentary sources for the period are far too incomplete to allow it to be confirmed or denied. Nevertheless, it does illustrate a certain local view of the British as administrators – arbitrary and harsh disciplinarians, who descended upon the village unexpectedly from time to time. One could never tell in advance whether their visit was to be peaceful or punitive. In the story of their final, peaceful visit, the emphasis on Nwatu's unexpected good fortune bears out Afigbo's account of the haphazard way in which warrant chiefs were selected. A warrant appears as the local equivalent of a medal or a schoolroom gold star.[28]

The incident is also illuminating in that there is a striking contrast between the way it was described in the official correspondence at the time, and recalled later by Mr Nwaogwugwu. The difference of opinion over personal and place names, for example, is by no means accidental. In the days following the repulsion of the court messenger, a debate took place between the local D.O. and the provincial commissioner as to the correct name of the village, and its precise location on the Protectorate map. It emerged that very little was known of the town, except that it had been visited in 1913 by the D.O.s of Aba and Bende, while demarcating the boundary between their districts. It was automatically assumed that the boundary position of the village lay at the heart of the dispute. Officials concluded that the villagers were confused as to which court they should be attending, and wished to have a court in their own town.[29] Having arrived at a settled view of the incident, they then proceeded to ignore it: Ngwa-Ukwu remained without its own court until 1923, when one was set up at Ayaba (Ahiaba-Ubi).[30]

In Mr Nwaogwugwu's account the question of boundaries does not arise. The origin of Nwatu's resistance to arrest is held to lie in the fact that he had been 'framed' in the first place. He had been falsely accused by the jealous former husband of his new wife. This man, Ahuchogu, came from Umu-

Ojima, in Umu–oha village-group, and was a warrant chief at Owerrinta. Nwatu feared that if his case was brought for trial at Owerrinta, his enemy would triumph. Once again, this story has not been verified, yet even if apocryphal, it reveals an interesting attitude towards warrant chiefs. A court prone to manipulation by powerful individuals would be a risky place for the powerless to bring their disputes. For the inter-war period, as will be shown in Chapter 7, more evidence exists to indicate that the courts were indeed used selectively by certain kinds of Ngwa people to settle certain kinds of dispute. Meanwhile, unofficial village councils or secret societies may well have continued to handle many cases, as Chanock has shown for Malawi and Zambia.[31]

These contrasting accounts of the Obikabia incident also illustrate that district officers were unable to monitor the actions of warrant chiefs closely enough to prevent abuses. This impression is supported by the D.O.s' annual reports, which display an overriding preoccupation with personal survival, the prevention of warfare and the constant need to respond to higher-level commands.[32] This last task was essential if colonial rule was to make any planned impact at the local level, to balance the unplanned impact of the warrant chief system. Yet it was a task which district officers found hard to carry out successfully, partly because of the financial constraints mentioned earlier, partly because of the difficulty of achieving any planned results within the warrant chief system of administration, but not least because of the very vagueness and frequent impracticality of the higher-level commands. In the final sections of this chapter, we will illustrate the last point with reference to policies relating to the export trade, domestic slavery and currency. It will be shown that the only area in which colonial officials achieved their stated economic aims was that of transport innovation, which was to make a major impact on the Ngwa region from 1904 onwards.

If the Niger Coast and Southern Nigeria Protectorates can be said to have had one clear economic aim, it was to foster the expansion of the import–export trade. Officials had justified the Aro Expedition by saying that it would promote the abolition of the internal slave trade and, as a logical corollary, 'open up' south-eastern Nigeria to 'legitimate commerce'.[33] Yet on closer examination this aim loses something of its clarity. Officials wavered in their views of what export products should replace internally traded slaves, and they all too readily lost heart when confronted with the practical difficulties involved in suppressing slavery itself.

During the late nineteenth-century depression officials despaired of the future of eastern Nigeria's staple oil palm export industry. They initiated a search for new economic crops, establishing a Botanic Gardens at Old Calabar in 1893. Coffee, cocoa, rubber, rice and other crops were cultivated experimentally at the Gardens, and the curator toured neighbouring hinterland regions to survey the existing crops and assess the area's potential for diversified commercial agriculture. By 1895 he had propagated several new plants and had produced some coffee seedlings for distribution to local farmers.[34] But he had time to do little more before there was a change of policy. In 1900 the Gardens were closed down. The small amount of finance made available was used to establish a Forestry Department to conserve existing rubber and timber resources.[35]

In 1906 the Colonial Office began taking a renewed interest in West African resources. A superintendent of agriculture for the British West African Colonies was appointed and visited south-eastern Nigeria to assess the prospects of cotton and rubber cultivation. In his report he mentioned the oil palm industry only as 'the industry which occupies the natives of Southern Nigeria to such an extent as to render the introduction of other agricultural projects nearly impossible'.[36] However, within the year there was a boom in European demand for palm produce and bands of officials were sent out to tour the villages of Southern Nigeria investigating the industry.[37] A split now appeared between on the one hand the local Forestry Department surveyors, allied to the Imperial Institute in London, and on the other hand Governor Egerton and Mr Dudgeon, the Superintendent of Agriculture, who continued to favour cocoa, cotton and other crops.[38] Meanwhile, little was done to influence the mix of crops actually cultivated or processed within villages. Official action was confined to monitoring the quality of traded palm produce; though here again official policy changed several times between the 1890s and the 1920s.

Dirty produce was a nuisance for European traders to handle, as it had to be cleaned before industrial use. Yet dirt tended to enter into palm oil in the normal course of production, and kernels could easily be spoiled by soaking during the canoe journey to the coast.[39] Traders found it hard to detect these faults in the markets, and clamoured for government assistance throughout the 1890s to the 1930s.[40] An ineffectual scheme using first the traders themselves, then district officers, then indigenous assistant produce inspectors, was in force from 1896 onwards.[41] It was never formally abolished, but by 1915 Governor Lugard was announcing publicly that the merchants should look after themselves, and in 1918 the district officer at Azumini refused to hear a case brought by Opobo traders against their Kwa suppliers.[42]

Just as officials wavered in their policies towards the export trade, so also they hesitated to implement the bold humanitarian aims towards the import and internal trades which had been avowed by Britain and other European states at the Brussels Conference. These included the abolition of the arms, liquor and internal slave trades.[43] The arms trade was suppressed with some vigour: imports of all except 'flintlock' guns were banned in 1894, and rifles and cap guns were seized and destroyed wholesale during the expeditions of conquest.[44] But the trade in liquor, which was vitally important as a source of revenue, was never suppressed. It simply halted with the outbreak of the First World War, when communications were broken with Germany and Holland, the two main suppliers.[45]

Finally, as is well known, colonial policy on slavery remained ambivalent. In 1901 two proclamations were enacted in the Protectorate of Southern Nigeria: the Slave Dealing Proclamation, which was designed to halt slave recruitment, and the House Rule Proclamation, which perpetuated the status of existing slaves. Many historians have commentated on the official fear of anarchy if slavery was abolished, and on the contemporary uses of slave labour both by chiefs and by officials.[46] In 1915 the House Rule Ordinance was repealed, but this move simply allowed slaves to free themselves without official hindrance: it did not allow for active official intervention on the side of the powerless. In 1934 an official investigating the slave trade in the Eastern Provinces concluded that the problem remained intractable.[47]

Further intractable problems confronted early colonial administrators when they attempted to reform the local monetary system. Eastern Nigeria had not undergone a late nineteenth-century 'currency revolution' and its traders still relied on 'transitional' currencies like manillas and cowries in the Ngwa region, brass rods and copper wires along the Cross River, and gin and iron bars at the coast.[48] Early twentieth-century officials wanted to replace all these currencies with a standard coinage, so eliminating the floating exchange rates which bedevilled trade within the region.[49] They banned the import of brass rods in 1899, of manillas in 1902 and of cowries in 1904.[50] From 1911 all government staff were paid in cash, and rods and manillas ceased to be legal tender in courts and government offices. In 1913 Birtwistle, the commercial intelligence officer, suggested that the newly established West African Currency Board, which supplied stocks of cash, should finance the buying in of all existing stocks of manillas.[51] However, the proposal was not taken up until 1948, when 32 million manillas were finally redeemed at a cost to the government of £248,000.[52]

Meanwhile, yet another floating exchange rate had been added to the many existing locally. The silver shillings provided by the Currency Board attained a limited popularity in local markets, but even by the 1920s officials had not succeeded in producing a subsidiary coinage which could rival the manilla in convenience and durability.[53] The manilla gradually appreciated in value against sterling, rising in the hinterland of Opobo from a rate of 20 per shilling in 1902 to 9 per shilling in 1909 and 6 per shilling in 1918.[54] The exchange rate fluctuated seasonally, as middlemen used manillas to obtain palm oil. This meant that African staff who were paid in shillings faced unpredictable cost-of-living changes: food was traded against manillas in the markets. Birtwistle argued in 1913 that instead of modernising the trading system, officials had succeeded only in provoking their own staff to acts of robbery and violence in the market place.[55]

Early colonial economic policy achieved real success in only one sphere – that of transport innovation. Following conquest, the Cross River became a highway for steamers, and the Imo River and its extension, the Aba River, were cleared so that steel canoes could travel up to Aba by 1907.[56] A programme of annual clearance was instituted on long stretches of the Imo, Otamini, Sombreiro and Kwa Ibo Rivers, to blow up the trees which fell across them in the rainy season and destroy the screw pine growth which recurred annually.[57] It will be shown in the next chapter that this work had a great effect on Ngwa trading patterns, although it was disrupted during the First World War and major re-clearance had to be carried out between 1924 and 1927. By 1927 the Imo River was navigable for large (eight to ten-puncheon) trade canoes up to Ife, which is near the Ngwa-Ukwu village of Ihie.[58]

Creek clearance was important, but slow and unspectacular. A more attractive policy to top-level administrators, but one which was more difficult to finance, was that of railway building. Various railway projects had been proposed for eastern Nigeria between 1902 and 1908, but none had attracted the necessary external funds.[59] Then in 1908–9 the area around Enugu was conquered and coal was found at Udi. This inspired a determined search for a suitable deep-water harbour, to be linked to the coalfields by rail. In 1912–13 a suitable site was found in the Bonny estuary and work began on the construction of a new town – Port Harcourt. Despite the strains soon imposed by wartime conditions, the railway line to Udi was completed by 1916.[60] By 1927 the line had been extended to Makurdi, running via Enugu, Jos and Kaduna.[61]

The building of the Eastern Railway ensured that Nigeria's public debt had risen to over £8 million by 1919. Nigeria had also received £4,700,000 in grants-in-aid, to cover the cost of expeditions of conquest.[62] Funds from the British Exchequer had clearly been of vital importance in financing major administrative ventures in the region; however, these funds had not been made available for lesser undertakings like the day-to-day running of government or the redemption of manillas. Hence a perennial scarcity of funds combined with vague and conflicting economic objectives, and the persistent uncertainty of control, to prevent officials from intervening effectively in the economic lives of Ngwa villagers. In the early colonial period railways and steamers drove narrow channels into the hinterland, along which Europeans gathered. But vast areas remained unvisited except by perennial military expeditions, and by district officers stationed in lonely outposts or passing through on tour. The administrators remained at a distance from their new subjects, and their policies were most effective where they dealt with the external circumstances of people's lives: in the establishment of a new superstructure of power, in the building of roads and in the clearing of creeks.

4

The expansion of the oil palm industry, 1884–1914

Eastern Nigeria's export producers began to feel the impact of the late nineteenth-century trade depression in 1885, when London prices for palm oil fell sharply from £30–40 to £20–24 per ton.[1] Liverpool prices fluctuated around the level of £25 per ton throughout the 1890s, recovering only in 1905–6, when a dramatic eight-year boom began.[2] Colonial government policies reinforced the effects of world market trends: the imposition of customs duties coincided with the depression of the 1890s, while the clearing of roads and creeks coincided with the early twentieth-century trade revival.

In this chapter we will examine the impact of successive phases of slump and boom upon the Ngwa and neighbouring farmers. During the depression, eastern Igbo and Ibibio farmers differed from those living to the west of the Niger in maintaining a high output of palm produce, rather than diversifying into large-scale rubber and cocoa production. Then, once the twentieth-century boom began, Ngwa farmers began encountering labour constraints more rapidly than their Ibibio neighbours. These regional differences will be explored below, and related to differences in local soils, climate and population density. The Ngwa–Ibibio contrast will also be related to the special position of the Ibibio as members of the Cross River food-trading network.

Within each region, women and men were affected differently by the trade depression of the late nineteenth century. Just before the slump began in earnest, a new export trade had begun in palm kernels, the women's perquisite which previously had had no cash value.[3] William Lever pioneered the industrial use of palm kernel oil in Britain, using it together with coconut oil to make a new 'self-washing' soap aimed at working-class consumers in hard-water areas.[4] During the 1890s palm kernel prices stagnated along with those of palm oil; but this trend represented a setback in the growth of a new trade, rather than a sudden slump within a well-established one.[5] Furthermore, as Colin Newbury has recently shown, the 1880s had seen a fall in the prices of cotton piece goods and trade spirits exported to West Africa from Britain, offsetting a rise in the prices of iron,

45

salt and hardware.[6] During the 1890s the prices of both spirits and salt rose slowly while others, for example of tobacco, stagnated.[7] These trends in import prices make it difficult to tell whether the real value of exports revived or fell further after the sudden slump in palm oil prices in 1885. For women, the existence of a new trade in palm kernels may well have outweighed the income effects of any decline which did occur.

Newbury has also shown that prices for rubber and ivory held up better than those for palm oil and kernels during the 1880s. He suggests that a switch from palm oil to palm kernel production in the region between the Niger and the Congo, 1875–85, was followed by a boom in rubber and ivory exports. By 1890, British rubber imports from western Africa accounted for 20 per cent of the region's trade with Britain.[8] The rubber boom was especially marked in the hinterlands of Lagos and the Gold Coast, where it was accompanied by a wave of early experiments with cocoa.[9] The Ngwa and their neighbours did not share in this process of export diversification: cocoa never became popular in the region, and exports of rubber stood at only 386,000 lbs per annum from the Niger Coast Protectorate in 1896, for example, as compared with 6,484,000 lbs from Lagos and 3,735,000 lbs from the Gold Coast in the same year.[10]

One reason why Ngwa farmers did not participate in the cocoa experiments and the rubber boom may be that local demographic and ecological factors prevented them. Rubber was produced from the *Funtumia elastica* tree and the *Landolphia owariensis* vine, both of which were wild plants found in the primary forest, and so were relatively scarce in densely populated eastern Nigeria.[11] Cocoa grows best on land which has recently been cleared from the primary forest, rather than on fallowed land. In the twentieth century, major cocoa-growing areas tended to have population densities of around 100 or fewer people per square mile, rather than the 200 or more which was characteristic of the main eastern Nigerian palm belt in the 1920s.[12] Finally, cocoa requires a rainfall of about 60 inches per annum, rather than the 80 inches or more which is typical of the Ngwa and neighbouring regions.[13]

While environmental and demographic factors handicapped the Ngwa as cocoa or rubber producers, they provided decisive advantages in the oil palm industry. Palms grew in abundance on fallowed farmland and in compounds, so that dense population was no handicap here. One official estimated in 1907 that there were six palms to the acre in Aba District, and ten to the acre in the even more densely populated Ibibio districts of Uyo and Ikot Ekpene.[14] In 1912 the Aba district commissioner complained that people planted raffia or wine palms, but persistently ignored his pleas to plant oil palms as well. Their actions were understandable given that raffia palms were scarce outside riverain swamp areas, but oil palms were abundant. In riverain regions where the reverse was true, people frequently planted oil palms.[15]

The Ngwa and neighbouring farmers also benefited from the fact that the local palm fruit was exceptionally rich in oil. In 1909 the Imperial Institute published an analysis of palm fruit samples which showed that the oil content of eastern Nigerian palm fruit was 26 per cent of the total weight; the corresponding kernel yield was 11 per cent. The comparable figures for the Western Province of Nigeria were 19 per cent for oil and 19 per cent for kernels; and for the Central Province, 16 per cent and 13 per cent respectively.[16] Eastern Nigerian palm fruit held a similar advantage over palm fruit from Sierra Leone, Dahomey and the Gold Coast.[17] This comparison helps to explain why eastern Nigeria rapidly became a centre of the palm oil export industry in the early nineteenth century, and also why farmers remained loyal to the industry in the twentieth century.

A continuing allegiance to the oil palm industry implied the perpetuation of a vent-for-surplus pattern of export production. Export production in the Ngwa region involved the exploitation of a tree which grew in symbiosis with food farming, and not in a plantation system demanding the clearance of virgin forest: therefore it involved no radical changes in existing patterns of land use. Oil processing absorbed labour in sporadic bursts which could be fitted in within existing patterns of labour use. This was also true of kernel production, which involved the cracking of palm nuts (the by-products of oil processing) between stones. Since each nut was cracked separately, the activity could be interrupted at will.[18]

For Ngwa women the most important economic change of the period 1884–1914 was that they began to earn cash in their own right from the export industry. Ngwa informants are unanimous in stressing the value of palm nuts as a woman's reward for helping in oil processing, and the usefulness of the kernel trade as a source of cash for women.[19] The fact that men did not take over the kernel industry as they had the oil industry once it became commercially important may reflect the fact that women's property rights in the nuts were firmly anchored in local conventions. Just as men could claim the right to yams which they had harvested and which had been grown on fields they had cleared, so they could claim the ownership of oil which they had helped to process, and which had been obtained from fruit they had harvested. Yet their ultimate ownership of land did not enable men to claim the ownership of cocoyams or maize grown by women on the fringes of yam fields or in compounds.[20] Similarly, their ultimate ownership of palm fruit did not enable men to claim ownership of the nuts left over from oil processing. Perhaps they could have attempted to make such claims if they had been willing to take over the work involved in cracking the nuts; but this was precisely the kind of monotonous, repetitive and long-drawn-out activity that was usually left to women.

We have no nineteenth-century evidence on the way in which Ngwa women used the cash which they now began to earn. However, in neighbouring Southern Igbo societies by the mid twentieth century there was a clear division of responsibility between the sexes: women provided most of the food for the whole household, while men provided palm wine and kola for entertaining strangers, and animals for sacrifices and public feasts.[21] Such a spending pattern could well have grown out of women's association with the private sphere and with the responsibilities of parenthood.

It is likely that women's share in the export income of Ngwa farmers continued to grow even during the trade depression of the 1890s. During the late 1890s the total export income earned from palm production and trade within the Niger Coast Protectorate remained stagnant at approximately £760,000 per annum. However, the share of palm kernels in this total rose from 38 per cent to 45 per cent between 1896–7 and 1899–1900, reflecting a rise in export volumes from 38,000 to 44,000 tons per annum. Meanwhile, the volume of palm oil exported had fluctuated around a level of 31,000 tons per annum.[22]

This period of stagnation in the oil palm industry was brought to a close by the revival of world demand for vegetable oils and oilseeds in the early twentieth century. In 1902, just as world trade was beginning to recover from the long slump, a new process was invented by which soft vegetable oils could be hardened and purified for use in top-quality soap and margarine manufacture. This was the process of hydrogenation, by which hydrogen was combined under pressure with more volatile elements; it revolutionised the position of palm oil and especially palm kernels within the world market. Palm kernel oil proved particularly amenable to the hydrogenation process and, along with coconut oil, became a staple ingredient in margarine.[23]

Liverpool palm oil prices rose from their 1890s level of under £25 per ton to over £26 per ton in 1906, and continued to fluctuate between £26 and £33 per ton from then until the outbreak of the First World War. Meanwhile, Liverpool palm kernel prices exceeded £14 per ton for the first time on record in 1906, and continued to rise relatively steadily to reach a pre-war peak of £24 10s.0d. per ton in 1913.[24] Thus, while palm oil prices regained the level they had reached before 1885, palm kernel prices reached unprecedented heights. In Nigeria, officials noted that Lagos palm kernel prices rose from an annual average of £9 15s.0d. in 1900 to one of £18 17s.8d. in 1913.[25]

In the Ngwa region the stimulating effect of rising world market demand upon palm production was reinforced by the early colonial programme of road and creek clearance. Between 1907 and 1912, traders from Bonny, Opobo, Ohambele and New Calabar began establishing settlements along the newly cleared Imo, Aba and Otamini Rivers: for the first time, Ngwa farmers no longer had to carry their palm produce overland to the Ndoki region.[26] However, the links between the Ngwa and Ndoki regions continued to be strong, for many settlers along the Imo River were Ndokis – known together with traders from Bonny and Opobo as the Ubanis. The Ubanis operated as independent middlemen, rather than as the agents of European firms.[27] Their settlements were initially exclusively male. In particular, the husbands and trading partners of Ndoki middlewomen seized the opportunity afforded by river clearance to break the women's stranglehold upon the palm produce bulking trade. Older men from Ohambele, for example, travelled up to Ihie, Akrika, Ife, Aba, Azumini, Owerrinta and Otamini, where they established waterside trading beaches and employed young relatives or local youths to man their canoes.[28]

In Ngwa-Ukwu, Ubani settlements were established at Ihie, Ahiaba-Ubi and Umuchima. Aba and Owerrinta also developed as markets serving the southern Ngwa region.[29] The canoe journey from all these entrepôts to the coast was slow. In 1916, officials estimated that the journey from Aba to Opobo took six to seven days; from Akwete to Owerrinta, five to ten days; and from Umuahia to Opobo, twenty days. Yet canoe transport had the great advantage of saving labour: seven men could move nearly 4 tons of oil at once, in a six-puncheon canoe.[30] Canoes were especially well suited to the transport of palm oil, which could float in its puncheons if the canoe overturned. Palm kernels could be ruined by soaking, so that kernel producers may have benefited less than oil producers from this phase of transport innovation.[31]

Between 1904 and 1913 it is likely that producer prices for both oil and kernels were rising rapidly in the Ngwa area. Transport costs were falling, prices at the coast were rising, and it is not likely that the Ubani middlemen were able to assume the role of ruthless exploiters, depriving hapless producers of their rights. As far as we know the Ubani were not united in a 'guild'. They probably competed with one another, and with the Ndoki middlewomen, for supplies of palm produce, needed to meet an ever-increasing demand. Moreover, the settled farmers of the Ngwa area were independent of their trading partners. The expansion of the oil palm industry did not require any large capital inputs, and so did not involve farmers in the invidious cycle of expansion, debt and dependency.[32] In their land transactions with the Ubani, the Ngwa are recorded as offering them kola tenancies (in exchange for token payments) rather than mortgages (in return for large loans) or freehold titles.[33] The Ubani were regarded with affection and respect by their trading partners, as by officials.[34] But they maintained a social distance between themselves and the neighbouring Ngwa farmers – although some of their customs in dress, dance and idiom are said to have entered into local culture.[35]

Contemporary written evidence also suggests that the real value of palm produce rose in the hinterland, as at the coast, during the first phase of the export boom. Palm produce was paid for in manillas, and the expansion of the trade (in conjunction with the import ban upon manillas) caused an appreciation in the sterling value and import-purchasing power of manillas.[36] At Opobo, one shilling could purchase twenty manillas in 1902, but only seven in 1913.[37] The import-purchasing power of the manilla also varied in accordance with short-term fluctuations in trading conditions. Contemporary officials observed that, while the manilla value of palm produce remained stable in the short term, a boom in the export trade was accompanied by a fall in the manilla price of imports. This produced the curious result that imports could be purchased more cheaply in the hinterland markets than at the ports – if the current coastal exchange rate for manillas was used in the calculation. This phenomenon was noticed at Uzuakoli in 1910, and at Azumini in 1912.[38] In 1912 the going exchange rate for manillas against sterling at Azumini was seven per shilling; but 'a bottle of beer worth 6d. at Opobo can be bought in the market at Azumini for three manillas'.[39] Thus, it seems that any windfall gains from sudden price rises in the palm produce trade were likely to accrue to producers and petty traders, as middlemen reduced the price of their imported wares in a desperate attempt to obtain manillas with which to purchase exports on the rising market. Such scrambles for manillas probably provided the driving force behind the slow appreciation of the manilla from 1902 to 1913.

Producers gained, not only from the rising real value of palm produce exports during 1902–13, but also from the widening range of attractive imported wares brought up-river by the Ubanis and also, possibly, overland by the Aros. Salt, snuff and stockfish were traded by the Ubanis at the waterside.[40] But, by 1911–16, a much wider range of imports was to be found in local markets: cotton cloth, lamps, kerosine oil, umbrellas, salt, gin, tobacco, soap, rice, biscuits, tinned foodstuffs, cycles, sewing machines, beer, watches, beads, iron pots, guns and powder, and patent medicines.[41] Some of these were long-established staples of the import trade – for example, cotton, gin and salt. Others were new – for example, stockfish, which appeared in the Protectorate's customs statistics for the first time in 1900, and accounted for just 2.13 per cent of the region's imports (by value) in 1913.[42] Others were beyond the range of most producers – for example, bicycles and sewing machines. But their very presence in Ngwa markets indicates that a substantial rise in prosperity had occurred during the early years of the export boom. It also indicates a growing integration of the export–import trade with the everyday commercial life of Ngwa farmers.[43] This may be linked with the increasing importance of women as purchasers of imports. Village markets were, after all, a mainly female preserve.[44]

The early colonial period also saw a dramatic rise in the quantity of palm oil and palm kernels sold to middlemen by Ngwa farmers. During 1903–13, while the volume of palm kernels exported annually from Southern Nigeria rose by 32 per cent, and of palm oil, by 53 per cent, the volume of both palm oil and kernels exported annually from Opobo alone rose by 70 per cent.[45] The volume of palm kernels exported from Opobo rose throughout 1903–9, and reached a pre-war peak of 18,645 tons per annum in 1911. The volume of palm oil exported from Opobo also rose during this period, but in two sudden leaps (in 1907 and 1913), rather than as a steady, cumulative process.[46]

Several phases of export expansion may be distinguished between 1904

50

and 1913. During the first phase (1904–7) Liverpool prices for both oil and kernels rose continuously. The volume of oil and kernels exported from Opobo also rose. By 1907, annual exports of oil from Opobo had reached a level 42 per cent above that of 1903: for kernels, the corresponding increase was 47 per cent.[47] Then, between 1907 and 1910 the Liverpool prices of both oil and kernels fluctuated just below the level of 1907. Meanwhile, exports of kernels (but not of oil) from Opobo continued to rise. In 1910 the Liverpool prices of oil and kernels rose again. This inaugurated a third phase (1910–13) during which oil prices fluctuated around a level of £30 per ton, as compared with their 1905–9 range of £25–£30 per ton. Liverpool prices for kernels fluctuated between £13 and £17 per ton between 1905 and 1909, rising to a level of £19 per ton in 1910 and rising above this to £23 per ton in 1913. In short, the Liverpool prices of kernels between 1910 and 1913 were higher in relation to previous levels than were the Liverpool prices of oil. This shift in the price ratio of kernels to oil was reflected in a rise in the volume of kernels exported from Opobo between 1909 and 1911; the volume of oil exported from Opobo continued to fluctuate around its previous level in those years. However, in 1912 the volume of kernels exported from Opobo fell. This fall continued in 1913 – a year which saw a sudden rise in the volume of oil exported from Opobo. The fall in the ratio of kernels to oil exported from Opobo was confirmed in the following year. This trend ran completely against the grain of contemporary price movements.

The pattern of the period 1911–13 was unusual. Between 1904 and 1911, export volumes from Opobo changed in general sympathy with contemporary price trends. The rise of kernel exports during a period of stagnating prices after 1907 can be seen as an extension of the general trend of vent-for-surplus expansion discerned in the 1890s export trends. The main points of interest about the export statistics of this period concern the peculiarities of the oil trade, and the limits of vent-for-surplus expansion in the kernel trade. The last point will be explored through an analysis of the puzzling trends which emerged after 1911.

From 1904 to 1911 the volume of oil exported annually from Opobo tended to fluctuate in a way which bears no apparent relation to price trends. The most likely explanation for these fluctuations is the annual variation in rainfall. Records kept in the Colony of Lagos in 1887–1903 (when produce prices were stagnant) demonstrate that oil exports rose and fell in each year in accordance with the level of the previous year's rainfall.[48] Rainfall variations presumably determined the oil content of the local palm fruit. This factor could help explain the suddenness of the rise in Opobo's oil exports in 1907, which followed on several years of rising prices. Another possible factor may have been the establishment of Ubani merchants at Aba following the clearance of the Aba River in 1904: we do not know exactly when they moved inland, and the trade at Aba may have taken several years to establish following the clearing of the river.

Throughout the period 1904–13 palm oil continued to dominate Opobo's export trade. In part, this reflects the high oil yield of eastern Nigerian palm fruit, as commented on earlier in this chapter. The unusual importance of palm oil in the trade of eastern Nigeria as a whole is shown by the following figures. In 1907, the ratio of oil to kernels in eastern Nigerian exports was 233 gallons to one ton.[49] The comparable ratio for Lagos (where import–export houses faced considerable competition from the railway trade in oil to the north)[50] was 67 to 1; for the Central Provinces of Nigeria, 123 to 1; for Sierra Leone, 18 to 1; and for the whole of West Africa, 117 to 1. Only the Ivory Coast, with a ratio of 473 to 1, exported more oil per ton of kernels than eastern Nigeria: and Opobo alone exported over three times as much oil per annum as did the Ivory Coast.[51]

Yet fruit yields alone cannot explain the overwhelming primacy of palm oil in Opobo's export trade. Within eastern Nigeria, more palm oil was exported from Opobo than from any other port. In 1903 the ratio of oil to kernels in Opobo's exports stood at 349 gallons to one ton. By 1906 the boom in the kernel trade had reduced the ratio to 312 to 1, and this ratio averaged 287 to 1 from 1907 to 1912. Then, in 1913, the sudden upsurge in the volume of palm oil exports brought it back to 353 to 1. Even at its lowest, between 1907 and 1912, this ratio was the highest in eastern Nigeria: the comparable ratio for Calabar was 180 to 1, and for Degema, 256 to 1.[52] Throughout the period 1906–29, Calabar remained the major centre for the palm kernel trade in eastern Nigeria.[53] Yet palm oil and palm kernels were joint products; and the hinterland of Calabar overlapped so closely with that of Opobo, in the districts of Abak, Ikot Ekpene and Bende, that it is hard to imagine that the composition of palm fruit in the two hinterlands would have been so radically different as to explain the difference in the ratio of oil to kernels in the exports from each port.[54] Two other arguments will be considered below: firstly, that the clearing of the Imo River benefited oil producers more than kernel producers; and secondly, that pre-existing regional differences between Ngwa and Ibibio farmers favoured the kernel industry in the Ibibio region. These regional differences helped to set the limits of vent-for-surplus production for both oil and kernels.

Contemporary officials held that transport problems were largely responsible for the low proportion of oil to kernels in Opobo's exports. They stressed the special problems involved in transporting kernels through narrow rivers and creeks by canoe. Whereas oil could be expected to float in its casks if the canoe capsized, kernels lost value and might be rejected by European buyers if they were soaked. Officials therefore anticipated a large increase in the volume of kernels produced in the Ngwa area following the construction of the Eastern Railway.[55]

This argument was supported by officials' direct observations of the produce trade in the Ndoki region between 1912 and 1916. Much of the palm produce destined for Opobo was brought overland or down the Aba and Imo Rivers to this region, where it was bulked and sent down the broader and safer reaches of the Imo River to Opobo. Officials observed that the only enthusiastic kernel producers in the region supplying the Ndoki markets were the Kwas (Anang Ibibios) of Abak District, who took their kernels overland to Azumini.[56] The Kwas had a special system for drying their kernels in all weathers, as Captain Burrough reported: 'The nuts are placed on a bamboo bed inside the house with a fire underneath.'[57] The Ngwa and Ohoho, who sent kernels down the Imo to Akwete, took less trouble in drying the nuts before cracking, and produced kernels of lower quality.[58]

Yet in the event the railway stimulated a greater increase in oil than in kernel production. The ratio of oil to kernels in the exports of Port Harcourt (the railway port) averaged 347 gallons to one ton between 1920–9 – by which time the ratio for Calabar had declined to 130 to 1; for Degema, to 210 to 1; and for Opobo, to 340 to 1.[59] The distance over which kernels had to be transported was probably a more important influence on the level of production than the means of transportation. Kernels, although as bulky as oil, had a much lower value per ton. Thus, transport costs would affect the relative producer prices of oil and kernels with increasing severity in regions further away from the coast. This point would become important once the limits of vent-for-surplus production were reached in each area – that is, once a choice had to be made between the use of labour in oil, kernel or food production.

It must be re-emphasised at this point that the limits on vent-for-surplus production were probably set in the Ngwa area by the supply of labour, rather than of land or palm trees. All the evidence cited earlier on this point was drawn from reports written towards the end of the period 1904–13. This, our earliest available evidence, indicates that land and palm trees were scarce enough to render their possession a source of economic power. However, they were not so scarce as to provoke a change from long-fallow to intensive cultivation, or from the harvesting of wild palms to the systematic cultivation of palms in plantations.[60]

Labour supplies posed less of a problem for Ngwa producers than for their counterparts in the sparsely populated Niger Delta.[61] However, even the Ngwa area was sparsely populated relative to the Kwa and neighbouring Ibibio regions, where population densities by 1927 were over 300 persons per square mile, as compared with the southern Ngwa average of just under 200 persons per square mile.[62] Some Kwas actually travelled as migrant labourers to the Ndoki region.[63] Their kernel-drying method, which may have been a twentieth-century innovation, could hardly be described as labour-saving compared with the Ngwa method of simply spreading the kernels out to dry in the sun. The Kwa method simply enabled women to spend more time cracking the dried kernels in the rainy season. In short, it can be taken as a sign of the relative abundance of labour in the Kwa region.

Ibibio farmers were at an advantage in the kernel trade not only because of their dense population (which in itself would not necessarily have affected the amount of labour available within each household) but also because the demands placed upon them in food production were eased by their involvement in the Cross River food trade. Future students of Ibibio economic history might well explore the question of why the Ibibio came to engage in this trade. Apart from the obvious motive of a gain from the principle of comparative advantage (ecological specialisation), Ibibio farmers may well have been forced to enter the trade as their population grew beyond the level which could be supported comfortably by long-fallow farming on the available land. They may also have used yam supplies from the upper Cross River to free them for palm production once the Atlantic trade began. Whatever their motives, the Ibibio were heavily engaged in a trade of yams and palm oil along the Cross River by the early twentieth century.[64] Yam imports may well have relieved local women of some of their time-consuming farming duties, and so freed them to produce more kernels for export, as well as more oil for sale to Afikpo farmers and European traders. In the long term, the Cross River trade probably diverted oil away from the Calabar market as well as allowing an expansion of kernel production, and so had a dual impact on the oil to kernel ratio in Calabar's exports. In the short term, the riverain trade may have facilitated the marked rise in Calabar's kernel exports which occurred between 1911 and 1913.[65]

At Opobo, as already mentioned, this phase of the 1904–13 boom saw a fall in kernel exports and a rise in oil exports, while kernel prices rose and export prices stagnated. The most likely explanation of this otherwise puzzling trend is that Ngwa and Ohoho producers, in particular, were unable to expand their production of both oil and kernels in response to the higher price levels of this period. A short-run solution to this dilemma was for men to insist on higher oil production, even though household income as a whole would have been maximised by higher kernel production. This solution, once adopted ensured that the level of income under male control was maximised. An alternative solution which would have achieved the same end was for men to enter the business of kernel production and lay claim to the proceeds. However, this solution would have posed a direct challenge to female property rights and would have upset the balance of reciprocity between the partners in oil processing. One further possibility was for men to take on more of the tasks involved in oil processing. This would have minimised the conflict between male and female interests which arose out of the strains placed on female labour resources within the status quo. Indeed, it will be shown in Chapter 8 that this option was taken up after 1914. It probably represented the most feasible long-term solution to the labour supply problem, given that it was combined with some labour-saving innovations in production methods. Such labour-saving innovations were apparently absent between 1904 and 1913.[66]

The fall in kernel exports from Opobo after 1911 thus signals a clash of economic interests between Ngwa men and women, grounded in an increasing scarcity of female labour. This clash was later resolved relatively' equitably. However, the initially biased solution indicates the continuing strength of the power exercised by senior men within households. During the early colonial period social conflicts and economic problems of this kind remained largely invisible to officials: they were glimpsed in fragments, and it is from these fragments that historians are obliged to reconstruct them. Officials noticed more about the oil palm industry than about the basic patterns of food production, social relations, ecology and local trade within rural eastern Nigeria. However, it has been shown that changes in the export sector cannot be explained without reference to the underlying ecological, demographic and commercial features of the domestic economy.

It has been assumed in this chapter that these basic features of village life remained unchanged between 1884 and 1914. However, towards the end of the period they began to come under strain from the increasing labour demands of the oil palm industry. Meanwhile, the colonial judicial system was taking shape and it was becoming apparent that colonial rule could not be resisted indefinitely. The new political order offered new opportunities to the different groups seeking power and wealth within village society; and the Ubanis entering the hinterland brought with them new possibilities of cultural and economic change. During the First World War and the decade which followed it, commerce and colonial rule at last began to affect the basic structures of Ngwa village life.

5

The end of the boom

In 1914 the prices paid for palm produce in Nigeria began a decline from which they never recovered. By 1920 the barter terms of trade for palm oil had slipped to 38 per cent of the 1913 level; and for palm kernels, to 30 per cent. Real export prices fluctuated below, but near these levels throughout the 1920s before falling sharply again in 1929–30 and 1933–4 to levels around 14 per cent of those of 1913 for both oil and kernels. The Second World War saw a further decline, to around 11 per cent of the 1913 level. Even during the boom which followed the Second World War, real price levels in Nigeria averaged only 28 per cent of the 1913 level for palm oil, and 22 per cent for palm kernels. After 1961 they began to fall sharply again.[1]

Colonial administrators gradually became aware that the First World War marked the end of a period in which rising returns to labour could be obtained within the oil palm industry without innovation in production methods. They did not begin to engage directly in commercial palm production and trade until the Second World War, a period which lies outside the scope of this chapter.[2] However, during and after the First World War they began reconsidering their policy towards the industry. It will be shown in this chapter that the seeds of later actions were sown in the policy debates and Agricultural Department experiments of this period. Two alternative strategies were developed, at least in theory; both of these were to be tried out in succession after 1939. Meanwhile, as will be shown in the four chapters which follow, different groups of Ngwa farmers were evolving their own alternative strategies for coming to terms with the end of the palm produce boom.

The end of the boom came most rapidly for palm kernels, which lost their German market on the outbreak of war in 1914. In 1913 77 per cent of the kernels exported from British West Africa had gone to Germany, while 83 per cent of the palm oil exported had gone to Britain.[3] Liverpool prices for palm kernels fell from around £23 to £17 per ton between January and October 1914.[4] Meanwhile, prices for palm oil were buoyed up when the munitions industry began to use large quantities of glycerine, a by-product

56

of oil processing. Liverpool prices for palm oil rose from around £29 a ton in 1914 to a peak of £41 in 1915.[5]

Liverpool traders and Nigerian government representatives campaigned vigorously to interest British manufacturers in the business of kernel-crushing, and by 1915 some firms in Hull had taken up the challenge.[6] Meanwhile, as imports to Britain of butter, margarine and other vegetable oils fell and demand for margarine and soap grew, the demand for palm kernel oil revived. British margarine production rose from 78,000 to 238,000 tons per annum between 1914 and 1918 – using palm kernels crushed in Britain. By 1917 Liverpool palm kernel prices had risen to £26 per ton, at which point a price ceiling was imposed by the British government.[7] A price ceiling of £48 per ton was also set for palm oil being sold in British ports; both ceilings were in force from 1 May 1917 to 1 April 1919.[8]

By 1916 it seemed to officials in Britain that the oil palm industry had passed the danger point. A committee which had been set up in 1915 to examine the British kernel-crushing industry concluded in June 1916 that the end of the war was likely to usher in a phase of intense competition between the various European crushing industries for limited supplies of palm kernels. The committee recommended the imposition of a differential export duty of £2 per ton on all British West African palm kernels shipped outside the Empire.[9] The proposal met with stiff opposition from unofficial interests, especially in the Gold Coast; but it was finally implemented in October 1919.[10] Meanwhile, officials at the British Ministry of Food were drawing up a scheme by which they would be able not only to control the destination of imperial palm produce, but also to cream off a share of the profits made in its trade. In 1917 Sir Charles Finlay proposed that the Ministry should fix palm produce prices in West Africa as well as in Britain, and that the British government should become a monopoly buyer of palm produce, using established merchants and shippers as its agents. West African governors combined to defeat the proposal on the grounds that it would associate their officials with wartime profiteers; but the scheme remains interesting as a forerunner of later Marketing Board proposals.[11]

While officials in Britain discussed the possible profits to be made from the oil palm industry, officials in Nigeria were realising that the industry had by no means weathered the storm. Shipping shortages curtailed the quantity of palm produce which could actually be shipped to Britain, no matter how high the metropolitan demand and prices. The years 1916–17 saw heavy British shipping losses. In June 1917 the British Ministry of Shipping requisitioned all available steamers and more than doubled the freight rates charged to commercial shippers; these had already risen from £1 10s.0d. to £2 8s.0d. per ton between July 1914 and June 1917.[12] Meanwhile, produce piled up at the Nigerian ports and merchants were able to obtain fresh stocks at very low prices.[13] As Liverpool prices for palm oil soared, Lagos prices remained below the levels of 1913–14 throughout 1917 and 1918; and

European traders began to break their defensive pooling agreement, which had been formed in 1897 by the African Association, the Niger Company and several smaller firms.[14]

While European traders in Nigeria made windfall profits, the colonial administration found itself struggling to maintain its revenues. The outbreak of war put an end to the import trade in Dutch and German spirits from which the government had derived 36 per cent of its revenue in 1913. After the war the temperance lobby succeeded in gaining a ban on all imports of cheap liquor into British West Africa, so that by 1921 the proportion of government revenue derived from liquor duties had fallen to 4 per cent.[15] Between 1914 and 1916, revenue shortfalls were met by withdrawals from government reserves; and the Eastern Railway attracted further external funds.[16] But in the long term it would clearly be necessary to search for fresh internal sources of revenue.

Governor Lugard, appointed in 1912, held strong views on revenue and favoured direct taxation wherever possible. He pressed in 1914 to be allowed to introduce direct taxation to Southern Nigeria, and was finally permitted to do so in south-western Nigeria in 1918. This move provoked the Egba rising, which required 2,600 soldiers to repress it and involved 1,000 civilian deaths.[17] Direct taxation continued to be advocated as the basis for local fiscal responsibility and indirect rule, but could not seriously be considered as a revenue-raising measure: indirect taxes still accounted for 92 per cent of government income in 1920.[18]

In the long term, the main effect of the wartime revenue crisis was to add urgency to the search for new forms of indirect taxation. The administration began to rely more heavily on railway revenues and on receipts from court fees and fines, from the tin mines and from Udi colliery.[19] To some extent these developments lifted the fiscal burden upon the oil palm industry and other agricultural export activities; also, there was a direct connection between transport services, for example, and government railway revenues. Yet customs revenue continued to be important: it accounted for 56 per cent of all government income in 1913, and 46 per cent in 1920, having risen from under £2 million to over £3 million per annum.[20]

Customs revenue was maintained after the collapse of the trade in spirits partly by increases in the rates of other import duties, and partly by the imposition of export duties for the first time in October 1916. Initially the export duties were levied at rates of £2 per ton for palm oil, £1 2s.6d. per ton for palm kernels, 10s. per ton for groundnuts and £2 6s.8d. per ton for cocoa; these rates were raised to £3 for palm oil, £2 for kernels and £1 for groundnuts in 1920.[21] The early rates represented a levy of about 10 per cent on Lagos prices for palm produce in 1917–18.[22] Meanwhile, the wartime tendency for import prices to rise was heightened by an increase in the rate of ad valorem duty on imported furniture, textiles, earthenware and hardware, from 10 per cent to 12.5 per cent in 1916. The specific duties on tobacco, salt, wines and spirits, matches, soap, kerosene, gunpowder and beads were raised by 25 per cent in 1919, and were raised again in August 1921.[23]

The net result of these changes for Nigerian palm producers was that the real prices of imported consumer goods rose further while the range of goods available continued to be restricted. The administration's response to the fiscal challenge posed by the war left producers in an even worse position than before. However, the administration itself was able to begin building up its reserves again in 1917–18.[24] In 1916–17 officials experienced a brief spate of concern about the possibility that farmers might start felling oil palms to obtain palm wine; but this concern was quickly removed by the discovery that farmers preferred the wine of the raffia or tumbo palm.[25] After this, official concern about the oil palm industry was focused not on the implications of the low real price levels of the present, but on the possible international competition of the future.

The first sign of the new concern over the industry's prospects came in the midst of the severe slump of 1921, which followed a heady post-war trading boom. In 1921 the barter terms of trade for cocoa, groundnuts and palm produce as against imports fell to a level even lower than those of the 1930s.[26] In the same year, a Committee on Trade and Taxation for British West Africa met in London and recommended the abolition of the differential export duty on palm kernels, which was duly achieved in 1922.[27]

The committee had heard in evidence that margarine manufacturers preferred coconut oil to palm kernel oil, because it gave a better flavour. Copra was also useful to crushers in that it gave a 64 per cent yield of coconut oil, as opposed to the 44 per cent oil yield of palm kernels, which left a large residue fit only for use as pig food.[28] Copra was exported mainly from Ceylon, Malaya, the British South Sea Islands, the Philippine Islands and the Dutch East Indies. Supplies from these regions had been curtailed by wartime shipping problems, falling from an annual average of 545,000 tons in 1909–13 to one of 430,000 tons in 1914–18.[29] However, during the inter-war period copra exports expanded again and, as the 1921 committee had feared, gained an increasing share of the world market.

By 1919–24 the annual average of world copra exports had risen again to 744,000 tons; and it continued to rise thereafter. In oil equivalent, world copra exports in 1909–13 had been 385,000 tons per annum or 260 per cent the volume of palm kernel exports. By 1929–33, although palm kernel exports had risen from 145,000 tons to 250,000 tons per annum in oil equivalent, copra exports had risen even more rapidly to 915,000 tons per annum in oil equivalent, or 366 per cent the volume of palm kernel exports.[30]

Surprisingly, given that there had been some official awareness of the threat from copra in 1921, the continued growth of copra exports in the 1920s and 1930s caused no further alarm in British official circles. In the relatively prosperous years of 1927–9, Lagos palm kernel prices were only 34 per cent of their average 1911–13 level in real terms, as compared with a corresponding figure of 39 per cent for palm oil. These differences could well be related to the fact that world supplies of coconut and kernel oil had risen by 90 per cent in this period, and of palm oil by the slightly lower figure of 80 per cent.[31] Palm oil also had a relatively strong position on the world market, since it was uniquely suitable for use as a flux in tin-plating and as an oil of intermediate 'hardness' in soap manufacture.[32] Nevertheless, it was upon palm oil that official fears now began to centre.

In South and South-East Asia, copra was produced both by smallholders and on plantations, with obvious differences in land and labour use but with few clear differences in processing methods, save for the occasional use of crushing mills to extract the oil at source on European estates.[33] The oil palm industry in South-East Asia was strikingly mechanised by comparison, and this may well be why it caught the eye of British colonial administrators concerned with Nigeria. Mechanisation, then as now, was considered the hallmark of development. Nigerian palm producers were commonly casti-gated for being 'crude and wasteful', not in their attitude towards oil palms but in their processing methods.[34]

While Western observers then saw the presence of mechanisation as the hallmark of progress, historians today might well argue that the absence of mechanisation has been the hallmark of patterns of agrarian change like that developed by the Ngwa. Centuries of patient experimentation to produce yams capable of growing on different soils and at different times of year; a long commercial experience involving the diversification of the cropping system, of local diets and of sources of income; generally low cash incomes – all combined to encourage the flexible use of resources rather than the pinning down of funds in machinery which could have only one fixed use.[35] It will be argued in the remainder of this chapter that British officials concerned with eastern Nigeria in the 1920s and 1930s were grappling with a choice between, on the one hand, designing new tools and developing new crop strains which would harmonise with the existing local pattern of innovation and, on the other hand, engineering a transformation of local patterns of resource ownership and use to permit experimentation with large-scale, mechanised forms of palm production.

Hancock, writing in 1942, thought that this choice was made once and for all in the 1910s, when William Lever applied for concessions over land, labour and palm trees in British West Africa, offering in exchange his technical expertise in the development of new mechanised industries. He failed to come to an agreement with the Colonial Office before 1912, and this failure was confirmed in 1915 by the decision of the British West African Lands Committee to support indigenous communal systems of land tenure.[36] Yet Lever's views on the technological superiority of mills and plantations had by no means been defeated. Officials were sure that they did not like Lever's demands for concessions, but they were divided in their views on the merits of machinery. Between 1915 and 1945 they searched for ways of raising productivity within the oil palm industry while retaining its smallholder basis. After 1945 the state itself began to assume some of the rights over land and palm fruit which Lever had demanded, and set up its own oil processing mills.[37]

Within the inter-war period the debate over technology was finely poised. On the face of it there was no reason why the oil palm industry should not prove amenable to mechanisation. Camels had been used in Roman North Africa to work olive oil presses; screw presses and mills had been used in the same industry in Roman North Italy.[38] However, Lever was not the only entrepreneur who had wished to try out machinery in British West Africa. Several others had tried without the aid of concessions before 1920, only to founder because of technical problems.[39] Meanwhile Lever's own mills, which had been established with strong land concessions in the Belgian Congo, made heavy losses during the same period.[40] By 1924, the orthodox Colonial Office view was that mechanical palm processing was costly and by no means certain to work in the region.[41]

This view was threatened by the emergence of a healthy oil palm plantation industry, using sophisticated machinery, in Malaya and Sumatra. The new machinery used centrifugal force rather than hydraulic pressure and was considerably cheaper to set up and more efficient in oil extraction than earlier designs.[42] Exports of palm oil from Malaya and Sumatra did not begin until 1923, and had reached an annual total of only 38,000 tons by 1929.[43] Yet no sooner had the exports begun than British firms requested the Colonial Office to reconsider its concessions policy.

This time it was the traders rather than Lever or other industrialists who clamoured for concessions.[44] The Colonial Office took their views sufficiently seriously to appoint a review committee and send two West African agricultural officials to South-East Asia. However, the review committee brought forth no new evidence, serving mainly as a vent for the traders' views; and the officials reported that the South-East Asian mills were not in themselves cost-cutting. Their prosperity was underpinned chiefly by cheap indentured labour and by the exceptionally high yields of oil palms grown in the local environment.[45]

A similar reassessment of views about the virtues of mechanisation and the future of the Nigerian industry was going on in Nigeria itself, led by the first Director of Agriculture, O. T. Faulkner, who was appointed in 1921. Two out of the four articles in the *First Annual Bulletin* of Faulkner's Department dealt with palm oil processing techniques. One drew attention to the high labour costs of soft oil production by existing 'native methods'.[46] The other, written by Faulkner, advocated the erection of central factories (mills) to meet the threat of competition from the East. In this article, Faulkner urged only that the administration should publish his figures on the profitability of mill production, and should employ a chemist to develop machinery for use in mills. However, in an unpublished memorandum written at this time, he went much further.[47]

Faulkner was greatly impressed by a mill which had been set up in about

1915 at Ibagwa, near Abak in Ikot-Ekpene Division; the mill was run by a firm called Nigerian Products Ltd.[48] Little is known about the origins of this firm, but by 1920 it had been absorbed into the powerful British-owned African and Eastern Trade Corporation.[49] The Ibagwa mill used centrifugal machinery, fuelled partly by palm kernel shells; but little more was known about its methods, for its owners were extremely secretive. Faulkner suggested that it be granted a monopoly concession forbidding the erection of a rival mill within 'a small area for a few years', in exchange for disclosing its secrets to the Agricultural Department.[50]

Faulkner's suggestion was rapidly dismissed by the Colonial Office, whose decision proved to have been wise, for two years later Nigerian Products Ltd exhibited their plant freely at the British Empire Exhibition.[51] Doubts about the efficiency of the mill had meanwhile been expressed by the local district officer, who observed that it produced oil of an F.F.A. content which was actually 'higher than that found in the Native Produce'.[52] This was not true of all mills: by the 1930s it had become clear that South-East Asian mills produced oil of an extremely high, standardised quality. But this high quality resulted from care in sterilising the fruit and from the high quality of fruit grown in the local environment, rather than from any intrinsic difference between West African and South-East Asian machinery. Indeed, some of the machinery used at Ibagwa and exhibited in 1924 was later adopted and used successfully by planters in Malaya.[53] Meanwhile, the Ibagwa mill was running into severe financial difficulties; in 1931 it closed down.[54]

Faulkner continued to lobby metropolitan officials on behalf of prospective mill-owners. In 1926 he won support from Thomson, the new Governor of Nigeria, and from the Colonial Office for a proposal to provide cash subsidies to the owners of mills like the one at Ibagwa.[55] However, the merchants themselves had little interest in this scheme, arguing that nothing short of plantation concessions or a government drive to improve smallholder fruit production could make the mills commercially viable.[56] In 1927 a Nigerian government committee of which Faulkner was a member recommended that European firms should be allowed to establish plantations in areas with few palms. Meanwhile, Agricultural Department officials were advised to establish experimental plantations in existing groves, allowing local people to harvest the fruit and use it as they saw fit.[57]

Gradually, merchants and officials were coming to terms with the fact that eastern Nigeria had lost its position as the greatest grove area in the world. It was still the greatest grove area in Africa, with the continent's best natural environment for oil palms.[58] However, following the first planting of West African palm seedlings, brought to Java in 1848 and to Singapore in 1875, a completely new strain of oil palm had evolved in response to the new soils and climate of South-East Asia. The Asian 'Deli' palm had high fruit and oil yields and was relatively short, so that it could be harvested by labourers using ladders. The fruitfulness of eastern Nigerian palms looked meagre in comparison.[59]

Not only had eastern Nigerian palm producers begun to experience the full impact of a secular downswing in prices; they had every reason to fear cheaper competition in the future. Officials, pushed by European traders into awareness of the threat, led the movement to regenerate the industry. Meanwhile, as will be argued in the following chapters, farmers began to act on their doubts about whether this was an industry worth regenerating. The result was that when officials began to follow the recommendations of the 1927 committee in establishing experimental plantations of 'improved' palms in existing groves, they met with considerable resistance. At Umuahia in 1927 they reported that 'the village communities as usual did not definitely refuse to enter into the scheme but kept asking for a few months more to consider the matter.'[60]

Officials persevered nevertheless, and the policy continued to be centrally important throughout the 1930s and 1940s. The 1927 committee's report had not ruled out the possibility of future mill-and-plantation development, but in the short term this was clearly not politically feasible. As Hancock re-emphasised in 1942, the best palm-growing areas were already densely populated. Given the poor economic performance both of mills and of plantations in other West African colonies during this period, the granting of land concessions to European entrepreneurs seemed neither profitable nor safe in the short term.[61] For the time being, the Nigerian government settled down to pursue their second option, that of developing new palm strains and providing technical assistance of a type which might prove attractive to smallholders.

An experimental palm breeding station had been established at Calabar in 1908, and seedlings from this station were supplied to farmers in the Ngwa and neighbouring regions from 1929 onwards.[62] By the end of 1929, twenty-seven small plots had been set out in Onitsha, Owerri and Calabar Provinces. Within these plots, local farmers worked under Agricultural Department supervision in thinning and tending the palms and in interplanting new palms among the mature specimens.[63] In 1935 a Cultivated Oil Palm Ordinance was passed, allowing farmers a rebate of their export duty on oil of high quality (less than 5 per cent F.F.A.) produced from the fruit grown on registered plots, of at least 15 acres in extent.[64] The number of farmers registered continued to grow steadily, from 704 cultivating 1,457 acres of improved palms in 1934, to 5,602 cultivating 10,551 acres in 1939. However, it is doubtful whether the ordinance encouraged this growth, as the average registered acreage per farmer remained only 2 rather than 15 acres.[65]

During the Second World War, planting continued but Agricultural Department officials became increasingly worried about a 'yellowing disease' which attacked palms cultivated even in small plantations. Eventually it was found that an application of wood ash would cure the disease, vindicating by implication the farmers who persisted in clearing and burning down the other secondary vegetation around wild palms, while clearing land for farming.[66] In later years this disease was found to be due to potassium deficiency and many other pests and diseases were discovered among plantation palms which were unknown to palms growing in groves, on farms or in compounds in eastern Nigeria.[67] Clearly it was not going to be easy to develop a local equivalent of the Sumatran plantations.

It also became clear during this period that it would be difficult to breed a local equivalent of the Deli palm. Indeed, from 1939 the Nigerian Agricultural Department abandoned their attempt to supply farmers with new seedlings bred from a Camerounian oil-rich strain, because 25 per cent of the seedlings supplied proved barren and the rest yielded a fruit with virtually no kernel. Palm producers were not willing to increase their oil yields at the cost of destroying the kernel export industry.[68] In 1939 a new Oil Palm Research Station was opened at Benin, but during the war it was run by only one botanist, and in the meantime Department-sponsored farmers continued to plant seedlings obtained from local thick-shelled, self-pollinated palms.[69]

This ill-fated policy of offering botanical advice to farmers was supplemented by a determined effort to develop small-scale presses for subsidised sale to Africans.[70] Officials began their systematic experiments with processing machinery only in the 1920s. Before then, they had largely been content to rely upon commercial firms to supply experimental machinery which they would try out with interest. C. A. Birtwistle, a former merchant who served as Commercial Intelligence Officer before the First World War, was especially intrigued by kernel-cracking machinery and staged a contest in 1913 between a Nigerian girl and a centrifugal contraption marketed by Miller Brothers, which had also been tested in the Gold Coast in 1903. The machine could produce 16lbs. of kernels per man-day, including time spent picking the kernels out of the splintered shell by hand; but the girl could produce 4lbs. of clean kernels in one hour.[71] Birtwistle learnt from this comparison; his own invention, which followed, was an iron dish and hammer for use in areas which lacked suitable stones for manual cracking.[72]

The officials of the 1920s were more ambitiously innovative, and had closer ties with the British scientific and engineering world. Initially, the leading figure was Mr A. C. Barnes, who arrived in Nigeria as Government Chemist in 1923 and joined the staff of Faulkner's Agricultural Department. Barnes' initial brief was to devise non-mechanical means of improving local palm processing methods, a task on which his colleagues had already made a start.[73] In 1924 Barnes began to take an interest in mechanical processing methods. He visited the Nigerian Products Ltd stand at the British Empire Exhibition and suggested a refinement of the firm's methods of cleaning the oil after extraction. On his return to Nigeria, he began experimenting with a cooker and press purchased from British manufacturers: fruit was steamed in the cooker, pounded as usual with pestle and mortar, and pounded to extract the oil.[74]

In 1925 the 'modified native' hand process of oil extraction and the cooker-press method were tested in the field at Loburo (Abeokuta Province). The 'modified native' process was a failure, but the cooker-press method was found to extract 60–65 per cent of the oil contained in the fruit pericarp, with a low F.F.A. content of 2.5–10 per cent. The cooker was praised as being labour-saving by the women who tried it out, but the press was said to be very hard work to use. Moreover, the press cost £25 even in England. The cooker was substantially cheaper at £15.[75]

Barnes now began work on a locally made version of the press, which used only a few imported parts and so was much cheaper than the version tested in 1925. The new version was worked by lever, rather than by imported screw. However, early tests revealed it to be less efficient in oil extraction, and work on the project had not progressed far before Barnes was transferred to Zanzibar in 1928.[76] Other officials continued his experiments; but the emphasis in Agricultural Department work thereafter shifted to the practical task of persuading farmers to use the screw presses.

They found this task only slightly easier than that of obtaining land for experimental plantations. The initial purchasers were men – perhaps significantly, not simply in terms of the official tendency to deal with men, but also in the fact that men often had more cash than women.[77] The men who bought presses may well have intended to hire them out or to employ others to work them, as is suggested by the social status of the first purchaser of a cooker-press, 'Chief Benstowe of Azumini'.[78] In 1928 three more farmers followed Chief Benstowe's example. By this time, the price of each press had fallen to £17 10s.0d., but this still left them beyond the reach of most people.[79]

Ironically, the onset of the renewed depression in 1929 seems to have been accompanied by a marked rise in local enthusiasm for presses, possibly related to the introduction of the more efficient Duchscher model – and a loan scheme for purchasers – in 1931.[80] By December 1932, 58 presses were in use in Southern Nigeria; four years later the total had risen to 390, of which 362 were in eastern Nigeria. By this time it was clear that most of the owners of presses were middlemen who had begun by buying in fruit, but now found it more profitable to hire out the machine or to allow farmers to come to their sheds and press fruit for a fixed charge. In Owerri Province, standard charges for pressing were 1s.6d. per 4-gallon tin in 1936, but were falling rapidly as more press owners began to offer their services. In early 1937 the charge was 7d. per tin.[81]

African interest in presses continued to grow and by December 1940 1,048 had been sold. At this point a new scheme of giving away presses began, funded by the United Africa Company which also supplied the presses. In 1943 57 of these were given away and there was a waiting list of 150 applicants for future supplies.[82] Major business interests were now beginning to join officials in trying to woo small-scale entrepreneurs into mechanisation, rather than implementing a large-scale policy over their heads.

It is difficult to tell what impact the new policy of Agricultural Department extension work had upon the Ngwa and neighbouring farmers before 1945, aside from offering fresh sources of profit to a few of the entrepreneurially minded people among them. The acreages of 'improved' palm groves and the numbers of presses in use were probably too small to have a profound effect on the structures of the oil palm industry throughout the region. Certainly the innovations initiated by officials during the 1930s and 1940s do not figure largely in the life-stories of the Ngwa farmers interviewed for this study.

Nevertheless, the official debates and perceptions of the First World War and the inter-war period are of great importance to an understanding of Ngwa economic history, because official sources offer a relatively clear view of the world market trends and events elsewhere in the tropical world, which provided the commercial framework within which the Ngwa were working. Official actions also affected this framework itself, in that customs duties and railway freight charges influenced the prices offered in Ngwa markets for palm produce and all imported items. In the long term officials saw themselves as working for economic growth and renewal; but in the short term they needed to raise revenue, and their actions here reinforced the end of the boom.

6

Cassava and Christianity

After the decade of prosperity which had ushered in the colonial period, the Ngwa found themselves confronted by a series of commercial crises. In this chapter and the three which follow, their reactions to these crises and to the long-term decline in palm produce prices will be explored. Initially, they attempted to improve their terms of trade for palm produce by boycotts and by produce adulteration. However, neither of these strategies proved viable even in the short term: in the long term the Ngwa needed to search for alternative sources of cash.

During the First World War, the Ngwa began to make two major changes in their way of life; they began to adopt cassava and Christianity. Both of these changes were slow to spread through Ngwa society, yet ultimately cassava was to prove an attractive alternative to palm produce as a source of cash, while the education which often accompanied Christian conversion offered an escape route from the rural community itself. Women and junior men were the first to seize these opportunities, which for them held the additional attraction of being outside the economic sphere controlled by senior men. This chapter will outline the causes of their early enthusiasm for cassava and Christianity, which lay both in the contemporary circumstances summarised above, and in the distinctive advantages offered by the new crop and the new religion within the existing Ngwa way of life. In later chapters the story will be followed through to show the way in which Ngwa men and women turned these advantages to practical use in meeting the challenges posed by export sector decline and changing national political structures.

The first reaction of the Ngwa to collapsing palm produce prices in 1914 was to organise a boycott of the export trade. They cut back their output of oil during the dry season of 1914–15.[1] Initially their neighbours followed suit, and palm oil exports fell not only from Opobo but also from Degema and Calabar. However, while oil exports from Opobo continued to fall in 1916, the trade at Calabar and Degema revived, thus undermining any effect which prolonged Ngwa resistance might have had on local prices.[2] The Ngwa were probably able to hold out longer than their neighbours

67

because of their relatively strong ethnic cohesion across a large area, and because of the economic strength derived from their self-sufficiency in staple foods. However, this strength was of little use given the failure of resistance elsewhere in eastern Nigeria.

While economic resistance was often short lived, armed anti-colonial risings posed a major problem to the British administration in Southern Nigeria throughout the First World War. Such uprisings were provoked not only by wartime price falls but also by official demands for carriers and soldiers.[3] The Ngwa region was again unusual in that it did not share in this final wave of resistance to colonial conquest, in which African middlemen and producers were able to make common cause against the Europeans. Instead, Ngwa producers and petty traders fought their own minor battle against fraudulent middlemen.

In September 1914 the Ubanis attempted to sell watered gin in Ama-Oji market. Local farmers promptly stormed the market, seized several of the offending bottles and chased the middlemen away. The Ubanis then denounced the farmers as rebels to the district officer at Umuahia. A patrol was sent to subdue the people of Ama-Oji, although its commander, Commissioner Walker, came to sympathise with them after hearing their story. His solution to the dispute was to punish the leaders of both sides.[4] In April 1915 a formal enquiry was held at which the people of Ama-Oji were more strongly criticised and fined £100 for 'taking the law into their own hands'; but official fears that the incident might presage a more overt challenge to the colonial order, for example a boycott of work on the Eastern Railway, were never justified.[5]

Falling levels of export production, market boycotts and revolts were essentially material reactions to material problems. Yet the most striking popular movement in which the Ngwa participated during the First World War was a spiritual one: a movement of mass conversion to Christianity, inspired by the teaching of the Prophet Garrick Braide. This movement was interpreted at the time by the colonial authorities as yet another form of anti-colonial protest, yet it is remembered by Ngwa informants not as a political uprising but as the time of 'the burning of idols'.[6] Clearly the movement needs to be seen in the contemporary context of political and economic upheaval, yet it was more than a simple reaction to material woes.

The Ngwa region lies within the 'triangle' of Bende/Okigwi, Owerri/Aba and Uyo divisions, which has been identified by Ifeka-Moller as the most extensively Christian region within Eastern Nigeria by the 1960s, and which was also the focus of Ekechi's study of missionary rivalries during the early colonial period.[7] Both Ifeka-Moller and Ekechi have emphasised material woes as a motive for conversion. Ifeka-Moller focused on the humiliation of conquest and on the disillusionment with cash crop production caused by falling prices, which in her view predisposed people to conversion as a means of gaining access to the sources of white power, especially education. Following Ekechi, she argued that mission rivalry led to redoubled efforts and inputs of resources within the 'triangle'. Ekechi emphasised a further aspect of white power, the practical ability of missionaries to protect individual converts from threats of imprisonment and from the arbitrary exactions of officials and chiefs.[8]

The timing of the Braide-inspired conversion movement in the Ngwa region undoubtedly bears out Ifeka-Moller's interpretation, but the details given below introduce some essential modifications to the materialist view. In particular, it should be emphasised that the missionaries operating in the northern Ngwa area during and after the Braide movement belonged to the African-run Niger Delta Pastorate, so that they could offer the Ngwa no power beyond that of their message and their skills. Yet the message itself carried distinctive attractions, especially in its offer of closer contact with a supreme being, whose existence was already admitted but who was perceived as a remote, inaccessible entity within traditional Igbo and Ibibio culture.[9] The message as expressed by Braide and his followers was particularly attractive in that it was highly accessible and, unlike mission Christianity, was oriented not only towards the salvation of the soul but also towards physical healing through faith. Braide's movement catered for the 'here-and-now' as well as for the hereafter.[10]

In its origins the Niger Delta Pastorate was a relatively radical body, whose members had seceded in 1892 from the Niger Mission of the Church Missionary Society, in protest at the worsening treatment of African clergy within it.[11] However, in its religious message it was conventionally Anglican. By 1914 it was a well-established Church with parishes throughout the coastal region of Owerri Province, and at Calabar and Ahoada. Its clergy were drawn mainly from western Nigeria and Sierra Leone, and maintained a strict policy by which converts were put through a rigorous course of instruction before baptism. No attempt was made to reach hinterland peoples like the Ngwa.[12] However, Delta converts including Garrick Braide were beginning to claim the right to exercise the ministry and to spread the Christian message beyond the coastal zone. Eventually it was to be Delta people, the Ubani, who brought Christianity to the Ngwa region, firstly within the context of Braide's charismatic movement and later as more orthodox ministers of the N.D.P.[13]

Garrick Braide was born of poor Kalabari parents in about 1882, and baptised in 1910. Following his confirmation by Bishop James Johnson of the N.D.P. in 1912, he became a lay preacher and quickly gained a local reputation for zeal and spiritual power. In 1915 he began his campaign of charismatic evangelisation and healing at Bonny, and rapidly acquired a large band of followers whom he commissioned to spread his message and share his healing powers.[14]

Braide and his followers viewed his healing ability as a demonstration of the superior power of the Christian God over indigenous deities; and they made the aid of this power readily accessible to all. They were silent on the issue of polygamy, and imposed no long courses of religious instruction on converts. Within Braide's movement the essence of conversion was the forswearing of all other gods and the burning of idols. After this dramatic act the convert was urged to give up alcohol and to observe the Sabbath with prayer and songs of praise.[15] Like his contemporary, the Prophet Harris who preached in the Gold Coast and the Ivory Coast, Braide made rapid mass conversion possible and offered tangible help with the problems of the age.[16] Ironically, he died of influenza in 1918, having been in prison since March 1916. However, his movement had an inspirational appeal which transcended the personality of its founder.

Braide's movement first touched the fringes of the Ngwa region in February 1916, when a wave of idol-burning and Church-building occurred in the Ndoki area. Enthusiastic young men began organising parties to destroy the shrines of their neighbours, at which point the district officer felt compelled to step in and restore order. By June 1916, however, the movement had gone so far that he reported 'there is not a member of Aba Native Court who does not call himself a Churchman, many . . . having turned within the last three months. The easy way in which the whole population has now thrown over "juju" is remarkable.'[17] Meanwhile the movement was carried northwards through the Ngwa area, both along the railway and along the older trade routes from Opobo to Bende.[18] Years later, H. G. Brewer of the Primitive Methodist Mission recalled that

> While knowing nothing of Braide, the towns of Bende caught the contagion. Space fails to tell of a historic Sunday morning when Mr. Dodds preached at Umuigu to 5,000 people, of the return to Ndoro from which town Mr. Christie had been squeezed out, of the triumphs from Uzuakoli to Umuahia down the west of the railway. There is a story of one wonderful week when a new church was opened every day, and two on the Sunday![19]

As Brewer hints, the main beneficiaries of the Braide movement were ultimately the established missions, the N.D.P. in the northern Ngwa area and the Methodists to the north. In 1921, by which time 9 per cent of the people in Owerri Province were estimated by officials to be Protestant Christians, only 22 per cent of these belonged to the Garrick Braide Church or to the related Christ Army and Niger Delta Native Churches. A further 3 per cent of the population belonged to the Roman Catholic Church, which had established a station at Aba following the opening of the Eastern Railway in 1916.[20] Braide's most important legacy may well have been the popularising of Christianity and the involvement of the Ubani in hinterland evangelisation, rather than the structure of his own secessionist Church.

The Ubani were important agents of change in the Ngwa region not only through their involvement with Braide and with the N.D.P., but also through their knowledge of suitable methods for processing cassava, a crop which was widely adopted in the decade after Braide's followers burnt the idols. Elsewhere in tropical Africa the spread of cassava was closely associated with the arrival of strangers: the Portuguese in coastal zones, European and African traders along the great rivers in the era of the slave trade, and emancipated slaves from Brazil and Sierra Leone in Yorubaland from the 1840s. Many varieties of cassava have a high prussic acid content, which makes the roots poisonous unless painstakingly processed by methods quite different to those in common use for yams, maize or other starchy staples. Hence the crop was unlikely to be widely adopted without the example of people willing to eat it, and the availability of direct demonstrations of processing methods within each hinterland area.[21]

In the Ngwa case, informants recall that they 'saw' cassava when it was grown by the Africans who followed the British inland. There is no mention of it in the early reports on the region's conquest used in Chapter 2, and it was not mentioned in a comprehensive list of crops being grown along the route of the Eastern Railway in 1917; but it was found throughout Aba and Bende Districts by 1928.[22] This evidence suggests a close link between the adoption of cassava and the establishment of Ubani trading settlements along the Imo River and the railway itself from 1907 onwards, coupled with the growing involvement of the Ubani in the lives of neighbouring village communities as pastors after 1916. Sierra Leonean pastors attached to the N.D.P. may also have been important in the southern Ngwa region, near the major railway and administrative centre of Aba, during the 1920s.[23]

D. C. Ohadike has provided an alternative explanation for the timing of cassava's adoption in the hinterland regions of eastern Nigeria, drawing upon evidence from the Lower Niger and linking the coming of cassava to the economic and political upheavals of the First World War. This argument echoes that of Ekechi and Ifeka-Moller about the adoption of Christianity, except that Ohadike links the adoption of cassava less to the traumas of conquest or to export sector fluctuations than to the manpower losses caused by wartime recruitment and disease, in particular by the influenza pandemic of 1918–19.[24] This world-wide disaster certainly had a dramatic effect throughout Southern Nigeria, not least among the Ibiono people of Ikot-Ekpene District, where it sparked off a widespread campaign of resistance to the authority of the court messengers and the police. The persecution of 'twin women' (the mothers of twins), which had been effectively discouraged by missionaries, began again. Wild rumours spread – that German shells had fallen on the tobacco stores and poisoned their stocks; that the white men were dying off; and that 'the Motors were breeding the sickness'. Government officers hastened to hold meetings to quell the rumours. The wave of panic quickly subsided, but the pandemic itself continued to rage. Within Southern Nigeria as a whole, officials estimated that 3 per cent of the entire population had died as a result.[25]

Ohadike argued that this death toll was highest among young men, exacerbating a labour shortage arising from years of resistance to colonial rule. His informants associated the adoption of cassava with the need to save labour while yet producing more food during a period of starvation. This argument has the merit of being based on local perceptions, and receives support from other case studies of the use of cassava in periods of

71

famine or social disruption elsewhere in tropical Africa.[26] Yet evidence from the Ngwa region and from western Nigeria suggests that Ohadike's argument is not universally applicable. As with the case of Christianity, it may well have been the attractions of the innovation within the context of established local practices, rather than the existence of a climate of despair, which prompted widespread adoption. In this case an increase in the accessibility of the new crop or religion, rather than a sudden disaster, may well have been the critical factor determining the timing of its adoption.

In the case of western Nigeria, cassava was cultivated in the nineteenth century mainly as a cash crop, which was sold in the form of *gari* (fine grains) to be eaten in prosperous urban centres like Lagos. A major reason for its popularity as a cash crop was its great adaptability, which enabled it to be fitted in with little disruption to a wide range of established cropping sequences.[27] Again, in the Ngwa and neighbouring regions cassava was initially welcomed because it could be harvested all year round, and so could be used to fill an existing hungry-season gap in the supply of yams, from May to September. It was usually planted during the same season, thus easing the pressure upon community labour resources during the months of bush clearance, water-carrying and yam-planting.[28]

Some support for Ohadike's emphasis on male labour-supply problems is provided by one Ngwa story of the coming of cassava. Mr A. A. Nwogu of Amiri holds that cassava was brought to his village by a widow, who accidentally discovered how to cook it and called it *j'akpu* (cf. *ji* meaning yam). Her neighbours wondered how such a woman, who might be expected to be poor, managed to eat so well. When they discovered her secret, they followed her example.[29] This story illustrates the importance of cassava as a crop which could be grown on the fringes of yam fields or on land entering into fallow, thus reducing the need for female farmers to depend on male labour in land clearance. However, while shortage of male labour was a problem for widows or elderly couples without sons, it was not a problem for Ngwa communities in general by 1918. Their situation was very different from that outlined by Ohadike for the Lower Niger region. Ngwa farmers had fought few battles against their new rulers during the early colonial period; instead, they had engaged in increased palm production and trade. As shown in Chapter 4, women bore the brunt of the strain placed by export production upon local labour supplies.

The adoption of cassava did little to relieve this strain, for it became a female crop. Although it was easier to plant, tend and harvest than the yam, women found they had to bear these tasks alone, for men scorned the new plant. Furthermore, women had to spend long hours preparing the roots for cooking. The method used initially was to peel and thinly slice the tuber, then leave it to soak in an earthenware pot for a week or so until it became soft. The slices would then be rinsed, drained, boiled and finally stirred to a pulp. This pulp, called *akpu*, could be eaten on its own or mixed with pounded yam. In all, the method is considerably more time-consuming than the usual method of cooking yams, which involves no very fine slicing, soaking or straining of the raw root.[30]

As the cultivation of cassava spread, women may even have found that they were taking on a greater share of the work involved in food production, as men delegated more of the responsibility for household food supplies to their wives. J. S. Harris noted that men were reserving part of their yam crop for storage and sale in the Ozuitem area in the 1930s, while women used cassava to augment the domestic food supply. When export prices were sufficiently high, Ozuitem men withdrew from food farming altogether to concentrate on palm oil processing. Similarly, Ottenberg observed in the 1950s that Afikpo men concentrated on long-distance trade, while women used cassava to feed their families. In the Mbembe region the balance of responsibility between men and women had tipped so far that women had difficulty obtaining male help with land clearance. Afikpo women also periodically resorted to hiring male labour and to buying the right to harvest crops of cassava planted by men.[31] These examples suggest that as the importance of cassava grew, strains on female labour supplies may have forced men into a greater role in export production, or indeed into a new participation in the production of cassava itself.

In the Ngwa area the importance of cassava grew slowly during the 1920s. Officials compiling tax assessments in 1927 noted that it was a minor crop, planted on yam farms during or after the yam season itself.[32] Nevertheless, a trade in *gari* was growing up with the nearby towns of Aba and Umuahia, and by the eve of the Second World War men were participating in this trade and in the hard labour of processing. In *gari* processing the hard raw root had to be grated, rather than sliced, then soaked. After the bitter juice had been strained off, the residue was fried to form a fine meal which could then be mixed with boiling water to form an ideal urban convenience food. Two Ngwa men who participated in the early stages of the *gari* trade recall helping in the preparatory grating stage of processing, in a way analogous to the participation of men at the pounding stage of the 'soft oil' method of palm processing.[33]

Before the Second World War the *gari* trade remained localised and small scale, and informants recall that the income from it remained firmly in the hands of women and junior men. Cassava did not enter into the category of produce controlled by the *ofo*-holders, the ultimate owners of land and palms. Introduced by outsiders and adopted by women, it remained within the category of crops grown by women in their own time, on land left over from yam farming. Its adoption reinforced the growth in female autonomy which had begun with the rise of the kernel export industry in the late nineteenth century. However cassava, being primarily a crop which women used for feeding the family, did not yet challenge the association between women's crops and supplementary foods for household consumption. Its full potential for transforming the balance of income and labour allocation within the rural economy was realised only after the Second World War.[34]

During the 1920s and 1930s, Christian conversion had a far more obvious impact than cassava upon Ngwa social and economic structures. As will be shown below, the missionaries did not challenge the identification of Ngwa women with the domestic sphere, but their message and the education which they brought had a thoroughly unsettling effect upon the relationship between senior and junior men. This effect was anxiously anticipated by colonial officials, who viewed with misgivings the steady increase in the number of Christian converts which occurred in eastern Nigeria after 1916. Some held that the new churches and schools were simply 'young men's clubs', the potential hotbeds of sedition. Others emphasised that the adoption of Christianity by young men threatened the income of *Okonko* and *Ekpe* secret society members, which was derived largely from their heavy entrance fees.[35]

The disturbing influence of Christianity was reinforced by the impact of colonial conquest and the artificiality of many warrant chiefs' authority at the local level. By 1920 officials were becoming alarmed by 'the almost complete absence of authority of the chiefs over the people they are supposed to control' and by 'the lack of respect or obedience the youths have now for the Chiefs and Elders, compared with what they had only three years ago'. Village elders were losing authority and being reduced to ignominious poverty because 'their old methods of enforcing their orders have been forbidden, their Courts in which fines were collected have been stopped'. This decline was in turn contributing to the difficulties which warrant chiefs were experiencing in the exercise of their new authority.[36]

In 1921 the tensions between senior and junior men were brought to a head by a severe slump in the palm oil trade. In November 1920 oil prices at Opobo began to fall, and by December they had sunk to a quarter of the previous level. Kernel prices also fell, but less sharply, to about two-thirds of their former level. By February 1921 oil prices had sunk so low that they equalled kernel prices – an unprecedented event. When this happened, some middlemen abandoned the oil trade altogether. Meanwhile, import prices remained high, and producers began to withdraw from the export market.[37] The slump was brief: its worst phase was over by March 1921. However, while it lasted it had an even more dramatic impact on producer incomes than the slump of 1929–30. Many farmers were driven to unearth and spend their cherished hoards of silver.[38] Meanwhile, affrays occurred throughout Owerri, Aba and Bende Divisions, as renegade *Okonko* members, now turned Christian, mocked the society and revealed its secrets and as branches of the *Okonko* society held defiant masquerades and attempted to punish any non-members who came to witness them. Less violent signs of rivalry also appeared between Ubani pastors and warrant chiefs. Contemporary officials, alarmed and bewildered by the bitterness of the strife, took the view that the leaders of both sides were endangering the peace of the region.[39]

Ultimately these conflicts proved to be short lived, subsiding of their own accord in mid 1921 and only reviving briefly in 1933 and 1950.[40] In the absence of open conflicts the social changes brought about by Christianity also tend to disappear from the official record; yet they continued to be important within village life, as oral information and the histories of specific missions operating in and near the Ngwa region indicate. By 1927, representatives of the Roman Catholic, N.D.P., Qua Iboe, Seventh Day Adventist, Primitive Methodist and African Churches were present in or near Aba District; the impact of the Anglican (including N.D.P.) and Catholic missionaries has been particularly well studied by historians, while Methodist records have been consulted for this study.[41] Information drawn from these sources confirms the view held by officials in 1920–1 that Christianity was most revolutionary in its impact on the lives and ambitions of junior men. Women were affected by changes in the customs surrounding puberty and childbirth, but had little access to the schooling which was of central importance to men in changing their way of life.

The main change which the Ngwa women interviewed for this study associated with the coming of Christianity was the ending of *mgbede*, a period of seclusion which marked a girl's entry into puberty and her preparation for marriage. During this time the girl would do no work of any kind, but would be well fed, anointed with oil and camwood, and possibly tattooed with elaborate designs in blue dye. Finally she would emerge to pay a ceremonial visit to the market, suitably adorned with body paint and, for example, iron leg rings. Known to outsiders as 'fattening', this custom was widespread within Igbo and Ibibio society, although not all families could afford to fulfil it.[42] With the arrival of the missionaries, even the wealthier families began to abandon *mgbede* in a move towards 'singlet-mindedness', with the Christian emphasis on decorum reinforcing the value of costly wrappers as a form of display. For example, Mrs Selina Danne Nwosu recalls that in the 1920s a young girl would acquire her first wrapper on puberty, with older married women wearing up to four wrappers as a sign of wealth. While the importance of puberty continued to be publicly recognised, the form of recognition had changed.[43]

A similar change occurred in the case of customs surrounding childbirth. The high value placed by the Igbo upon fertility was indicated by the fact that a wife did not acquire her own kitchen until the birth of her first child. At this time her own mother would present her both with a set of cooking utensils and with the symbol of her *chi* (personal god) which would then be installed formally in her husband's compound. Today the secular part of this ceremony is still widely observed – sometimes in conjunction with a church service of thanksgiving for the birth of the child.[44]

While some aspects of women's lives were affected in this way by their contact with Christianity, other aspects remained virtually untouched. For example, in the sphere of healing, *dibias* (diviners) continued to be important throughout the Igbo area during the 1930s, and continue to work alongside herbalists, bonesetters and Western-trained doctors in the Ngwa area today. Furthermore, missionaries had great difficulty in persuading local men to accept their ideals of monogamous marriage or even to participate in church weddings, which continue to be perceived as a sign of great wealth, sometimes to be undertaken as the final seal upon a marriage after the birth of one or more children.[45] Women continued to be involved in polygamous marriages, and had little access to the mission schools which prepared a few girls for companionate relationships with evangelist husbands. White women missionaries did establish classes for prospective mission wives at Ebu Owerri and at Bende during the 1920s, providing instruction in sewing, drawing, cleanliness and Bible-study.[46] However, the numerous schools established during the 1920s in the Ngwa area appear to have catered solely for boys, and I met very few Ngwa women over the age of thirty who had attended school, as compared with the many men over the age of fifty who had done so. In Harris's budget studies of the neighbouring Ozuitem area in the late 1930s, school fees appear as a routine item of expenditure – but only boys are recorded as attending school.[47]

For those Ngwa boys and men who were able to attend school, Christianity was to bring not only a profound change of spiritual outlook and a modification of customs, but also a certain emancipation from social obligations imposed by their seniors, and ultimately the opportunity of working away from the land. The importance of education and growing off-farm employment, as the main secular consequences of conversion in this region from the 1920s, stands in direct contrast to the experience of those parts of West Africa where Christianity had taken root during the nineteenth century and had been associated with the search for new 'legitimate' agricultural exports to provide alternative sources of income to the slave trade. In western Nigeria during the early twentieth century Christianity had again been associated with the spread of cocoa, which was used by several churches as a means of achieving economic independence.[48]

A major reason for this contrast is that south-eastern Nigeria in the 1920s offered little scope for the achievement of independence through new kinds of agricultural work. As has been shown in Chapter 4, diversification into cocoa was not a viable option in south-eastern Nigeria for reasons of ecology and land scarcity; while the oil palm industry itself lay firmly within the control of *ofo*-holders and *Okonko* members. Furthermore, the industry's entry into a phase of falling real prices meant that only limited profits could be gained from any battles over the income generated within it. After the 1921 clashes between Christians and *Okonko* members, no further challenge to the authority of senior men was made. It will be shown in Chapter 7 that senior men were able to use the Native Courts during the 1920s to reinforce their control over the labour and natural resources used in palm and food production. These underlying economic and political realities meant that education became an essential means of economic as well as intellectual emancipation for junior Ngwa men. In Chapter 8 a variety of life-stories will be given to illustrate the wide range of uses to which a mission-school education could be put by ambitious young men in the early colonial period.

While junior men began to seek independence outside the village economy with the aid of Ubani trading contacts and Christian education, Ngwa women were beginning to use cassava to meet existing responsibilities within the domestic economy. As a result of this and of the increased palm production by which households attempted to maintain their cash incomes, women found that their responsibilities and labour burdens were becoming ever heavier. In Chapter 9 their responses to these pressures and to continued trading fluctuations within the oil palm industry will be explored. Ultimately, however, the regional trade in *gari* which began during the 1920s and 1930s was to offer Ngwa women brighter prospects of an independent income, and relief from the problems of the faltering export sector. By the 1960s, as will be shown in Chapter 10, the full emancipating effects of both cassava and Christianity were being felt.

7

Authority, justice and property rights

Ngwa palm producers found themselves in an awkward situation when the terms of trade turned against them. The ecological considerations which had earlier tied them to palm produce, rather than cocoa or rubber, remained relevant. Furthermore, during the inter-war period it became increasingly evident that newer export industries like cocoa were almost as vulnerable as the oil palm industry to declining terms of trade. Nigerian import prices soared well above U.K. wholesale price levels during the post-war trading boom of 1918–19. In subsequent years, as U.K. wholesale prices and Lagos export prices collapsed, Nigerian import prices declined far more gently. Even in the depths of the 1930s depression, when U.K. wholesale prices were at 1913–14 levels, Nigerian import prices were 50 per cent above these levels. This phenomenon, combined with a secular decline in nominal export prices, ensured that the barter terms of trade fell as severely for cocoa as for palm produce between 1910 and 1940.[1] Within Nigeria, only groundnut prices remained near their pre-war level throughout this period: but groundnut cultivation was hardly a viable option for Ngwa forest farmers.

Faced with these commercial realities, senior Ngwa men showed little inclination to switch their land, capital and labour resources into fresh uses. Instead, they concentrated on issues of ownership and power, and began to re-establish their claims to land and palms within the new colonial judicial system. In this chapter we will follow their fortunes during the 1920s and 1930s. It will be argued that the *ofo*-holders continued to use pre-colonial institutions and informal means to assert their ownership over land and, especially, palm trees; but the colonial courts became important arenas within which men began to define the means by which cash could be used to gain rights over land and people. Neither colonial officials nor *ofo*-holders had a decisive influence over the workings of the courts: they formed a new kind of institution, within which wealth, literacy and patronage were the keys to power. In the closing sections of this chapter, the family history of one of the most powerful men within the court system, a warrant chief, will be outlined. This case shows that such power could be transitory, and illustrates the general tendency of senior and wealthy men to use their wealth in acquiring more clients, wives and property rights – all of which could easily be dispersed upon their death. This pattern of investment will be contrasted with the colonial ideal of investment in cost-cutting innovations to revive an export industry under threat.

Colonial officials had relatively little influence over the changes in property rights which occurred in the Ngwa area during the 1920s. In part, their hands were tied by the decision of the West African Lands Committee in 1915 to maintain indigenous land laws.[2] After 1915, the only way in which the colonial administration effectively interfered with eastern Nigerian land laws was by demanding land for its own purposes – for railway construction, botanical experiments and urban expansion. In this sphere, there was no clearly defined colonial land law, although Southern Nigeria had originally been a Protectorate, whose rulers had a right to be consulted over land concessions of any kind.[3]

The desire to respect local rights was evident in the instructions which the secretary for the Southern Provinces issued to district officers during the construction of the Eastern Railway in 1914. They were obliged to obtain the consent of local chiefs to all land acquisitions; the resulting negotiations proving extremely complex and lengthy.[4]

Officials were less careful of local rights after this experience. During and after the First World War, they became especially eager to acquire land in eastern Nigeria for the establishment of botanical stations and forest reserves. Here, they were able to make use of the British Land Committee's edict that governments needed special legal powers to protect endangered regions from deforestation.[5] In 1917, Lugard was able to pass a Forestry Ordinance, first prepared in 1915, which empowered him to impose restrictions on the use of endangered land without the consent of its owners.[6]

Despite Lugard's high ambitions, he and his successors met with sustained opposition to this attack on indigenous land rights. Even before the ordinance had become law, it had been vigorously attacked by the women of Calabar. They claimed in a petition in 1916 that the proposed regulations would 'oppose the building of our houses in our native ways . . . verge upon the extinction of the cultivation of our land . . . pave way for the starvation of our Country . . . retard the Education of our children . . . ' and 'deprive us of our right in our native land'.[7] Once the ordinance had been passed, sustained opposition by communities all over eastern Nigeria deterred forestry officers from making extensive use of it.[8] Between 1924 and 1927 villagers near Umuahia failed in a campaign of resistance to the establishment of an Agricultural Station, but successfully obstructed official plans to obtain use rights over oil palms for experimental purposes.[9] Officials feared to invoke the compulsory powers available to them under the 1917 ordinance, and instead spent four years negotiating to obtain land for the Imo River Forest Reserve (1925–9).[10]

The limitations of colonial control at the local level were reflected again in the character of the local colonial courts – the Native Courts. In the years immediately following the conquest of eastern Nigeria, district commissioners presided over these courts (at least in theory) and hoped to persuade local people to settle all their disputes there. They devoted considerable effort to suppressing rival judicial institutions, especially the Arochukwu 'Long Juju' and other oracles.[11] District and (in 1914) Provincial Courts were set up to handle major and controversial cases.[12] Yet many regions were remote from the early courts. The northern and eastern Ngwa had no local Native Courts until the establishment of courts at Ayaba (Ahiaba-Ubi) and Umuaro in 1923.[13] In such areas, many pre-colonial legal institutions and practices may well have survived without official recognition until well into the 1920s. Even after the establishment of local Native Courts, many people may well have chosen to settle their disputes elsewhere. Meanwhile, within the Native Courts the local warrant chiefs operated without even formal supervision by district officers after 1914.[14] Appeals could be made to the District and Provincial Courts in hotly contested cases, but even here the district officer tried to reach judgments which would accord with 'Native Law and Custom' – as defined by the petitioners and the warrant chiefs. After the Women's War of 1929, officials began to make a systematic study of the legal traditions of each community, with the aim of ensuring that these were reflected rather than transformed by the verdicts reached in the courts.[15] However, before 1929, the courts functioned largely as an arena within which the wealthy, the literate and those with official connections could settle their disputes more or less as they chose.

These general points will be illustrated below through a discussion of Ngwa court cases from the late 1920s and early 1930s involving land, debts and dowries. It will be argued that the courts helped to channel wealth into the hands of the powerful, but that they probably handled only a small proportion of all the internal disputes which arose in the Ngwa area at the time. Furthermore, it will be argued that court judgments were most significant in underpinning a relatively new category of property rights – those involved in cash transactions – rather than in transforming the basic local structure of kin-based property relations in land, palm trees and people.

The land disputes handled in the courts may be divided into two categories – border disputes between villages and disputes about inheritance or cash transactions between individuals. Border disputes were dealt with in the District and Provincial Courts. The settlements reached here were rarely accepted without question. Cases were often appealed, and final settlements could take years to reach.[16] The people who chose to claim land from neighbouring villages through the courts were often warrant chiefs – a point which casts some doubt on the impartiality of the system.[17] On the Ngwa–Ibibio border, farmers continued to settle disputes in their own way: 'affrays' occurred regularly here throughout the 1920s.[18] The absence of affrays between Ngwa villages may reflect the existence of unofficial methods of conciliation and adjudication of land disputes within the 'clan'. It may also reflect the relatively low population density of the Ngwa region.[19]

Land disputes between individual members of one village or village-group were dealt with in the Native Courts. The court records were kept in English, and the strong emphasis which district officers placed on this written record placed an additional hurdle in the way of those who wished to appeal against the verdict of the chiefs. For example, in 1933 an illiterate farmer, Enweremadu Owunna of Ahiaba-Okpuala, brought a case at Ahiaba Native Court against a 'stranger', Ihedacho of Ihie-Oji, who (according to Enweremadu) had obtained some land on pledge from his grandfather and now refused to let him redeem it. His case was initially allowed, but was dismissed on appeal on the grounds that Enweremadu could not prove his grandfather's ownership of the land. In September 1935, Enweremadu hired a letter-writer and petitioned the district officer, only to have his case shelved indefinitely because he could not produce a copy of the original proceedings in the case.[20] This case illustrates both the tangled logic of land disputes – Ihedacho had produced a witness from Ahiaba who swore that he (the witness) had originally owned the land, and had made a present of it to Ihedacho – and also the crucial role of written records and depositions in all dealings with district officers.

How far did the biased operation of the court system affect the balance of economic power at village level? Possibly only marginally; for remarkably few land cases seem to have been brought before Ahiaba Native Court, for example. Out of a total of 548 summonses issued by this court in civil cases between September 1931 and December 1932, only 33 related to the ownership of land or palms.[21] These cases tended to involve pledged land, rather than questions of birthright.[22] This pattern of litigation reflects, firstly, the fact that land was still relatively abundant in the Ngwa area. In 1929, the fallow period was four to six years, and land sales were unheard of.[23] Transactions in land of a kind which gave rise to court cases were highly visible, but probably touched only a minute fraction of the land under cultivation in the Ngwa area. In the second place, the pattern of visible litigation indicates the limitations of colonial courts as an arena for the settlement of disputes. Disputes over use rights in communally owned land (not involving pledging or members of other villages) do not appear in the Native Court records. These, and other internal village disputes, may well have been settled outside the courts – by village elders, rather than by officially appointed warrant chiefs. Green witnessed the settling of a case of false accusation, and another of theft, by open village meetings in Umueke-Agbaja in the late 1930s.[24] At the same time, she found that customary law regarding use rights in oil palms and the regulation of grazing on farm land was being modified through a continuous process of public debate, conducted outside the courts.[25]

In the Ngwa region, such unofficial law-making appears in the official records in the 1930s, when renewed enquiries into the ownership of oil palms revealed a number of recent changes and disputed claims. The *ofo*-holders were continuing the process, begun in the nineteenth century, of laying claim to palms growing both in the bush and on farmland. They were using their village councils, gatherings which had no recognition from the colonial administration, to decide collectively the dates on which 'village' palms could be harvested, but other village members were appealing to the colonial administration to contest this right.[26] Meanwhile, compound heads were making a fresh claim to all the palms growing on abandoned family compound land, under the rule of '*Nkwo Okpulo*'. Originally, this rule had applied only to palms growing on the compound of the original founder of a village section. Under the new rule, an *ofo*-holder could lay claim to all the palm groves near his compound, and treat the fruit harvested in them as his personal property.[27]

J. G. C. Allen, the district officer who made detailed investigations into many aspects of Ngwa society in the 1930s, supported the local faction which was seeking to restrict the rights of the *ofo*-holders.[28] However, his opinions had little effect on the course of events. Several Ngwa informants recalled in 1980–1 that palms had been strictly controlled by compound and village heads in the 1930s; and by the 1960s, the system of ownership by compound heads had become the norm within the region.[29] *Ofo*-holders had fought a successful battle to consolidate their hereditary property rights.

It is interesting that this battle was fought outside the colonial courts, which elsewhere in Africa have been seen as a major arena for the making of customary law, and for struggles between senior men, women and junior men.[30] Perhaps the key reason why Ngwa land law-making continued to be carried on outside the courts was the relative stability and homogeneity of the Ngwa lineage system. In place of the shifting balance between matrilineality and patrilineality which Chanock sees as being characteristic of colonial Malawi and Zambia, the Ngwa retained a firmly patrilineal system.[31] Thus there was little scope for the courts to act as a forum for disputes over the rules of the lineage game. Instead, they acted as a forum for disputes involving cash. Of course, the balance between rights of purchase and lineage rights of access to land and labour resources could ultimately have become as controversial, and so as rich a source of litigation, as the balance between matrilineality and patrilineality in Chanock's example. However, during the 1920s and 1930s in the Ngwa region cash remained firmly subordinate to seniority as a source of economic and social power.

This explanation of the marginality of court cases within Ngwa economic life stands in direct contrast to the standard argument of Nigerian critics of the colonial legal system, who allege that it was quite simply ineffectual. In their view, central problems like theft and adultery could not be coped with following the abolition of domestic slavery. Imprisonment had little deterrent value compared with the sanction of enslavement. Furthermore, the principle of individual responsibility weakened the effectiveness of campaigns against debt defaulters, whose families could no longer be penalised too.[32]

While this argument has been made powerfully for the case of criminal law, it is more difficult to apply it in the area of civil law, where pre-colonial Ngwa sanctions had usually fallen well short of enslavement.[33] Yet it was civil rather than criminal law which was most critical in regulating the everyday conduct of economic life and the underlying distribution of power and wealth within Ngwa society. The court records here indicate, not that the colonial legal system was seen as completely ineffectual, but that it was used selectively. Substantial numbers of debt cases, in particular, were brought before the Ahiaba Native Court. Among the 548 civil summonses issued by this court in 1931–2, 314 referred to debt cases between individuals and a further 72 to the affairs of contribution clubs. Finally, 62 cases involved dowry payments or refunds due.[34]

One reason for the high proportion of debt cases in this sample may well be the contemporary crisis in the import–export trade, which will be discussed further in Chapters 9 and 10. However, an examination of the cases themselves reveals that they fitted a pattern of trade disputes which had long been common in the higher courts, for which we have earlier records. These cases often involved Ubanis or European firms, and revolved around the workings of the Trust System, by which cash and imported goods were advanced to middlemen on the understanding that a given quantity of oil would be returned.[35] Similarly, most of the cases heard at Ahiaba Native Court involved people from different villages, and the detailed accounts of specific cases often mention advances of tobacco or expected repayments in tins of palm oil.[36] One major reason why the colonial court system was relatively well equipped to tackle such trade-related debt cases was that these cases straddled the boundaries of lineage-centred judicial systems.

Trade-related debt cases also suited the operating methods of the colonial courts themselves, in that the plaintiffs were often able to produce a written agreement to back their claims.[37] The court often had great difficulty in deciding cases relating to verbal contracts, for example over transactions in yams or in the long-term exchange of cash for labour services (pawning). Pawning raised further complications, as it was a grey area of colonial law: recognised but not approved of.[38] In general, officials disliked the idea of colonial courts getting involved in these and other cases in which the evidence consisted solely of verbal assertions by the interested parties and their families.[39] In one such case, the court had to be adjourned while the parties prepared to 'swear juju'.[40]

83

A few verbal transactions nevertheless continued to enter the courts, especially in the form of contribution club and dowry disputes. Through the regulation of these disputes, the courts may have played an important role in reinforcing the position of wealthy men. For example, certain clear patterns of judgment can be discerned in the records for Ahiaba Native Court in the early 1930s. In twenty-eight of the thirty-two contribution club cases in which a verdict was reached in 1932, judgment was given for the plaintiff (usually the head of the club).[41] Again, judges seem to have adopted a severe attitude towards dowry defaulters and debtors. Claims for a refund of dowry in cases where a wife had left her husband were generally viewed with sympathy by the courts, and a man could sue a wife's lover for 'unlawful detention'.[42] The official policy, as spelt out by C. J. Pleass, the D.O., Aba, in 1935 was to 'deter women from lightly leaving their husbands and going to live with other men'.[43] In one recorded case, a dowry refund claim was not fully met; but this case seems only to prove the general rule that men (and especially traders and chiefs) gained most from the legal opportunities offered by the new courts. In 1932, Ihediacho Njoku Adighku, of Abayi, petitioned the district officer, Aba, against his local chief, Ekwekwuo, who had adjudicated the petitioner's claim to a dowry refund on a wife from Ekwekwuo's own family. Ihediacho alleged that Ekwekwuo had not only demanded and accepted a bribe, but had also delivered a final judgment in favour of his own family.[44] This allegation illustrates the popular view that chiefs could take advantage of the system; and the case itself illustrates a key point about dowry disputes in colonial courts.

Court cases about dowry refunds usually involved claims made against the families of runaway wives, and not against the women themselves. This may have involved some modification of pre-colonial law, in that the women could no longer be sold to provide funds for this purpose.[45] However, it did not involve as profound a modification as has sometimes been alleged, both by colonial officials and by their critics. These critics focus on the provision made under colonial law for a discontented wife to bypass the usual procedure for divorce – by which she had to persuade her family or new husband to repay the original dowry – and, instead, repay the dowry herself, through the courts.[46] Observers assumed that many women would take advantage of the new law, at a high cost to the 'morals' of women in general.[47] However, the Ahiaba Native Court records cited above contain no evidence of divorce applications being made by young women who were prepared to refund their own dowries. In two cases, women were asked to pay money through the courts to husbands whom they had deserted. But both the marriages in question had lasted over twenty years, and the women were not being asked to repay the original dowry. Instead, they were being asked to reimburse their husbands for gifts made to them during the marriages. Moreover, in both cases the wife protested vigorously against what she saw as a harsh decision.[48]

These cases provide a fresh perspective on the colonial courts. While the courts did not exclude women, and in theory gave them new openings for legal action, in practice many women may have been too poor to pay fines imposed on them by the courts, let alone to prosecute cases on their own account. This impression is reinforced by the evidence of Jack Harris's budget studies. Five out of the six women included in his survey had cash incomes of between £1 and £3 per annum; the remaining one had an annual income of £5 16s.6d. On the other hand, none of the ten men surveyed had an annual cash income below £3. Eight had incomes ranging from £3 8s.9d. to £7 16s.3d., and two had incomes of £16 14s.0d. and £19 1s.9d. respectively. None of the women spent any money on court fees, except through gifts to men (which formed part of a reciprocal pattern of cash gifts between the sexes). Two men with very low cash incomes had been forced to pay fines to the village authorities in the year of the survey (1938–9). But only those with incomes above £6 a year had actually embarked upon court actions on their own behalf.[49]

In Ozuitem in 1938–9, court actions cost at least 7s. to initiate – 5s. for the official fee, and 2s. in bribes to court members.[50] This fact may help to explain a curious feature of the Ahiaba Native Court records: the prevalence of male names (Obasi, Wogu, Samuel, Obonna and Okereke, to name but a few) in the records of contribution club disputes.[51] This feature appears strange in view of the evidence collected at the time of the Women's War that many of the women's meetings which were common in the Ngwa area were actually contribution club meetings.[52] Some of these clubs met at eight-day intervals; others, which were associated with the churches, met after the weekly service.[53] Meetings like this are still held in Ahiaba-Okpuala.[54] They provide a means of saving on a small scale, often for a specific purpose: for example, in the 1930s, to pay for a burial, or to buy a bicycle. The process of saving was often painfully slow: Nwannedie Chigbundu recalls that it took her nine years to save enough to buy a bicycle, for £10, just before the Second World War.[55] Not all the clubs were exclusively female, and in some each member contributed as much or as little as she liked to the common fund.[56] In one such club, contributions ranged from 4d. to 1s.4d. every seven days.[57] Clearly, in all such clubs there was plenty of scope for dispute; but only men seemed inclined to take such disputes to the colonial courts.

All this evidence builds up to create the cumulative impression that the colonial courts were patronised mainly by the well-to-do – essentially the same people who could rise to eminence in the *Okonko* society, which itself continued to exist (though maintaining a low profile) after the spectacular disturbances of 1921.[58] The courts also provided a means for some Ngwa men to become wealthy by collaborating with colonial officials and acting as warrant chiefs.[59] In this way, the establishment of the Native Court system gave an advantage to those who were wealthy or politically astute, as against those who were merely senior within their lineage. However, the persistence of a land tenure system which gave precedence to those who were senior by birth rather than by wealth meant that there was probably a strong correlation between wealth and seniority. The warrant chief system added a new set of people to the group of senior and wealthy men which had previously dominated the rural Ngwa economy; it achieved no further changes in the basic structure of Ngwa society.

This point is reinforced by the fact that, as far as we know, no attempt was made by the warrant chiefs and other wealthy men to form themselves into a self-perpetuating 'class'. There is little direct documentary evidence on their activities and aspirations. However, we may read between the lines of the evidence given above, and draw on oral evidence regarding the fortunes of chiefly families, to suggest that chiefs at least did not succeed in consolidating their position. Chiefly income from court fees and bribes was essentially rentier income, and the position of chief was not necessarily heritable – there was some difference, in particular, between the first generation of 'warrant chiefs' and the members of the Native Councils set up after the Women's War.[60] In order to pass on his status to his sons, the colonial servant needed either to build up an economic enterprise which could survive him, or to invest in the education of his children, so that they too could aspire to positions within the increasingly bureaucratic, European-managed sectors of large-scale trade and government. Yet the evidence cited in this chapter regarding the use of courts to reclaim debts and acquire land, and regarding early colonial changes in the system of ownership of oil palms, suggests that chiefs and wealthy men were building up only the kind of enterprise which could be dismantled easily on their death: investing in land and people, using funds as working capital for trade or making loans, rather than fixing funds in machinery or plantations of tree crops. One chief in Abak District was riding a bicycle and had bought a lorry by 1923;[61] but there are no parallel reports relating to Aba or Bende Districts. There, informants mentioned that some chiefs entered into trade at Nbawsi as agents of European firms, but others concentrated on building up large farms and acquiring many wives, male clients and slaves.[62] Such large agricultural enterprises were likely to have generated a stable income, and allowed their heads to keep up a high standard of living despite the low export prices of the 1920s and 1930s. But these enterprises were not stable units. On the death of the chief, his land, wives and followers were likely to be shared out among several of his senior male relatives.

For example, Nwogu of Amiri (otherwise known as Umu Iri, or Ndiri) succeeded his brother Osundu as warrant chief at Umuaro Native Court in the early colonial period. Nwogu had eleven wives, and numerous children and male clients. He farmed thirty barns of yams, and exercised the right to declare palms 'open' or 'closed', although he did not take any fruit other than that cut by his own labourers. When he died in the late 1920s, his two eldest sons were young men; the eldest, aged about thirty, had already been given a wife by Nwogu. But the sons could not keep up the cultivation of their father's land, which was pledged out to his brothers and never fully redeemed. Warrant Chief Nwogu had disapproved strongly of Western education, and thus had not left his sons in a position to secure lucrative jobs as court clerks; they had to make their own way in life.[63]

Why did the senior and wealthy men in Ngwa society react to Agricultural Department offers of new seeds and machinery with caution, and show little inclination to develop capital-using innovations on their own initiative, preferring instead to invest in power over people and over natural resources? Sara Berry has recently raised this question for sub-Saharan Africa in general, arguing that the uncertainties created by the existence of parallel systems of land rights in the colonial period actually fostered such a pattern of non-innovative capital use.[64] While colonial authorities sought to preserve existing systems of land tenure, seeing them as static and so providing no forum within which they could be modified, the colonial courts were actually being used to establish new kinds of claims on resources. Within this setting the use of capital to acquire personal standing or to influence the outcome of court cases, could bring great rewards. Nevertheless, such rewards were risky, for title to land could be challenged in a variety of ways. The acquisition of wives, children and clients was possibly safer, and was also essential to the successful pursuit and use of property rights. Hence, patronage became vitally important within the colonial authority structure, and 'strategies of accumulation were directed toward building up power over resources rather than increasing productivity'.[65]

The main problem with this analysis in the Ngwa case is that lineage land tenure rights were not fundamentally challenged within the courts, or eroded outside them by commercialisation, during the early years of colonial rule. The use of cash to finance trade became more important – and more risky – as evidenced by the debt cases noted in this chapter. However, the development of a market in land had not gone far by 1930, while the use of cash to acquire labour continued to take the forms of clientage and pawning, both of which stood outside the mainstream of the literate colonial legal system. In short, there is little evidence that the colonial courts themselves stimulated the development of new forms of claim upon resources. The conflicts evident within Ngwa society during the 1930s remained similar in nature to the conflicts of the late nineteenth century, with one major exception: conflicts over trade.

The reasons for this limited commercialisation of land and labour in the Ngwa region during the early twentieth century are broadly the same as those relating to the same phenomenon in the pre-colonial period. The staple Ngwa export industry continued to rely upon a natural resource, the oil palm, which grew in symbiosis with food farming; and high population densities maintained the value of local land at a level which imposed prohibitive costs on would-be palm plantation owners. Meanwhile, most of the work in palm production continued to be done by women, whose low status was reinforced by Christianity and by court decisions. Marriage rather than contractual wage relationships continued to be the mainstay of labour recruitment, just as food farming rather than palm production continued to be the central use of land.

Within this system, wealth could be accumulated both by *ofo*-holders and by those with political power, from *Okonko* members to warrant chiefs. However, the opportunities for investing it profitably in production were technologically limited. The new oil palm seed strains and machinery tried out by colonial officials during the 1910s and 1920s were highly experimental. To invest money in these would not only have been risky, but from the perspective of the inter-war period would also have tied investors in to a rapidly declining industry. Indeed, as shown in Chapter 5, the early palm oil presses were most popular with middlemen, who were already committed to the palm produce trade and who saw in them a means of entering a new sector of the market. Farmers were less eager to enter into unequivocal commitment: they had learnt the value of flexibility from their experience of life within the harsh Ngwa environment, with its dry-season water scarcity and hungry season which only diversified cropping could alleviate.

In her recent book on the processes of accumulation and social mobility in twentieth-century Yorubaland, Sara Berry has argued that there too, there was little radical change during the early colonial period. She argues that despite the new demands which cocoa placed on land resources, there was little commercialisation of land and little development away from the smallholding model of export agriculture. In the Yoruba case, restrictive social and cultural factors combined with difficulties in labour supervision on a large scale, and with the absence of economies of scale, to discourage the development of large plantations and the growth of a landless class.[66]

This suggests that the Ngwa example is not unique. In the early colonial period, both new and long-established export economies allowed senior men to acquire wealth, but did not produce the material basis for a transformation either of production techniques or of relations of production. In the absence of new possibilities for consolidating agrarian estates, the wealth gained by the early warrant chiefs from the state tended to be dispersed after their deaths. Meanwhile, more junior men who had capital to invest tended to put it into trade, as we shall see in Chapter 8.

In the short run these investment strategies contributed to the rise of bicycle and lorry transport, which completed the transport revolution begun by the Eastern Railway and stimulated both export and commercial food production within the Ngwa region. However, in the long run the lack of investment in agriculture has limited the ability of Ngwa farmers both to increase production and to cut their costs in the face of keen competition on the world market. As will be shown in Chapter 10, the terms of trade facing Ngwa palm producers continued to decline after the 1930s and in the absence of successful cost-cutting innovation, their most attractive option was to exit from the market.

The bleaker side of this situation is explored from the point of view of

Ngwa women in Chapter 9. Ngwa men felt the problems less keenly, as they had more escape routes: initially trade and, later, clerical work. As Sara Berry has pointed out, ultimately the most significant contribution of the colonial state to the processes of class formation in Nigeria may have been made during the period of decolonisation, when the size of the bureaucracy and the teaching profession began to grow. Education then became not only a passport to a job, but also a means of passing on this right to one's children.[67] From this perspective, it may be argued that the warrant chiefs failed to consolidate their privileged position, not because of their conservative attitude to farming, but because of their proprietorial emphasis on farms and followers rather than on the education of their sons.

8

Trade, credit and mobility

Despite the low real price levels of palm produce during the inter-war period, exports from eastern Nigeria continued to increase. The volume of palm oil and kernels exported in 1935–9 was almost two and a half times the level of 1909–13.[1] In the following two chapters, we will examine the role of the oil palm industry in the lives of the main producers: women and junior men. It will be shown that while colonial transport innovations provided junior men with fresh opportunities to travel and enter into trade, women remained tied to their homes and families, both in their daily lives and in their loyalties. In this chapter, we will follow the fortunes of junior men. An initial discussion of the transport innovations which paved the way for change will be followed by a survey of the trade and credit structures of the inter-war period, within which aspiring Ngwa middlemen played a growing, but still subsidiary role. A number of individual life stories will then be related to illustrate the range of opportunities which junior men were able to take up, and the way in which they used the limited profits which they were able to make from palm production and petty trade before the Second World War.

The Ngwa differed from their Southern Igbo and Ibibio neighbours in that they did not get heavily involved in the agricultural labour migrations which became important in many regions of Nigeria during the inter-war period. Labour migration could be seen as the natural replacement for the pre-colonial escape route for junior men, the colonisation of fresh lands, which was now frowned upon by colonial officials anxious to fix boundaries and prevent armed struggles over land.[2] Alternatively, labour migration could be seen as the result of the development of commercial agriculture in a few favoured regions, attracting labour from neglected areas elsewhere.[3] Probably there is an element of truth in both interpretations: as Map 7 illustrates, migrants mainly travelled from densely to thinly populated regions, and travelled both to palm producing areas and to those which specialised in the commercial production of yams to feed the Cross River trade.[4] There is a strong similarity between these movements and the pre-colonial movements of slaves to the upper Cross River and to the areas engaged in palm produce canoe trading.[5]

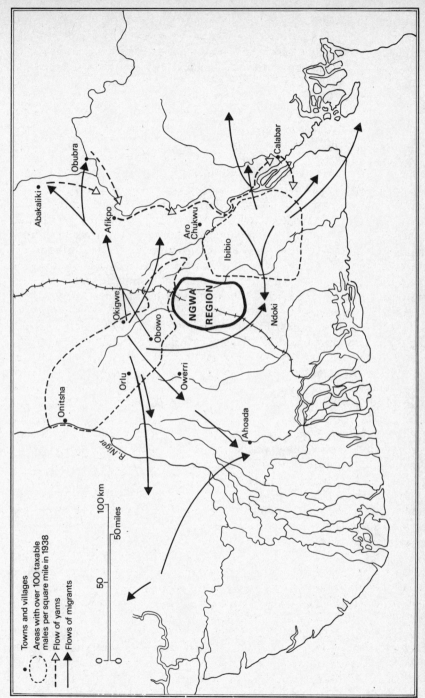

Map 7. Population densities and flows of yams and migrants, south-eastern Nigeria, to 1938

Towns and villages

Areas with over 100 taxable
males per square mile in 1938

Flow of yams

Flows of migrants

Obubra

Abakaliki

Afikpo

Aro
Chukwu

Calabar

Ibibio

NGWA
REGION

Ndoki

Okigwe

Obowo

Owerri

Orlu

Onitsha

Ahoada

R. Niger

100 km

50 miles

50

During the colonial period, the Ngwa remained firmly outside the network of long-distance labour movements, and had little to do with the regional trade in yams. Their position as a cohesive ethnic group, with a population density which was neither light nor exceptionally heavy, was probably the main cause of this relative stability and self-sufficiency. However, from 1916 onwards the attractions of the Ngwa region itself grew. The opening of trading stations along the Eastern Railway, in the heart of the region, offered restless junior men the chance to pursue their ambitions without cutting off their ties with the village economy. This mitigated the pressures which population growth and colonial land policies jointly exerted in favour of labour migration.

The Eastern Railway was opened in 1916, just as produce prices began to revive following the early wartime slump. At Opobo, prices rose steadily between 1916 and 1918, from £17 to £20 per ton for palm oil and from £8 to £14 per ton for kernels.[6] The tempo of the export trade soon quickened. The rate at which manillas could be exchanged for shillings rose from 10 to 7 manillas per shilling between April and June 1916.[7] By December 1918, the early wartime hold-ups in the hinterland had been succeeded by a glut at the ports: 4,898 tons of palm oil and 2,409 tons of kernels were lying in store at Egwanga.[8]

During the boom which followed the First World War, the quantities exported from Opobo and Port Harcourt (which now shared a hinterland) rose exceptionally fast. Exports from this region rose by 75 per cent between 1910–13 and 1920–3, as compared with a rise of 50 per cent for Degema, whose hinterland received most of the new migrant labourers; and a fall of 15 per cent for Calabar, which drew its palm produce supplies from the Ibibio region, now a major source area for migrant labour.[9] Clearly the railway had given a strong stimulus to palm production in the central palm belt. It will be argued below that this stimulus arose essentially from the vigorous competition which now developed between African middlemen, based along the Imo River, and European firms stationed along the railway.

The railway was not a very cheap form of transport. Although its freight rates were initially set to compare favourably with the estimated costs of canoe transport to Opobo, they soon rose. Between 1916 and 1922, the rates for rail transport from Aba to Port Harcourt rose from 10s.6d. to 18s.8d.[10] The railway posed no immediate threat to the prosperity of riverain traders, who continued to operate in the northern Ngwa region until at least the early 1930s. Few Ubanis chose to abandon their canoes and set up business on their own account in the new railway towns.[11]

European firms proved more enthusiastic than local middlemen in entering the rail-borne trade. Miller Brothers and the 'French Company' (C.F.A.O.) began buying produce at Umuahia in 1916.[12] By 1918, the Company of African Merchants, G. B. Ollivant, H. B. W. Russell and W. B. MacIver had joined them; and Miller Brothers, C.F.A.O., John Holt, the African Association and the African Traders' Company had established factories at Uzuakoli, as well as Umuahia.[13] The firms agreed not to extend their operations to the southern stations until adequate shipping facilities had been made available at Port Harcourt.[14] But by 1919 the African Association, the African Traders' Company and Miller Brothers had established buying stations at Imo River, and these firms, together with John Holt, C.F.A.O., G. B. Ollivant and H. B. W. Russell, had established themselves at Aba.[15] By 1921, Aba had 29 Europeans, in addition to 50 'Native foreigners' and 325 people from northern Nigeria among its population.[16] Omoba and Nbawsi were the last stations in the palm belt to attract the firms' attention: G. B. Ollivant was the first firm to establish itself at Nbawsi, in 1924, and was followed by U.A.C., the 'French Company' and John Holt.[17] By 1929 European firms were also to be found at Omoba.[18]

The expansion of rail-borne trade was closely linked with the establishment of the European factories. In 1918, 5,508 tons of oil and 3,558 tons of kernels were railed to the coast from Umuahia, while the level of trade in palm produce at the other stations remained low. In 1919, following the opening of factories at Aba and Imo River, shipments from these stations began to rise rapidly, as did shipments from Nbawsi after 1924, and Omoba after 1928.[19] The European firms may well have stimulated trade by attempting to outbid one another for produce. Having bought out their German rivals on the outbreak of war, the major British trading firms had proceeded to fall out amongst themselves. The pooling agreement between Miller Brothers, the African Association, the Company of African Merchants and the Niger Company broke up in 1917.[20] In 1919, the African Association, Miller Brothers, and the Gold Coast firm of F. and A. Swanzy merged to form the African and Eastern Trade Corporation (A.E.T.C.).[21] However, this firm had many independent rivals. Five firms were established in competition against it at Aba alone between 1919 and 1924.[22]

The firms established along the railway faced further fierce competition from African traders on the nearby Imo River. As we have seen, it was by no means certain that traders using water transport suffered a cost disadvantage in this competition. In contrast to Nwabughuogu's picture of the supersessions of old by new trading networks, the picture which emerges from the Ngwa evidence is one of a finely balanced rivalry between the two.[23] In 1918 officials interpreted the rapid growth of exports from Port Harcourt as a sign of the competitive strength of the railway as a means of transport.[24] However, much of the oil which supplied the merchants of Umuahia in 1918 came from the Okigwe District and from the northern parts of Bende and Owerri Districts. These regions were poorly served by water transport, especially between 1914 and 1924, during which period no colonial clearing parties visited the local rivers.[25] Thus, the stimulus which the railway gave to the export trade was probably twofold. The western Ngwa (including the people of Ngwa-Ukwu) probably benefited most from the competition between railway and waterside traders. Their neighbours to the north and east probably benefited more directly from the establishment of trading posts which were closer than ever before to their own villages. The construction of the railway performed the same service for these farmers as the clearing of the Imo and Azumini Rivers had done for Ngwa farmers a decade before.

This comparison between the opening of the railway and the clearing of the Imo River may be extended to illuminate the question of why it was the European firms, rather than the Ubanis, who exploited the new opportunities offered by the railway. The Ubanis, with their riverain skills and 'canoe house' system of labour organisation, were well equipped to extend their operations along the rivers of the hinterland after 1903. But the railway trade called for bureaucratic skills in handling transactions with railway officials, on the one hand, and with coastal combines, on the other, if the middleman was to avoid the need to travel with his own produce on the railway. The payment of railway freight charges in cash required the use of large stocks of working capital, while the obligations of a riverain middleman towards his canoe-paddlers were almost certainly more flexible, and may have included a substantial element of payment in kind. Finally, the vertical integration which was emerging among the European combines enabled their railway agencies to sustain direct links with the principals in Britain: once European factories were established along the railway, indigenous middlemen probably found it hard to enter into direct competition with them. European firms were peculiarly well suited to the large-scale railway trade. However, they usually employed African agents to buy oil and kernels, sometimes sending them into village markets outside the main railway trading centres.[26]

In the northern Ngwa region, the railway trade continued to grow in the 1920s, with the rise of Nbawsi as a trading centre. By 1927, five European firms were operating there and about 2,000 tons of palm oil, with 800 tons of kernels, were being railed southwards annually.[27] Some Ngwa men were able to join the Ubanis in working as agents at the European trading stations.[28] But most Ngwa farmers benefited simply from the increased competition among railway and river-borne traders: very few attempted to become middlemen at this level themselves.

Most of the informants whose life-stories will be given below took up trading at a much humbler level – the level of petty trade: buying oil in the villages for sale in railway towns or buying imports from the railway traders for retail sale in the villages. This kind of trade received its greatest stimulus from the transport changes of the 1920s and the 1930s: the widening of the roads and the coming of the bicycle.

There had been some road improvements in the period 1891–1914, but these had been geared mainly to administrative needs, and consisted essentially of path widening. During the inter-war years, on the other hand, there was a drive to construct roads of all-season motorable quality.[29] In 1921 lorries owned by Miller Brothers, Weeks Transport, and Holt Brothers were already transporting produce along the main road between

Aba and Itu. Lorries were also operating in the Abak District.[30] In 1923 work on a motor road to link Aba and Umuahia was begun; in 1924 a bridge over the Imo at Umuokpara was completed; and by 1925 there were all-season motor roads between Umuahia and Angana (via Umuokpara), Owerri and Itu (via Owerrinta, Aba and Ikot Ekpene), Aba and Asa, Aba and Opobo (via Azumini), and Ikot Ekpene and Erriam.[31] The pattern of these roads largely followed that of the pre-war Public Works Department roads, save for the route out of the new railway town of Umuahia. However, by 1935 an extensive network of 'motorable roads' had sprung up, oriented towards the railway as well as towards the rivers, serving new administrative centres (Ayaba, Utu Etim Ekpo, Abak) and forming a network linking centres of population – not just of trade and government (see Map 8).[32] The roads served a particularly useful function for traders in the Anang Ibibio area, which was poorly served by the snag-filled Achacha and Kwa Ibo Rivers, but which was linked by the new roads to Azumini, Aba and Itu.[33]

Even in the 1930s, many 'motorable' roads were probably more suitable for bicycles than for cars: local officials mention lorries only as plying along the Owerrinta–Ikot Ekpene, Umuahia–Angana and Aba–Azumini routes.[34] However, the bicycle was in itself a great innovation in the palm produce trade. Over 100,000 bicycles were imported into Nigeria between 1922 and 1929.[35] Clearly, the numbers were small relative to the total population of Nigeria; and only richer farmers could hope to buy one. In 1918 bicycles retailed at between 12 and 16 guineas each, and although their price fell gradually over the period 1922–9, it still stood at about £5 10s.0d. at the ports on the eve of the Great Depression.[36] Despite the cost, bicycles became very popular in flat areas with well-cleared roads such as Ngwa-Ukwu and the Anang Ibibio area. By the early 1930s many officials were commenting on the frequency with which young men and court members were to be seen riding bicycles.[37] For the latter, the bicycle was a symbol of prestige; for the former, a means of trade and personal emancipation.[38] It is notable that no women were reported as riding bicycles in the early 1930s, although the role of women in village-level trade was remarked by several observers.[39] There are two possible reasons for this. One is that junior men had more opportunity than women to earn sufficient amounts of cash to buy bicycles. But this seems unlikely in the case of men who remained within the rural economy. Here, women had at least equal opportunities to earn cash through the sale of palm kernels. A more likely reason for men's monopoly of the bicycle trade is that women had more alternative claims on their income than junior men had. As mothers, many women may have felt obliged to spend a fair part of their income on their children. Cultural constraints of the kind which inhibited women from climbing palms may also have inhibited them from riding bicycles.[40]

Women's failure to acquire bicycles deprived them of an ideal opportunity for small-scale capital accumulation. Once obtained, the bicycle

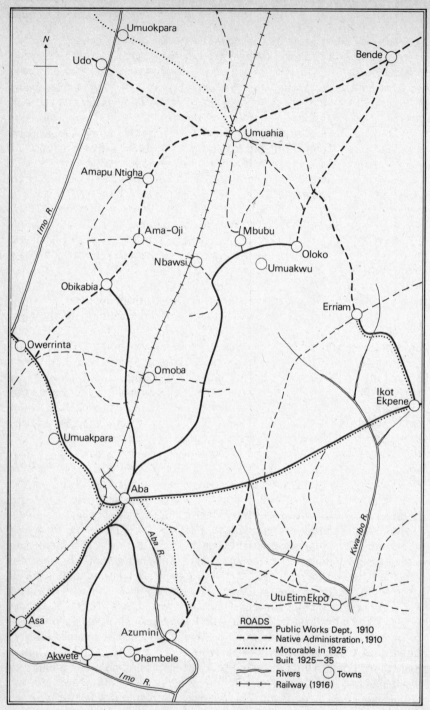

N

Umuokpara

Bende

Udo

Imo R.

Amapu Ntigha

Umuahia

Ama-Oji

Mbubu

Oloko

Nbawsi

Umuakwu

Obikabia

Erriam

Owerrinta

Omoba

Ikot
Ekpene

Umuakpara

Aba

Aba R.

Kwa-Ibo R.

Asa

Azumini

Utu Etim Ekpo

Akwete

Ohambele

Imo R.

ROADS
————— Public Works Dept, 1910
– – – – Native Administration, 1910
·········· Motorable in 1925
– – – Built 1925–35
〰〰〰 Rivers   ◯ Towns
+++++ Railway (1916)

Map 8. Communications in the Ngwa region, 1910–35

enabled a petty trader to double the quantity he could take to market – two four-gallon kerosene tins of oil, instead of one – and, of course, to travel more quickly and so economise on his own time.[41] While the railway brought European traders into the hinterland, the bicycle enabled Ngwa petty traders to venture further afield in search of better terms for their palm produce.

As Ngwa men accumulated cash from bicycle trading, they may well have begun to think of going further into trade and of becoming palm produce middlemen. However, the prospects for new groups of African middlemen seeking to break into the palm oil trade at this period were bleak. It has been argued above that the Ubanis held their ground against the European railway traders during the 1920s. Yet it will be suggested below that changes which occurred in the credit system in the 1920s made the terms of entry into the palm produce trade much less attractive. African middlemen had always been vulnerable to falling produce prices. However, the new terms of credit offered to them by the European firms threatened in addition to rob them of windfall gains in times of rising prices.

In the mid 1920s, a marked shift occurred in the bargaining-power of African middlemen *vis-à-vis* European traders in the palm produce trade in the Ngwa region. This shift was closely linked with changes in the local currency system. It will be recalled from Chapters 3 and 4 that colonial currency policy in 1891–1914 effectively restricted the local money supply. Imports of manillas and cowries had been banned and the new cash currency which had been introduced failed to win acceptance in the markets. As trade expanded, the cash value of the manilla gradually rose. Middlemen hastened the process by rushing to dispose of imports at low manilla prices whenever the cash price of palm produce rose suddenly. Manilla exchange-rate fluctuations infuriated officials and government staff, who were paid in cash but could only buy food with manillas. Meanwhile, the manilla price of food and of palm oil tended to remain constant.

The manilla remained the main currency of village-level trade in the Ngwa area throughout the 1920s.[42] Yet this period saw an increasing acceptance of cash by middlemen and European agents in the palm produce trade. This acceptance was only grudging and partial in 1917.[43] A major milestone in the process may have been the post-war boom of 1919–20, during which manillas rose in value to 4 per shilling in Calabar Province.[44] Cash currency was in use at European factories, government stations and even at the major produce markets at Aba and Umuahia by 1925.[45] It came into circulation through the payment of cash salaries to government staff, and through the issue of cash to traders through the banking system. African traders very rarely had direct access to the banking system.[46] By contrast, European traders found it much easier to obtain cash (for example, by exchanging British for West African currency or by transferring assets within the banking system) than they had found it to obtain

97

manillas. One of Birtwistle's original criticisms of the brass rod, which was similar to the manilla in being a 'transitional' currency, was that British traders and officials could not supply it themselves. The use of the manilla, cowrie or brass rod in hinterland markets meant that British traders became dependent on African middlemen to supply their currency needs.[47]

As cash became the main currency used in large-scale trade, the strain on manilla supplies was barely relieved. The manilla continued to appreciate against sterling. In 1924 the exchange rate was 6 or 7 manillas per shilling; in 1926 it stood at 5 manillas per shilling; and even during the slump of 1929 it remained as high as 7 or 8 manillas per shilling.[48] These exchange rates indicate that manillas were still in short supply, as one would expect given that they were still popular for small-scale village-level transactions.

The use of cash may not have relieved the strain on the manilla, but it relieved a certain strain on the European firms. In their dealings with African middlemen, they were now the suppliers of the staple medium of exchange. They were no longer under a great pressure to offer credit in goods in order to avoid the need to accumulate large stocks of manillas before the buying season. Yet African middlemen, especially those who were just entering the trade, continued to need credit either in goods or in manillas to finance their initial purchases of oil and kernels. In short, the balance of power between European creditors and African middlemen had shifted. This shift was reflected in a change in the terms on which credit was offered by European firms to African middlemen.

In 1913 Birtwistle recorded that European traders usually offered their African agents a combination of credit in manillas and credit in goods. The firms also held stocks of manillas in readiness for direct purchases. If oil prices rose, middlemen gained, for they were only obliged to sell their creditors oil to a certain cash value. They could supply less oil than the firms had expected under their credit agreement. The firms were then forced to draw on their stocks of manillas and buy the rest of the oil available at high manilla prices.[49] Within this system, middlemen stood to lose if prices fell, for they would then be obliged to sell large quantities of oil at low prices in order to fulfil their credit obligations. On the other hand, they could make sizeable windfall gains when prices rose. The extent of middlemen's gains depended largely on their skills in selling imports in local markets at the maximum possible manilla price: and on their skills in choosing the right moment to release stocks of manillas in buying in oil.

In the late 1920s European firms switched from offering credit in manillas and goods to offering credit in cash and goods. Within the new system, African agents were obliged to supply their creditors with a certain minimum quantity of oil. In addition, if the price of oil fell, they were obliged to supply oil or goods and cash to the value of the goods originally advanced.[50] Under this system, the middleman remained as vulnerable to a trade depression as he had been before. This was especially true given the increasing effectiveness of the colonial courts as a forum for debt cases. Thus, creditors were attaining a much stronger position in the late 1920s.

The vulnerability of middlemen to a trade depression may be illustrated with reference to the circumstances of 1929 in the Ngwa region. Between November 1928 and October 1929, the average price of palm oil bought at the European factories at Umuahia fell from £24 10s.0d. to £19 4s.0d. per ton: and of kernels from £13 2s.6d. to £10 2s.6d. per ton.[51] If middlemen were to fulfil their credit obligations, they needed to buy in almost one-third as much extra oil and kernels above the amount they had planned. Yet if they were to make a profit, they needed to offer worse terms of trade to producers and to petty traders. As far as we can tell from the court records, they were not able to force such terms of trade on producers by using the weapon of credit in their turn. In the Ahiaba Native Court records for 1930 there are very few cases which involved agreements to supply oil (rather than cash). In each debt case which directly involved palm oil, the defendant had agreed to supply a certain quantity and not a certain cash value of oil. Many of the other debt cases appeared to be straightforward cases of money-lending with no overtones of trading obligations.[52] In short, there is no evidence that the credit system which operated between European firms and middlemen also operated at village level. Middlemen were caught between two strong interest groups. The European firms had strength from their position of creditors. Meanwhile, Ngwa farmers drew strength from their continuing self-sufficiency in yams and vegetable crops. They had shown in 1914–15 and in 1921 that they were capable of withholding produce in response to falling prices, and they did so again in 1929 and 1931.[53] Their intransigence rendered the middlemen highly vulnerable.

For the ambitious Ngwa farmer, the main alternative to entering into a credit agreement under which his windfall gains would be creamed off and under which he would bear most of the risks involved in trade was to avoid the large-scale palm produce trade altogether. Petty trade was less lucrative than large-scale trade, since the value of each transaction was relatively low and much time might be spent haggling over prices. However, an independent entry into petty trade could be financed with the modest savings of a small-scale farmer. There was scope even at village level for making windfall gains from trade, especially in the import trade where prices fluctuated most severely.

The business of petty trade may well have been beneath the notice of the senior men whose fortunes are discussed above. Given their strong control over land, trees and female labour, many senior men may have preferred to rely on farming and on the proceeds of *Okonko* fees, court cases and bridewealth exchanges for their cash income. While they used their bicycles to ride to court, junior men used theirs to carry palm oil. It will be suggested below that this contrast reflects the fact that for junior men any source of income was welcome. Petty trade was important because it fell outside the agricultural sphere and outside the control of senior men. It was also important as a source of the cash with which they acquired senior status and access to productive resources.

Relatively little cash was required to gain access to land itself. Land rights came automatically with senior status and could be obtained temporarily for a small sum. A junior man could rent a plot of land for 10s. or 13s. a year or obtain it for 30s. on pledge in Ahiaba Native Court area in the early 1930s.[54] But he could not farm it alone. An outlay of some £4 was required to secure the labour of a male debtor or pawn.[55] Even heavier outlays were required to secure the permanent services of a wife. The dowries mentioned in divorce cases at Ahiaba Native Court in the 1930s ranged between £17 and £25. These sums were paid out over a period of years, and sometimes included payments for the father-in-law's second burial.[56] The balance between initial payments and later gifts is hard to estimate from the available evidence. In the southern Ngwa region, informants recalled initial payments ranging between £10 and £20.[57] Harris found that initial bride-price payments in the Ozuitem area in 1938–9 could amount to only £5 10s.0d., and that even this sum was often paid in instalments of 5s. to £1 15s.0d. per annum.[58] However, the initial payments made in the Ngwa area may have been higher; and Harris also noted that a prospective husband had to convince his father-in-law that he would be able to pay the full sum, or else the marriage would be cancelled and the early payments returned.[59]

Young men who worked for their fathers, or entered into a senior–junior relationship with other men, could expect to receive substantial help with their bridewealth payments from their patrons.[60] But those who wanted to earn cash and live independently were faced with a long, hard struggle. In the rural Ngwa area, their best chance lay in using resources left over from the production of yams and palm oil, in which their seniors took a direct interest. They could help mothers and sisters in *gari* production, and in the processing of oil from the fruit of communal palms. They could tap wine palms. They could also engage in freelance farm work, although this usually yielded payment in kind, rather than cash.[61]

Documentary evidence also indicates that some junior men may have begun producing palm oil independently of other household members during the inter-war period. During the slump of 1920–1, Liverpool merchants complained to the colonial authorities that 'in many localities where formerly good soft oil could be relied on, the stuff brought in today is hard oil which has been vilely prepared'.[62] This hard oil fetched prices which were about 20 per cent lower than those paid for soft oil at Calabar, Port Harcourt and Opobo in 1922.[63] However, producers in the Ngwa and neighbouring areas appear to have turned towards hard oil in increasing numbers after 1921. This trend was noted at Aba in 1925; and by 1938, 'semi' oil (which Farquhar described as a blend of hard and soft oil) was being sold at Nbawsi, Omoba, Aba and Owerrinta (see Map 9).[64]

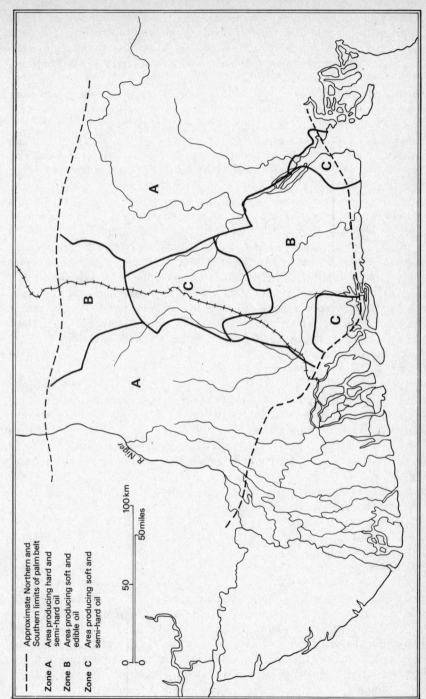

Map 9. Regional variations in palm oil production methods, south-eastern Nigeria, 1938

Legend:

— — — Approximate Northern and
         Southern limits of palm belt

Zone A   Area producing hard and
         semi-hard oil

Zone B   Area producing soft and
         edible oil

Zone C   Area producing soft and
         semi-hard oil

R. Niger

0   50   100 km
0   50 miles

Hard oil was usually produced exclusively by men. In the processes observed by colonial officials, they softened the fruit by fermentation, then pounded it and left it in a tilted vessel partly filled with water: the oil would trickle downwards from the pounded mass, and could then be skimmed off the water.[65] Because the process involved no boiling stages, it could be carried out without the co-operation of women. However, it is not certain that junior men were able to obtain access to sufficient fruit from unclaimed palms to be able to carry out large-scale processing without their fathers' or patrons' consent. Struggles over this issue may well have lain behind the gradual changes in property rights documented in Chapter 7: and that evidence indicated that senior men ultimately triumphed.[66]

In the context of a stagnating world market and of the strong grip held by senior men over the yam and oil-producing sectors of the village economy, it may well be that junior men needed to look outside the mainstream of agricultural production if they were to retain their connection with the Ngwa area, while earning enough money to achieve the position of husband and senior man without parental help. The old men interviewed for this study recalled that their main ways of making money in the 1920s and 1930s were to tap wine palms, engage in the sale of *gari* and palm kernels, engage in retail trade or money-changing and engage in paid work for the Ubanis or the Europeans.[67] It is particularly striking that none recalls engaging in hard oil production as a gesture of independence. Indeed, the palm produce trade itself appears only as an early stage in the careers of all the men interviewed.

Thomas Nwadike of Ovungwu, for example, started life at a disadvantage because he was orphaned at the age of five. He went to his mother's village, Umuagu, near Omoba, and spent many years in service with various kinsmen. These men gave him a series of 'dashes' which enabled him to begin trading in palm kernels, which he bought from local women in their houses and took to the middlemen at Aba. He soon began to buy soap and crayfish at Aba to retail in the village market. Eventually he began to travel to Port Harcourt by lorry to obtain these goods, and retail trade became his main activity. By the early 1930s, when he was in his twenties, he was able to buy a bicycle and was no longer engaged in farm work for his patrons, though it was still some years before he was able to marry.[68]

Augustine Amaeze Nwogu, of Amiri, had a slightly better start in life because he was already past adolescence when his father, Chief Nwogu, died; and he was able to co-operate with his mother in farm work. In the early 1930s he began travelling to Omoba to sell palm kernels and to Aba to sell *gari*. He went on to Okrika and Port Harcourt to invest his earnings in dried Niger Delta fish, which he retailed in local village markets. By the mid 1930s he had saved enough money to buy a bicycle, and was able to sell his kernels at Azumini and his *gari* at Owerrinta. But the wealth which enabled him to redeem some of his father's land was accumulated finally through money-lending within the framework of an *oha* contribution club.[69]

A similar career pattern was followed by Edward Uche Uche of Umuode-Nsulu, the grandson of a warrant chief, who had again been very young when his father died. In the early 1930s, when he was about twenty, he began selling fowls in the local market, and used his profits to set up in business as a money-changer, dealing in cash and manillas. He spent some time in domestic service with white doctors at Umuahia. Then, in the late 1930s, he began travelling by train to Aba, Umuahia and Port Harcourt to buy stockfish for resale at Nbawsi. By the 1950s he was married and had been able to redeem the pledged family land. He had begun trading on a larger scale in matchets, umbrellas and hardware.[70]

Rufus Erondu, of Umuakwu-Nsulu, who was about fifteen at the time of the Women's War, was also left fatherless while young, but was fortunate enough to have had an uncle at Calabar who found him a job there as a domestic servant. In his early youth he had attended the local mission school at Nsulu, and so had already had a varied career before settling down to farm with his mother and sisters in Nsulu in the early 1930s. He harvested communal palms and sold the oil produced by the family directly to the European agent at John Holt's, at Nbawsi. He was soon able to buy a bicycle, which he used in the oil trade. Later he began buying cattle at Umuahia and selling the meat in small quantities in the village market. This trade financed his marriage, which took place in the early 1940s.[71]

Mr Erondu's life-story, like that of Mr A. A. Nwogu, illustrates the point that the early death of his father could actually emancipate a junior man, providing that his mother and sisters were able to help him with farm work, and that he himself was old enough to claim access to land and palms. Several other informants whose fathers or elder brothers remained in positions of authority over them long after their adolescence, recount stories of rebellion and emphasise the importance of the new urban centres as refuges for ambitious junior men. For example, Mr J. W. Nwogu, senior brother to Mr A. A. Nwogu, spent much of his youth first in Port Harcourt (c. 1917–23) and then in Lagos (c. 1923–32). He worked there as a domestic servant, picking up a working knowledge of English and Yoruba which stood him in good stead when he returned to the Ngwa area. By the early 1930s his father had married a wife for him. But the father then died. Much of the land he left was seized by other members of the family. Mr J. W. Nwogu began to earn a low income by selling *gari* and firewood at Aba. He saved enough money from this activity to begin selling palm kernels at Aba, eventually setting up in business there as a regular middleman for U.A.C. He continued to live at Aba, renting a house and farm land, until the Civil War.[72]

Another Ngwa informant who spent many years at Port Harcourt is Mr S. O. Nwaogwugwu of Ahiaba-Okpuala, a junior son who had been forced to shoulder the farm-labour obligations of his elder brother, Isaac, who was a retail trader in stockfish. Samuel attended the mission school at Ahiaba-Okpuala for a couple of years around the end of the First World War, and then left for Port Harcourt, where he experimented with a dazzling variety of occupations: gardener, bricklayer, housepainter, riveter and sawmill worker. In the late 1920s he settled down and established a practice in herbal medicine, and also began to engage in part-time farming on pledged land at Ahiaba. After his father's death, in 1938, he returned to Ahiaba permanently. By this time he had three wives and sufficient capital to hire labourers. He concentrated his efforts on yam and oil production, and in 1943 took the *Eze-Ji* title.[73]

One feature which all these life-histories have in common is the importance of farming as the main career for married men. All the men interviewed are now full-time farmers, and several of the stories above culminate in the use of savings to redeem or obtain fresh land. Thus, even for the most adventurous men (none of the stories above reflects the experiences of those who simply stayed on the land and waited for parents to finance their marriage), yam farming and oil processing continued to be staple economic activities, and long-term investment patterns were dominated by marriage and land acquisition. But the careers outlined above do indicate an important change in the character of the regional economy. Commercial farming continued to be a safe haven and a staple occupation, but some men were beginning to use money earned in this sector to make risk-taking innovations elsewhere. Adventurous young men perceived accurately that trade, currency dealing and wage labour were the main sources of rapid, if unpredictable, earnings within the colonial economy. The bicycle was the major innovation in which they chose to invest.

Finally, in old age and as senior men, nearly all those whose life-stories are outlined above chose to invest substantial sums outside the agricultural sector, and outside the oil palm industry. All farmers spent money on consumer goods, on wives and on land; a few of those interviewed are now involved in the World Bank Smallholder Oil Palm Project.[74] However, in addition, Mr A. A. Nwogu, Mr J. W. Nwogu and Mr E. U. Uche spent large sums on the schooling of their children. Mr S. O. Nwaogwugwu, who had no sons, invested much of his capital in the construction of a fine two-storey cement house with a zinc roof, which was completed in the late 1950s. Finally, Chief I. W. Ebere, of Nbawsi, whose early career was spent trading in imports at Port Harcourt and Calabar, invested in a shoe-making business and became a nationalist politician in the 1950s, and then settled down to a life as a building contractor and local dignitary at Nbawsi after the Civil War. His daughter, an accountant, now lives in Texas.[75]

The keynote of all these life-histories is variety. Yam and oil production remained the basic source of income and the stable centre of a man's career, but the growth points of the regional economy were clearly moving elsewhere – towards trade (especially retail trade) and towards the increasingly literate formal sector. In the later colonial period it seems likely that farmers directed their innovative investment towards these sectors, much more than towards the plantations and oil presses which colonial officials were keen to promote. Meanwhile, in the 1920s, a heady atmosphere of change and commercial opportunity was generated by the rise of towns, the expansion of the import–export trade into new regions following colonial transport innovations and the coming of the bicycle. These changes helped to soften the impact upon junior men of the increasingly strict control which senior men were levying over the natural resources used in food farming and palm production. They may also have helped to soften the psychological impact of the depressed palm produce prices of the 1920s, by offering an escape route from full-time farming. Thus, while senior men sought to maximise their share of the falling income from palm production, junior men pursued their ambitions elsewhere.

9

Production and protest: the Women Riot, 1929

For Ngwa women the 1920s saw an increase in labour burdens combined with growing threats to their autonomy in marketing and use of income. As the barter terms of trade for palm produce stagnated following the major decline of 1914–21, women struggled to maintain their incomes. Unlike junior men, they remained closely tied to food and palm production. At a time when the adoption of cassava was increasing their farming and cooking duties, they managed to increase their production of kernels and to retain control of the income obtained from selling them, and they began carrying oil and kernels to the railway trading agencies. However, as shown in Chapter 8, women's social roles and in particular their responsibility for spending on household needs had held them back from buying bicycles and joining the ranks of the enterprising and ambitious retail traders.

All this meant that as European firms became increasingly cartelised and introduced new pricing and measuring arrangements in the late 1920s, among the small Ngwa traders it was women who felt the changes most keenly. They relied upon income from produce sales, and had little opportunity to offset losses there with gains on the swings and roundabouts of retail pricing. Their one remaining consolation was their exemption from the direct tax which was levied on all Ngwa men from 1927.

In 1929 this small privilege – and with it the autonomy of the women's sphere within the male-administered colony – came under threat. At Oloko, women and children were counted by tax assessors; the revolt which followed spread like wildfire through the Ngwa and neighbouring regions and has become one of the most famous events in Nigerian history. Known variously as the Aba Riots, Igbo Women's War or simply (as in the Ngwa region today) Women Riot, the revolt provoked a major re-examination of colonial administrative policy and a series of detailed enquiries into women's views and social roles. The event has continued to fascinate historians and anthropologists, white and black, for it provides a rare opportunity for an outsider or a descendant to hear the voices of women caught up in the changes of the colonial period, speaking at the time in a passionate expression of contemporary grievances and desires.[1]

106

The main aim of the present chapter is not to provide another interpretation of the causes or symbolism of the 1929 rising, since most of the possible views are eloquently expressed in the available literature, and that of Nina Mba in particular is fully in accord with the further evidence on Ngwa history provided here.[2] Instead, the aim is to reveal the light shed by the women's rising on their own views of the regional economy and of their place within it. We will also draw together the threads of earlier chapters to provide a complementary view of the economic circumstances of Ngwa women during the 1920s, seen through the lens of official sources. Special attention will be paid to the contrasting situations of Ngwa and Ibibio women since, although both participated in the revolt, Ngwa women formed the bulk of those involved from start to finish.[3]

The broad statistics of eastern Nigeria's export trade during the 1920s indicate that women, as kernel producers and traders, remained worse off than men, who owned the oil which household members of both sexes produced jointly. The barter terms of trade for palm kernels had fallen even further than those for palm oil during the slump of 1914–21, and although they rose slightly faster during the recovery of the 1920s the rise was not fast enough to fully compensate. Between 1925 and 1929 kernel prices stood at only 33 per cent of their 1911–13 level in real terms, while the comparable ratio for palm oil prices was 37 per cent.[4]

Within the region serving Opobo, Calabar and Port Harcourt, both men and women struggled to keep their incomes up through increased production: the volume of both palm oil and kernel exports rose by 30 per cent between 1920–4 and 1925–9. As a result, the real value of the region's oil and kernel exports rose by 49 per cent and 57 per cent respectively over the same period, representing a partial recovery after the dramatic slump of 1914–21. The region's income terms of trade for palm oil in 1925–9 were on average 70 per cent of the 1911–13 level; and for palm kernels, 57 per cent.[5]

These regional figures conceal marked differences in local experiences. As shown in Chapter 4, patterns of local trade combined with a basically similar sexual division of labour to provide contrasting constraints and opportunities for Ngwa and Ibibio women. The heavy labour burdens which Ngwa women bore in palm oil and food production limited the extent to which they could increase kernel production to maintain their incomes. By contrast, the involvement of Ibibio farmers in the Cross River trade in yams and palm oil not only gave them a buffer against export sector fluctuations, but also allowed Ibibio women to choose relatively freely between food farming and kernel production. While men in the Ibibio region obtained Cross River yams in exchange either for export sector earnings or for palm oil, men in the Ngwa region tended to spend their cash mainly on imported luxuries and dietary supplements like fish and salt, rather than on substitutes for home-grown starchy staples. Thus, the availability of Cross River yams relieved some of the pressure on Ibibio women as food producers, leaving them freer to concentrate on palm kernel production if they so wished.

These contrasting patterns of regional trade continued to affect the choices of Ngwa and Ibibio producers during the 1920s. A breakdown of the eastern Nigerian kernel export figures by port reveals that Ibibio women in the hinterland of Calabar increased the volume of their exports of kernels by 51 per cent betwen 1920–4 and 1925–9. Meanwhile, exports of kernels from Opobo and Port Harcourt, which were served by the Ngwa and other Imo River peoples, rose by only 13 per cent. The corresponding figures for palm oil are not comparable across the regions, because there had been a substantial diversion of Calabar oil into the Cross River trade during the 1914–21 depression. This diversion can be traced in the export figures by charting changes in the ratio of oil to kernels in Calabar's exports, which had stood at a fairly typical level for that region of 6 to 9 in 1913, but which fell during the war and after to reach a level of 1 to 2 by 1919–20, and then recovered slowly to reach 5 to 9 in 1929.[6]

The regional contrasts revealed by these statistics could in theory have been modified by the opening of the Eastern Railway, which like the Cross River ran north–south and crossed the boundaries of the major eastern Nigerian yam and palm-producing regions. But in practice the opportunities for local trade along the railway route were slow to be taken up. We have some statistical evidence on the extent to which palm oil was sent northwards by rail. In 1921–2 and 1928–9 railway consignments of palm oil from the five main 'palm belt' stations exceeded exports from Port Harcourt by some thousands of tons. The extra oil could well have been sent north. But this pattern was unusual: in all other years between 1918 and 1929 there is a close correspondence between the two sets of figures.[7] Any oil or other produce that was sent northwards was probably exchanged for cattle, rather than for yams or grains. A thriving trade in cattle had arisen at Umuahia by 1927.[8] In its early years, the rail-borne trade within eastern Nigeria thus exhibited the same characteristics as the export–import trade: palm produce was exchanged for luxuries or dietary supplements which did not replace items produced within the region. Trade enhanced the quality of the Ngwa diet, but it imposed a heavy cost in labour terms.

The slow rise of palm kernel exports from Opobo and Port Harcourt during the 1920s supports the view expressed in Chapter 4 that by the early 1920s the labour resources of the Ngwa region were being strained to the limit. Women in particular had little extra time to spare for kernel-cracking. As shown in Chapter 6, any extra time which they were putting into production was devoted to food, and especially to cassava. Meanwhile, men were taking more interest in palm oil production, as indicated in Chapter 8 where the rise of 'hard' palm oil was documented. However, men's involvement in palm oil production during the 1920s and 1930s was essentially a contribution at the margin, sufficient to raise the volume exported but not to replace previous female inputs. In the late 1930s the bulk of oil purchased at trading stations in the Ngwa region was 'soft'.[9] Women continued to work hard in food and palm oil production, and had little time in which to increase their independent incomes through kernel production.

A final activity which absorbed large amounts of women's time was local trade. As shown in Chapter 2, this was an established female sphere, connected with the basic female responsibility of obtaining extra ingredients like leaves and salt for preparing soups. While at market, women could also engage in the sale of palm oil and kernels, and during the 1920s many extended this role by travelling on foot to nearby railway and riverside entrepôts, where they sold oil by the 4-gallon kerosine tin and kernels by the bushel.[10] However, Ngwa women who recalled engaging in this trade also emphasised that they spent most of their income on food and clothing for the family; they did not see trade as a means of accumulating wealth to be spent, for example, on bicycles or on stocks of imports for time-consuming retail trade.[11] As noted in Chapters 7 and 8, Ngwa women were not prominent among the bicycle traders and litigants of the 1920s and 1930s. Furthermore, in contrast to women along the coast or at Oguta who were large-scale import–export dealers, Ngwa women do not seem to have become dealers in cloth or other imports.[12] In short, they remained confined to the sectors of trade within which there was relatively little scope for windfall gains to be made as prices and manilla–sterling exchange rates fluctuated. They came into contact with European firms and were directly affected by changing prices for palm oil and kernels; but they had little opportunity of manipulating price fluctuations to their own advantage.

The other side of this coin of powerlessness and dependence was the considerable autonomy enjoyed by women within their own sphere of childcare and household management. As shown in Chapter 6, the coming of cassava had heightened this autonomy in that, as with many newly adopted crops over previous centuries, women assumed control of the process of production right through from planting to cooking. Meanwhile, Christianity gave further ideological reinforcement both to women's confinement within the domestic sphere and to their authority within it. However, palm production and trade provided points of contact between this sphere and the wider world.

During the 1920s, women were given increasing cause for concern about the ways in which other traders' actions restricted their incomes and limited their autonomy within the sphere of trade itself. Finally, they discovered that the colonial administration could not be trusted to leave their central sphere of food production and domestic spending alone. Their feelings of frustration and discontent culminated in the Women Riot of 1929. In the remainder of this chapter, we will examine the documentary evidence of growing colonial intervention in village life, and growing manipulation and deterioration of trading conditions facing Ngwa women during the late 1920s. We will then take up the story of the Women Riot and show how the rising, and the women's public statements made during and just after it, support the interpretation of women's roles and grievances outlined above.[13]

As we saw in Chapter 3, official incursions into the domestic and local trading spheres had been largely ineffectual during the first twenty years of colonial rule. The corrupt actions of warrant chiefs and court messengers weighed heavily on some villagers; but white officials' concern about domestic slavery, manillas, the felling of palm trees or the adulteration of produce failed to generate effective policies of intervention at village level. Revenue was raised mainly by customs duties and railway freight charges, which had only an indirect effect on producer incomes. Meanwhile, the role of foreign firms in manipulating the terms of import–export trade was largely concealed from producers who traded only in the local markets. Petty traders experienced price changes mainly as changes in the manilla price demanded for imports by middlemen. In the late 1920s all this began to change. Officials began to take land by force where necessary. Interventionist policies towards the oil palm industry were finally implemented. Meanwhile, Ngwa traders came into direct contact with firms along the railway. In 1928 a new round of price-fixing agreements and mergers began. Finally, direct taxation was introduced to eastern Nigeria in 1928 – on the eve of the Wall Street Crash.

As shown in Chapter 7, Agricultural and Forestry Department officials began to make more open claims on Ngwa and neighbouring peoples' land in the 1920s. They found it extremely difficult to obtain land for experimental palm plantations and forest reserves, but they did succeed in establishing an Agricultural Station at Umuahia despite considerable local opposition. Such ventures posed a direct and unpredictable challenge to local autonomy. One particular case demonstrates the arbitrary and wilful character of official interference with local land rights. In 1923 a large area of land at Aba was seized by local officials who said they wanted to use it to establish a 'Stranger Traders Quarter'. Four years later, this land was placed at the disposal of the Agricultural Department, following the refusal of local farmers to volunteer palm groves for experimental work.[14]

Meanwhile, traders in Aba Division were being confronted with a new form of official interference: produce inspection. This policy had been on the statute books since 1894; and by 1918, produce was being inspected regularly at the ports. Ubani traders protested vigorously against this practice, arguing that the real culprits were the Kwa and Ibibio traders who sold oil at Azumini, and that inspection should be carried out there if adulteration was to be prevented.[15] By the mid 1920s, foreign firms and officials were beginning to concur in this view; their actions deprived Ngwa women of one of their few opportunities to manipulate the terms of trade.

Produce adulteration was one of the main ways in which petty traders softened the impact of low and falling produce prices. During the early 1920s, as before, produce was customarily bought by measure rather than by weight. This practice left scope for petty traders to soak palm kernels or add potash and water to palm oil in order to increase their bulk. However, as it became clear that the oil palm industry had entered on a long period of low real prices and restricted profit margins, European traders became increasingly concerned to minimise costs of this kind. As shown in Chapter 8, by the late 1920s they were beginning to impose more restrictive credit terms on middlemen. At about the same time, in 1926–7, they began to move against the petty traders too. Buying agents from Aba and Oguta complained to the local officials about soaked kernels which had been found to shrink rapidly after purchase; while several people were brought to court and convicted for adding potash and water to palm oil.[16] In 1926 the European merchants established at Opobo introduced buying by weight, an effective counter to most known types of adulteration. By early 1929 they had extended this system to Imo River and Itu.[17]

Not to be outdone, the colonial administration was simultaneously introducing a system of hinterland produce inspection. In 1926, a scheme suggested by the Liverpool Chamber of Commerce came into operation in western Nigeria. Agricultural Department inspectors were to test palm produce for purity, and examine and grade all cocoa offered for sale to exporting firms. In return, they received fees of 9d. a ton for palm kernels, 1s. a ton for palm oil and 2s.6d. a ton for cocoa. After further merchant pressure, the scheme was extended to the Eastern Provinces in August 1928.[18]

Officials were surprised at the strength of farmers' reactions to the scheme. In the east, many 'held up their produce' for several months 'in the hope that inspection was only a temporary measure'.[19] While clearly not on the scale of the 1930s cocoa hold-ups, this temporary boycott indicates the growing discontent of petty traders and farmers with the conditions of trade open to them. The railway hinterland of Port Harcourt was a major focus of discontent, since it was here that the produce inspection scheme had been introduced. Here also, as mentioned above, greater labour strains were involved in increasing palm production to compensate for the effects of low prices and extra charges. Indeed, export volumes from Port Harcourt and Opobo fell by 5 per cent for palm oil, and 6 per cent for kernels between 1923–5 and 1927–9; while from Calabar export volumes rose by 31 per cent and 26 per cent respectively.[20]

By the late 1920s it was becoming apparent that while the railway had brought the Europeans closer to the farmers and petty traders of the Ngwa region, and had caused a once-for-all trading boom there, many long-term problems and conflicts of interest were developing within the export economy. In 1929 the ability of European traders to emerge as victors in any outright conflict was enhanced by the merger of A.E.T.C. and the Niger Company to form the United Africa Company. Several firms remained outside the new combine, notably Holts, Paterson Zochonis, G. B. Ollivant and the two French companies. However, A.E.T.C. and the Niger

111

Company had been the two most powerful firms operating in eastern Nigeria. One indication of their size and power is that they each had an agreement with Elder Dempster to ship produce to Europe at preferential rates.[21]

Within eastern Nigeria, the collective power of the European firms was further enhanced by a number of localised produce-buying agreements. One such agreement had been concluded by the Umuahia agents in November 1928.[22] The high degree of unity thus secured enabled the European firms in theory to pass on the full impact of world price fluctuations as they occurred; and they did not have long to wait before putting the theory to the test. In March 1929 the U.K. prices for palm oil and kernels dropped sharply, followed immediately by those at Aba and Umuahia. After a decade and a half of low and fluctuating prices, farmers were faced with yet another drop in their standard of living.[23]

All Ngwa farmers, male and female, were affected by falling prices, by the growing power of the European firms and by the new interventionist policies on land and produce inspection. However, women as food farmers and petty traders may well have felt especially threatened by official interventionism. Women also experienced conflicts of loyalty and great pressures on their time as the labour resources of the Ngwa region came under strain. The spark which finally provoked their revolt was a rumour that women were about to be taxed: the female sphere of earning and spending on household needs, already beleaguered, was about to be invaded.

Women were already being taxed before 1929, but not in a way which was easily perceived. Customs and excise revenue provided 46 per cent of the Nigerian government's total income between 1922 and 1929, and represented a substantial tax on palm producers' incomes. An average of £544,000 per annum (or 7 per cent of export values) was provided by export duties on palm produce; while import duties, which are less easy to apportion by industry, absorbed 17 per cent of the value of all Nigerian exports.[24] These levies, though substantial, were invisible to producers: it is striking that the widespread West African tax protests of the 1930s were aimed only at direct hut, poll or income taxes, and the Women Riot of 1929 was no exception.[25]

Within Nigeria the Eastern Provinces were the last to be subjected to direct taxation, in 1927. The delay was caused partly because in this region revenue could be raised relatively easily by other means, and partly because British officials were aware that their local agents, the warrant chiefs, held only a tenuous grip on village affairs. Their fears that the warrant chiefs would have difficulty in collecting taxes were soon justified by a rising in Warri Province in 1927.[26]

Within Bende and Owerri Divisions, the initial process of assessment of local incomes and property holdings caused great alarm. Many farmers assumed that the count had something to do with further government plans for seizing their land and palm trees.[27] The news of taxation did little to soothe their feelings. When the real purpose of the count was announced to the Bende chiefs after the event, in April 1927, they threatened to resign *en masse*.[28] In Aba Division, people asked pointedly whether the Bonny and Opobo traders were also to pay tax.[29] Nevertheless, the assessment process continued and officials finally decided to levy a flat-rate annual income tax of 7s. per adult male in Aba Division, 5s. in the Ngwa areas of Bende Division, and 7s. in Ikot Ekpene Division. At contemporary prices the Aba and Ikot Ekpene taxes represented roughly one 4-gallon tin of palm oil or one bushel of palm kernels.[30]

These taxes were collected for the first time in 1928, without overt resistance. Women were not taxed, and men seemed to have accepted their fate. District officers were asked to keep a look out for 'any seditious or subversive influences' in each division, but none was visible. On 8 December 1929 John Jackson sent a report from Aba in which the only dark note was a sense of the rapaciousness of Native Court members and middlemen, which he felt was likely to alienate them both from ordinary townspeople and from upright white officials. He did not mention taxation as a possible cause of unrest.[31] Yet there had already been a women's demonstration at Oloko on 23 November, following a renewed attempt at tax assessment in which, for the first time, women had been counted. Over fifty women from Bende Division had gone to Port Harcourt on 27 November to receive top-level assurances that women were not about to be taxed; yet already the rumour that taxation was imminent was spreading like wildfire through the Ngwa and Ibibio areas. On 2 December there was another women's demonstration at Ukam, and on 9 December a crowd of women invaded Owerrinta Native Court, seizing the chiefs' caps and demanding a hearing for their views. The Women Riot was well and truly under way.[32]

The tax rumour was undoubtedly the main cause of the rising. Anger at this threat recurred as a central element of demonstrations at Owerrinta, Aba, Imo River and Owerri. By the time the rising reached Opobo on 16 December, the women were demanding not only the firm denial of the rumour but also the abolition of the existing tax on men. Older Ngwa women who recall participating in the movement continue to stress that the tax rumour was their main grievance.[33] However, once the movement began many other grievances surfaced. Women began to express their views on market regulations, produce prices, European firms and court messengers, as well as on the notorious warrant chiefs. This variety of themes and expressions has made the Women Riot an event of inexhaustible fascination for historians: an event which stimulates reflection on the wider evolution of the region's economy and society up to that time. As one Umuakpara woman said in evidence after the event: 'We had grievances and Okugo [the Oloko warrant chief] came and exposed the whole thing. He brought about the trouble that made us feel more to air our grievances.'[34]

During the rising itself the women indicated the full range of their grievances partly by choosing a variety of targets for their demonstrations. At Aba they converged not only on the Native Court, but also on the Company of African Merchants' Store and the Niger Company compound; and while on the march they attacked cars, lorries and a train leaving for Port Harcourt. Merchants' factories were also attacked at Umuahia, Aba, Imo River, Nbawsi, Omoba and Opobo; while Native Courts were invaded throughout the region shown on Map 10.[35] The strength of economic grievances was attested not only by the attacks on factories, but also by a boycott of the Umuahia agents by female produce traders throughout December 1929, and by the women themselves in declarations made at Owerrinta, Owerri, Obowo, Itu and Ikot Ekpene at the height of the rising. At Opobo the women forced officials to type out their demands, which have thus been preserved in detail. Besides abolishing direct taxation and replacing the local head chief, officials were asked to promise not to count personal property; not to levy market tolls; not to charge fees for permission to hold plays; and not to arrest prostitutes – in short, not to interfere in women's lives.[36]

The varied demonstrations which made up the Women Riot were generally peaceful. The women did not carry arms, and the worst wave of looting broke out after a woman was accidentally knocked down and killed by a European's car at Aba on 11 December. While several Native Courts were destroyed, very few physical injuries were inflicted on Europeans. The worst injuries were suffered by the women themselves when police fired on crowds at Opobo, Utu Etim Ekpo and Abak, between 14 and 16 December. Over fifty women were killed, and many more were injured.[37]

These deaths and injuries provoked questions in Parliament and two major official enquiries in Nigeria. Women were invited to give evidence at informal sessions with their local district officers, and at the second and more important enquiry. Their contributions, as preserved in the district officers' reports and in the Aba Commission's 'Notes of Evidence', have clearly been influenced by problems of translation and by leading questions from officials. However, officials were genuinely concerned to find out what had gone wrong, rather than to identify culprits for punishment, and the women responded with clear and forceful statements. Again, the general point of view which they expressed and the variety of topics which they raised shed valuable light on the issues discussed so far in this book.

The major market at Umuakpara and the railway towns of Aba and Umuahia had been key centres of unrest during December 1929. Women interviewed here and at Ayaba after the Riot protested vigorously about low produce prices and official land seizures, as well as the tax threat and the corruption of local chiefs.[38] A large number of Ngwa women then gave evidence before the Aba Commission, in whose 'Notes of Evidence' their remarks are directly preserved. Many complained about the low produce prices, one in particular saying bluntly: 'Trade was bad and that was why

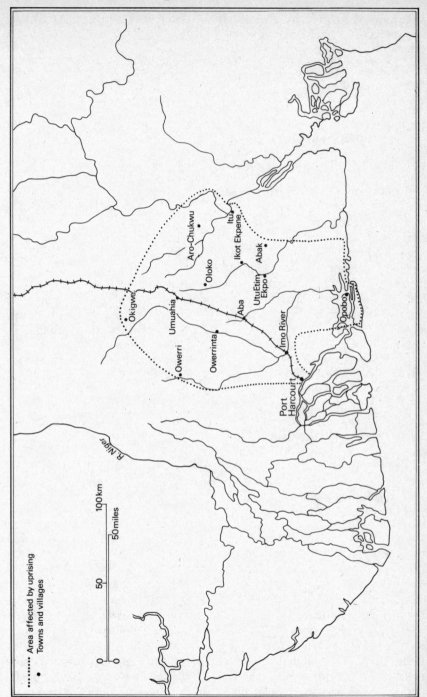

Map 10. The Women Riot, 1929

Area affected by uprising
Towns and villages

Aro-Chukwu
Itu
Ikot Ekpene
Oloko
Abak
UtuEtim Ekpo
Okigwe
Umuahia
Aba
Opobo
Imo River
Owerri
Owerrinta
Port Harcourt
R. Niger

100km
50miles
50
0

women moved about.'[39] However, their arguments were particularly vivid and direct when they spoke about the tax threat, saying:

> Women are subject to men, and any such levy should be on men and not on women.
> Men had to provide for our food and clothes. We had no money to pay for tax. Who ordered women, who have no yams but who are dependent on their husbands, to pay tax?
> What have we, women, done to warrant our being taxed? We women are like trees which bear fruit. You should tell us the reason why women who bear seeds should be counted.[40]

One point which these comments reveal and which does not emerge with such clarity from any other documentary source is the extent to which the women were prepared to work within the ideology of female dependence – despite their acknowledged fruitfulness and the fact that in practice they provided much food and clothing for their children as well as themselves.[41] They had been prepared to fight for the autonomy of their own sphere, but were not willing to challenge the overall authority and supremacy of men.

The same attitude underlies the women's statements about the Native Court system. Many of the female witnesses before the Aba Commission complained vigorously about the corruption of warrant chiefs and court messengers, but all were reluctant to state their own preferences for a new system of local government.[42] When pressed, some women asked that district officers should sit in the courts.[43] These and others argued that: 'women are not judges'; 'It is not for us to appoint Chiefs, nor do we women expect to be appointed Chiefs'; or, more positively: 'Women are not claiming to be made Chiefs. New men should be appointed. If the old Chiefs are taken away, then we who have goats will find that the goats will have kids.'[44] The women interviewed for this study were equally reluctant to be drawn into discussions on political systems.

Given the women's reluctance to challenge men's control of the courts and of village politics, they had little choice but to ask others to solve the major macro-economic and political problems which impinged upon their lives. These problems were summed up by Nwoto of Okpuala, as follows:

> Our grievances are that the land is changed – we are all dying . . . We don't want women to be taxed and we want tax on men to be abolished . . . Since the white man came, our oil does not fetch money. Our kernels do not fetch money. If we take goods or yams to market to sell, Court Messengers who wear a uniform take these things from us.[45]

The women who participated in the 1929 Riot and expressed their grievances afterwards were caught in a grave dilemma. They were disturbed by all the contemporary problems which are revealed in statistical and other documentary sources: by low produce prices, colonial incursions, corrupt warrant chiefs and monopolistic trading firms. However, they wanted neither to withdraw from trade and society, nor to seize control of the more powerful local institutions. Lacking power, they could only demonstrate and hope that their voices would be heard.

The Women Riot did achieve one major result from the point of view of the women concerned, which was that they were never taxed; although colonial officials maintained that they had never intended to tax women in the first place.[46] Male taxation remained steady at 7s. per head in Aba Division and 5s. per head in the Ngwa areas of Bende Division throughout 1929 and 1930, despite the severe fall in producer incomes which occurred then. By December 1930 the Aba tax was equivalent to the value of two 4-gallon tins of palm oil or two bushels of palm kernels, roughly double its real value in 1927–8.[47] Meanwhile, the women's grievances regarding the produce trade were simply ignored. A particularly callous attitude to the suffering caused by the slump was expressed in the Aba Commission's Report:

> Fluctuations are as old as trade itself and a period of depression inevitably brings its crop of complaints . . . This is not to be wondered at, for the question is ever present. It affects the daily necessities and the daily luxuries of life; and is ordinarily a principal subject of discussion at every market. Its importance therefore gets magnified and comes to be put in the forefront of grievances. That is what happened on this occasion.[48]

Produce inspection, which has been discussed earlier in this chapter as restricting petty traders in their attempts to combat the income effects of low prices, surfaced as a grievance in 1929 and was later denounced by numerous local officials as a system which saved the firms work at the producer's expense.[49] Yet a committee set up to investigate the system in 1931 concluded that it should be preserved; and by the 1940s it had become a national institution.[50] Here, as in the case of produce price fluctuations and men's taxation, the women's demands were heard but not acted upon. As will be shown in the next chapter, the main response made by colonial officials to the Women Riot was to carry through their long-meditated reform of the warrant chief system. This reform caused further shifts in the balance of power between senior and junior, wealthy and poor Ngwa men, but it did little to address the women's grievances relating to trade and to the interference of colonial employees in their everyday lives. Indeed, after the 1930s this interference became more pervasive than ever before, backed by an evolving philosophy of development and a growing capacity of the state to tax farmers indirectly through the Marketing Boards.

To some extent, the women who demonstrated in 1929 were expressing sentiments shared by most West African cash crop producers at the time, whether male or female: opposition to taxation, dismay at falling produce prices, dislike of oligopolistic foreign firms. The fact that it was women rather than men who protested in this case can partly be explained by the fact that women in eastern Nigeria took an unusually high share of the work involved in cash crop production.[51] Yet even here, men too were affected by produce price trends and by taxation. The fact that it was the women and not the men who were driven to protest indicates the strength of the women's resentment of taxation as an encroachment on their domestic sphere, just as their statements to the Aba Commission indicate the strength of their identification with that sphere. Again, women's concern with produce price fluctuations was all the more intense because the structure of their lives gave them very little room to manoeuvre in response to price falls. Ngwa women in particular had little free time to devote to extra production, and little spare cash to spend on bicycles or stocks for the retail trade. Migration into the growing towns and entry into large-scale produce trade were primarily male options: and after 1928 even the avenue of produce adulteration was being closed. While the young men voted with their feet, Ngwa women were driven to a single desperate protest; and after the deaths of 1929 they retreated back into the household economy and out of the official documentary record.

10

Cash cropping and economic change, 1930–80

After 1929, the political and economic framework within which Ngwa farmers operated underwent a complex series of changes, which will be surveyed chronologically in this chapter. The period 1930–80 is given unity by the fact that the real producer prices offered by import–export traders for palm oil and kernels continued their remorseless decline. However, the causes of this decline and the nature of the colonial response to it changed as the 1930s Depression was succeeded by the Second World War and by the rise of Marketing Boards and development planning. The pace of change hastened after 1940, as the state came into increasingly close contact with Ngwa villagers through the agency of tax collectors, produce inspectors and extension workers. Meanwhile, the creation of new institutions of representative government at the local and national levels brought increasing numbers of Ngwa men into the official political arena. This kind of politics now began to join trade as a means by which wealth might be used to gain eminence, irrespective of lineage-based seniority. In the trading sector, the increases in European monopoly power achieved during the 1920s were consolidated and then preserved within the Marketing Board system.

After the Second World War, the rapid expansion of Nigerian towns and of state employment created additional means by which the Ngwa might escape their confirmed export sector impasse. Christianity and cassava, which had been widely adopted during and after the First World War, became increasingly important within the changing regional economy which emerged from the Second. Western education became increasingly useful as a qualification for employment within the rapidly expanding state sector; and cassava became a major cash crop within the flourishing town–country trade. The new kind of development involved a heavy use of scarce land resources in rural areas, and was precariously founded on the use of government revenues to sustain the urban sector. However, the oil boom concealed these flaws, and it was not until the early 1980s that the fragility of the gains made earlier became evident.

The apparent prosperity of the Ngwa region in 1980 contrasted sharply in farmers' memories with the poverty and suffering of two previous periods:

that of the Nigerian Civil War, and of the late 1920s and 1930s. We will begin our survey with the earlier period, during which suffering was clearly less severe, but more prolonged. Following the slump of 1929, palm produce prices and incomes continued to fall relentlessly. The oil palm industry was even more severely affected than most of Nigeria's export industries. During the worst two years of the world Depression, 1933–4, the barter terms of trade for groundnuts were 55 per cent of their 1912–13 level; for cocoa, 23 per cent; and for palm oil and kernels, just 17 per cent.[1]

The groundnut and cocoa industries were still relatively young and had been growing vigorously just before the slump. World supplies of cocoa had risen by 120 per cent between 1909–13 and 1926–30; of groundnuts, by 140 per cent; of palm oil, by 84 per cent and of palm kernels by 72 per cent. Nigerian cocoa and groundnut exports had risen even more rapidly than world supplies: by 1,314 per cent in the case of cocoa, and by 2,295 per cent in the case of groundnuts.[2] Within northern and western Nigeria, which by this time drew most of their export income from the cocoa and groundnut industries, the falling barter terms of trade of the Depression years constituted a major setback, but did not prevent the income terms of trade from rising to unprecedented peaks. By contrast, within eastern Nigeria the Depression continued a phase of struggle and decline which had begun during the First World War. The volumes of palm oil and kernels exported from this region rose modestly by Nigerian standards between 1909–13 and 1926–30, by 80 per cent and 72 per cent respectively. The further rises in export volumes which occurred between 1926–30 and 1935–9, of 31 per cent for palm oil and 43 per cent for kernels, were only just enough to maintain the region's pre-Depression income levels.[3]

In the Ngwa region there were many continuities between the 1920s and the 1930s, as has been shown in Chapters 5 to 9. Junior Ngwa men continued to look outside the village economy; women continued the struggle to feed their families and increasingly made use of cassava and of palm kernel revenues in doing so; and senior or wealthy men continued to struggle for the control of resources. Meanwhile, Agricultural Department officials continued to focus their attention on the supply of oil presses and palm seedlings to farmers. The only new official response to the deepening of the trade depression was a slight modification of the tax structure. In 1933 a specific import duty rather than an *ad valorem* charge began to be levied on textiles, thus stabilising the income from one of the government's key revenue sources.[4] In 1931 the rates of direct taxation levied in eastern Nigeria began to fall, and by 1936 they had reached 4s. per man in Aba Division, as compared with 7s. in 1930.[5] In 1937, as produce prices began to revive, the Aba Division tax rate was raised again to 5s. per man; but in 1938, produce prices fell sharply and there was a tax rising in Okigwi Division, in northern Owerri Province. Throughout eastern Nigeria, direct taxation remained a measure to be pursued with extreme caution, and not a staple source of central government revenue.[6]

120

The history of eastern Nigeria during the 1930s stands in direct contrast to that of French West Africa, as described in general terms by Catherine Coquery-Vidrovitch. In her view the 1930s were a major watershed for rural export producers because governments shifted the burden of taxation away from trade-dependent customs duties and towards capitation taxes. This meant that farmers bore the full burden of government revenue demands regardless of their level of income from export production. This, rather than falling export prices, drove them out of the countryside to seek their fortunes in the towns.[7] By contrast, in eastern Nigeria colonial institutions of control remained too weak at the local level to allow administrators to stabilise their revenue by increasing direct taxation as export and import values fell.[8]

During the 1930s, officials in eastern Nigeria sought to remedy this problem. They gradually restructured the Native Court and Native Authority system, with the aim of eliminating the corruption inherent in the warrant chief system. Their reforms inaugurated an era of frequent changes in the system of local government, which may well have contributed to the impermanence of the chiefly fortunes outlined in Chapter 7. After 1929 periodic and unpredictable changes of personnel within the courts and the Native Authorities inhibited the formation of dynasties. Local political power was also broken down and diffused more widely by the first set of reforms. The functions of judge and administrator, which had been combined under the warrant chiefs, were separated by the Native Authority Ordinance and Native Courts Ordinance of November 1933. These decrees also paved the way for the creation of varying forms of council throughout eastern Nigeria, each to be based on local traditions of collective administration.[9]

In preparation for these reforms, district officers prepared a series of Intelligence Reports on local administrative traditions. In his definitive report on the Ngwa, Assistant District Officer J. G. C. Allen echoed the contemporary official emphasis on the constructive role played by unofficial village councils in settling local land, civil and matrimonial cases. He proposed that the councils should be allowed to continue their work unsupervised, and should be used as the models for the new system of Native Courts, to which they could refer particularly contentious cases. He also noted, but did not approve of the growing role of the *Okonko* club in settling village disputes. The club was ignored in his proposals for a new official system. The Native Courts now established in each village group were to consist of a 'massed bench' of elders, selected by the villagers in any way they chose. Each village group was also to have a group council, its Native Authority, whose members were to be selected by the village council from within its own ranks. Village councils were to include the oldest man from each *Ezi* together with any junior men they chose to co-opt.[10] These proposals were approved in December 1933, and twenty-four new Group Courts were set up in 1934. In 1937 the Ngwa Clan Council, whose members were delegates from the Group Councils, was given the right to use local tax

121

revenues and act as an all-Ngwa Native Authority. Its new offices and Treasury were opened in 1938.[11]

The workings of the new administrative and judicial system in the Ngwa region, as elsewhere in eastern Nigeria, would make a fruitful subject for research. Mr J. E. N. Nwaguru, himself a local man and for many years an archivist at Enugu, has covered the topic briefly in his excellent general history of Aba Division.[12] The information he has gathered provides a tantalising glimpse of the struggle for control of power and financial resources in the 1930s and 1940s. By this time, given that senior men had consolidated their control over palms, control of the courts was the most obvious way of increasing their power to appropriate wealth.[13] Allen's proposals gave them new openings, although the looseness of his classification of those fit to sit on councils – 'eldest men and their nominees' – left plenty of scope for debate at the village level. District officers did not supervise the process of nomination or election of members for the village, group or clan councils, so they left no records of the power struggles involved. However, the records of periodic enquiries into irregularities within the system, combined with Mr Nwaguru's personal knowledge of the region, provide some insight into the results.

The new administrative and judicial system provided both for the accumulation of wealth and power by individuals, and for the distribution of power across a much wider range of Ngwa men than before. The courts continued to be dominated by wealthy and senior men, probably with a growing overlap between seniority and wealth given the new official liking for elders. Some men continued to hold public positions for many years, despite the official intention that group council members should reselect the court and clan council members every three months.[14] However, a vast number of jobs were created by the establishment of twenty-four separate courts and the Okpuala-Ngwa Native Authority. During the 1930s and 1940s, many junior men or 'youths' were able to gain employment as 'office clerks, court clerks, interpreters, market masters, dispensers, nurses, messengers, and artisans'.[15] By 1942 the D.O., Aba was aware that the court reforms, far from eliminating bribery, had simply expanded the number of people who could claim bribes.[16] It was not clear how far the court members were able to secure jobs for their own sons or clients within this expanding network, so beginning a process of class formation centred upon access to the state. However, access to the state was clearly becoming an increasingly important source of wealth within Ngwa society as a whole.

During the 1930s, Ngwa economic life outside the state sector continued to develop along lines established earlier; but during and after the Second World War radical changes began to occur. As palm produce prices plunged repeatedly in 1939–41, to levels well below those even of 1921, Ngwa farmers began to look seriously towards the internal food trade and towards education as means of escaping their export sector impasse.[17] Not all farmers were able to maintain participation in the food trade, because population was growing rapidly at this time and land scarcity was developing in the northern Ngwa region, in particular. The combined pressures of land scarcity, export sector depression and political change were to transform Ngwa society during the later 1940s and 1950s.

The volume of palm kernels exported from eastern Nigeria during the Second World War was maintained at a level slightly above that of the late 1930s, partly owing to official compulsion and propaganda from 1943. However, the level of palm oil exported fell steadily.[18] One reason for this was that oil production in western Nigeria had fallen sharply with the development of cocoa, and a substantial road trade had developed in palm oil from the Eastern Provinces.[19] As export prices fell on the outbreak of war, this domestic market may well have become increasingly attractive. Railings of palm oil from the Eastern Provinces to the north also rose from 4,857 to 8,575 tons per annum between 1942 and 1944.[20] Meanwhile, the scarcity of imported stockfish had encouraged an increase of the railway trade in cattle. Between 1938 and 1940 the volume of dried and salt fish imported into Nigeria (mainly for consumption in the east) fell from 200,000 to 21,000 tons per annum. Between 1939 and 1940 the number of cattle railed annually to Umuahia from northern Nigeria doubled, to over 30,000.[21]

Gari was now one of the items exchanged for northern cattle. The trade had begun by road, following the opening of the Benue Bridge in 1931, but by 1944 the railway was also an important means of transport. Official fears that *gari* production would crowd out palm production, together with a more immediate awareness of localised food shortages in Aba and Umuahia, led to a temporary ban on railings to the north. On the farmers' side, feelings ran so high over the issue that there was a series of demonstrations involving up to 5,000 women in Ikot-Ekpene Division that November. As with the Women Riot of 1929, a major cause of the 1944 rising was a rumour – this time, that the government intended to seize cassava farms.[22] After the war, *gari* rail shipments from eastern to northern Nigeria continued without restriction, and rose from 15,778 tons per annum in 1948 to 16,992 tons per annum in 1950.[23]

Though the Ngwa region had shared in the northern *gari* trade during the war, its role in this trade was reduced following the development of cassava production near Enugu and Onitsha during the late 1940s and 1950s. By 1954, the main markets for Ngwa cassava and *gari* were the growing towns of Aba and Port Harcourt, together with the Ibibio area to the east.[24] The population of Aba had grown from 13,000 to 58,000 between 1931 and 1953, and was estimated at over 130,000 in 1963. Meanwhile, the population of Port Harcourt grew from 15,000 to 72,000 between 1931 and 1953, reaching 200,000 before the outbreak of the Civil War in 1967.[25] Many of the people living in the towns were 'strangers', traders and government clerks who had come from other areas within eastern Nigeria. Some rented land from local farmers in less densely populated areas like the Ndoki, Asa and Ahoada regions to the south and west of Aba, and a few Ngwa residents were able to rent land to grow food in or near Aba itself. But most had to buy food, offering a lucrative market to local Ngwa women. Some Ngwa women developed a profitable brokerage trade, for example Mrs Virginia Nwanne-die Akwarandu, the senior wife of a very wealthy man at Umuakpara, midway between Aba and Owerrinta. Mrs Akwarandu's husband gave her a bicycle on their marrage, and she used to buy *gari*, oranges and yams from Owerri District traders at Owerrinta for resale at Aba.[26]

In 1954 cassava was beginning to take the position of a joint staple, together with yams, within the Ngwa farming system. It was interplanted with yams, being introduced to the fields in July and August, by which time the yams were already well established. At Ahiaba-Okpuala it was still eaten as *akpu*, rather than as *gari*, so that it could be combined with yam in one meal. In the neighbouring Ibibio region, observers commented that *akpu* (or *fufu*) was also more filling than *gari*.[27] Yet despite this dietary conservatism, cassava was clearly growing in importance as a foodstuff, not least because it could tolerate short fallows. By this time, the population density of the northern Ngwa region had almost doubled, from the 1931 level of 345 per square mile, to between 490 and 700; for Aba Division as a whole, the level had risen from 214 to 413 between 1931 and 1953. The fallow period had fallen from the 1930s average of seven years, to five years, which Morgan estimated to be just adequate for soil regeneration.[28]

In 1959–64, the Federal Office of Statistics conducted a series of sample agricultural censuses in Eastern Nigeria. Cassava was found to be the main food crop in the Ngwa region, though yams, cocoyam and maize were still important there, in contrast to the Ibibio region where cassava had crowded out all other starchy staples except a little yam.[29] Much light is shed on the reasons for these regional distinctions by a study conducted in 1964–5 by the geographer T. C. Mbagwu. His main aim was to study the prospects for a renewal of the oil palm industry, not the reasons for the rise of cassava, yet he produced a detailed and rounded examination of farming and oil palm production throughout the Ngwa region.[30]

Mbagwu drew a major contrast between areas of dense population and areas with relatively abundant land and access to urban markets. He emphasised that by this time both Aba and Umuahia were poles of attraction. At the 1963 census Umuahia had a population of 155,000 – representing an exceptionally rapid growth from under 20,000 in 1953.[31] Cassava production for the Umuahia market was most important in the north-eastern Ngwa region, which at the time of the survey had a population density of about 400 per square mile, and 6–8 cultivated acres of farmland per household. Here and in the southern Ngwa region, cassava provided a higher proportion of farmers' cash incomes than palm production. Cassava from the southern Ngwa region was sold both in Aba and in the food-scarce Ibibio region. Land was plentiful on the borders of this region, which had a population density well under 400 per square mile, farms similar in size to those in the north-east and fallow periods of five years or more. The yam was still highly valued as the staple food crop for domestic consumption; cassava was grown either on the fringes of yam plots or in separate fields. Some fields were rented by the season to people wishing to grow food for sale.[32]

By contrast, in the north-western Ngwa region (including the village of Ahiaba-Okpuala) Mbagwu's survey revealed that the pressure on land was intense. Here, the rise of cassava was a reflection less of its income-earning potential than of land hunger. Population density had risen above 600 per square mile and each household was able to farm less than 4 acres each season, with a fallow period of only two years. Cassava was cultivated not only in separate fields, but also between the rows of yams in the main fields. However, the commercial cassava industry was relatively poorly developed: cassava was often sold unprocessed, whereas in the southern village of Obegu it was usually sold in *gari* form. In Obegu there were twenty-four cassava-grinding machines, which were taken on hire to the homes of *gari* makers; in the north-western village surveyed, Amapu, there were none.[33]

Shortage of land may have prevented north-western Ngwa farmers from developing a fully commercialised cassava industry: but it was no barrier to continued palm production. The north-western Ngwa region had concentrations of oil palms ranging from 60 to 120 per acre in 1964–5, as compared with 30–60 or even less in the south-eastern region. Seventy-one farmers surveyed in the northern Ngwa region in 1964 produced on average 275 lbs. of palm oil and 166 lbs. of palm kernels per household per annum; in the southern Ngwa region, the corresponding figures for eighty-nine respondents were 125 lbs. of oil and 81 of kernels.[34] Two relatively wealthy households from the two regions, including four wives in each case, had comparable incomes of £190 per annum, indicating that palm production was still potentially as lucrative as *gari* production. However, Mbagwu was unable to conduct detailed budget studies and so to discover whether northern Ngwa farmers needed to buy cassava or yams in order to supplement their diets.[35]

Some indirect evidence on this point was provided by Anne Martin in her study of Ibibio palm producers in 1952–3. The sixteen households surveyed spent an average of 55 per cent of their income on local food, of which 16 per cent went on *gari* and cassava, and 18 per cent on yams. However, landholdings in this area were considerably lower than in the north-western Ngwa region, with a similar fallow period of two years or more, but with total holdings, including compound land, of only 1.4 acres per household.[36] This suggests that Ngwa farmers, even in the north-western region, remained closer to self-sufficiency in basic starchy foods than their Ibibio counterparts.

Martin's work also provides interesting comparisons with Mbagwu's in that the incomes which she recorded in 1952–3 are higher in real terms than those recorded by Mbagwu in 1964. Between 1952 and 1964 the wholesale prices of imported goods at Port Harcourt rose by 45 per cent, but Mbagwu's estimate of the nominal incomes of relatively wealthy Ngwa farmers in 1964 is very similar to Martin's estimate for 1952–3.[37] The wealthiest household in Martin's survey had thirteen adult members and an annual income of £266, but the next four (out of sixteen), with approximately seven adult members each, had an average annual income of £193.[38] This estimate, compared with Mbagwu's estimate of an income of £190 for large households with at least five (and probably more) adult members, suggests either that Ngwa farm incomes were lower than those of their Ibibio counterparts; or that farm incomes had been falling overall during the 1950s and early 1960s.

It is possible that Ibibio farmers aimed at higher cash incomes than did Ngwa farmers, if only to cover their greater outlays on staple foodstuffs. However, it is more likely that the period 1950–64 saw an overall decline in the incomes of eastern Nigerian palm producers. Helleiner estimates that the real value of palm produce exported from Nigeria fell by 56 per cent between 1952 and 1964.[39] This decline was related to two factors. The first was the turning of producers to other occupations, reflected in a 20 per cent decline in the volume of palm oil exported and an increase of only 5 per cent in the volume of palm kernels exported over the period. However, at least for Ngwa cassava farmers the shift away from palm produce did not necessarily bring wealth, as shown by Mbagwu's income estimates. The shift was probably prompted by the declining value of palm produce itself, the second factor affecting their incomes within the industry. Between 1952 and 1964 the real producer price of palm oil fell by 54 per cent, and of palm kernels by 42 per cent.[40]

The problem of declining producer prices was common to palm producers and to groundnut and cocoa producers, for whom real prices declined by 24 per cent and 51 per cent respectively over the same period.[41] It had its origin in the post-war pricing policies of the Marketing Boards, which have been criticised by many authors, from Bauer to Bates.[42] In the case of the Nigerian oil palm industry, official control over marketing had been established in 1942, after the fall of South-East Asia to the Japanese made it imperative to safeguard and increase supplies. Initially, firms who had been engaged in the produce trade just before the war were appointed to act as buying agents for the new West African Produce Control Board, which set the prices to be paid both to local traders at hinterland buying stations and to its agents at the ports of shipment. The produce was then sold by the Board to the British Ministry of Food.[43] This scheme is virtually identical to the one put forward by the Ministry of Food during the First World War.[44]

In 1949 control over the marketing of Nigerian palm produce was transferred to the newly created Nigeria Oil Palm Produce Marketing Board, which continued to sell all its available produce to the Ministry of Food until 1953.[45] During the period 1947–9, the West African Produce Control Board had accumulated surpluses of £11.5 million from palm produce transactions alone. The Nigeria Oil Palm Produce Marketing Board inherited these reserves and added a further £21 million from trading surpluses accumulated between 1949 and 1954. The interest which it earned from holding its reserves in U.K. securities added a further £2.5 million to its stock of funds.[46]

Effectively these surpluses represented an immense tax on producers' incomes. Helleiner emphasised that the Marketing Boards were an 'extremely effective . . . instrument for the mobilization of savings for government sponsored economic development', rivalling export and import duties in their revenue-raising power.[47] The tax levied by the Marketing Board was even more severe for palm kernels than for palm oil. The temporary elimination of South-East Asian copra supplies from the world market, together with the acute post-war food shortage, placed palm kernels in a relatively strong position. Of the Board's £21 million surplus, 1949–54, £18.7 million was accumulated from palm kernel transactions, while subsidies of £6.9 million were paid to stabilise the producer price of palm oil in 1953–4.[48]

The Marketing Board reinforced this transfer of income from the palm kernel to the palm oil processing sector by pursuing a programme of investment in hand presses and oil mills, and in plantations designed to serve them. In the long term West Africa was acknowledged to have the advantage over Sumatran and Malayan plantation economies in the production not of palm oil, but of kernels. The 1947 Oilseeds Mission found that little progress had been made in developing a West African palm which could match South-East Asian varieties for oil yields, and debated whether more attention should be given to developing existing natural assets through the kernel industry.[49] However, engineers still had not developed an effective kernel-cracking machine. The main emphasis of post-war development policy lay in the refinement and introduction of techniques and seed strains developed beforehand, and this implied investment in oil mills and in plantations of relatively oil-rich palms.[50]

In the earlier phase of post-war planning, producers received some return for their forced investment. From 1949 to 1952, the prices offered by the Marketing Board to palm producers rose steadily. The increase was especially marked for the two highest grades of oil, with a free fatty acid content ranging from zero to 9 per cent.[51] At the same time, an official loan scheme provided funds for some of the farmers who wished to buy hand presses. By 1950, thousands of these screw presses were in use and thousands more farmers were applying for loans.[52] The hand presses did not make it easier for farmers to produce high-grade oil: a low F.F.A. content could be achieved only by using fresh fruit and boiling or steaming it before pressing.[53] However, they did enable farmers to save labour. In a 1964 village study in Abak, Miller found that the screw press method required 3.5 woman-days and 0.8 man-days to produce a hundredweight of oil, as compared with 7.3 woman-days per hundredweight for the purely manual method.[54]

127

However, government enthusiasm for the improvement of smallholders' processing techniques was dampened by the emergence of the Pioneer oil mill, which offered new hope for large-scale innovation. The Pioneer oil mill was developed in the 1930s by U.A.C., with the aim of bridging the gap between techniques suitable for plantations and for smallholders. It was much smaller than the mills tried out before the 1930s by Lever and others, but it was power-driven and could perform all stages of oil processing from the steaming of the fruit to the clarification of the oil. Hand methods still needed to be used for removing the fruit from the bunches and the nuts from the 'digested' fibres. In theory, the mill could be supplied adequately by fruit sold by local smallholders, and if no kernel-cracking machines were installed it could sell the nuts back to local women for hand-cracking.[55]

Between 1946 and 1949 five Pioneer mills were set up by the Nigerian government, the number swelling to 145 by 1960. Their establishment was financed by Marketing Board funds at a total cost of over £2.3 million by 1960.[56] Nearly 80 per cent of the mills were located in Eastern Nigeria, where they met fierce initial opposition from farmers. In 1948 there were riots in the northern Ngwa region, where women opposed a bid by Josiah Wachukwu's Nsulu Group Council to obtain one. Ibibio women followed suit in 1950, protesting against the threat which they believed the mills posed to their ownership of palm kernels. Their fears proved justified, as men soon began buying palm nuts from the mills and 'entering the palm kernel trade for the first time'.[57]

The mills almost certainly altered the balance of economic power in the areas where they were erected. They provided job opportunities for local men as wage labourers and technicians; for example, Mr J. D. Owuala of Umuobasi-Amavu in the Ngwa region, who began work at the local Pioneer oil mill as a labourer in 1950, and eventually became its manager.[58] Some men may have made economic gains from selling fruit at the mills, thus evading the need to participate in processing and to share the proceeds with their wives. However, some men gave fruit to their wives on credit, so that the women took the fruit to the mill and could claim a share of the proceeds of sale.[59]

The introduction of the Pioneer oil mill thus shifted economic power further towards those who were willing to participate in the cash economy as labourers or traders, rather than as processors and farmers. In some cases the first group could include women, although women were both less likely to get wage employment and more likely to retain their independence, if not through palm production, then through cassava cultivation. The growing cassava industry allowed women to maintain cash incomes without loss of autonomy in those areas where sufficient land was available and where men remained aloof from the new cash crop. However, in regions as densely populated as the Ibibio area, women may have suffered real hardship when their husbands began selling fruit to the mills.

In the long term, the main effect of the government's investment in

Pioneer oil mills was probably less to cause hardship to particular sections of village society, than to undermine the oil palm industry itself. All commentators agree that the new mills were dogged by the same problems which had rendered their predecessors unprofitable. These problems included operating inefficiency, high cost of spare parts and lack of skilled management. None were satisfactorily overcome before the Nigerian Civil War. Yet between 1950 and 1967 those Marketing Board funds which were not used outside the oil palm industry altogether, were used only to finance the establishment of more mills, and of the plantation and grove rehabilitation schemes designed to increase their supplies of palm fruit. The loan scheme to finance purchases of screw presses had been ended in 1950; then, as producer prices for palm produce continued to fall, farmers found it less and less worthwhile to make the investment on their own account. In 1964 Miller observed that some owners of press manufacturing plants in Uyo had switched to the manufacture of iron bed-frames.[60] The further growth and development of smallholder production had been sacrificed to the mirage of mill-based modernisation.

Helleiner estimates that other Nigerian export producers suffered as greatly as the Ngwa and Ibibio did from taxes made in the name of development after 1945. Export duties, Marketing Board surpluses and produce purchase taxes accounted for between 20 per cent and 32 per cent of the potential incomes of cocoa, groundnut, palm produce and cotton exporters during the period 1947–62; and this estimate does not include the impact of import duties, which continued to provide a high proportion of customs revenue. These taxes effectively reduced farm incomes which were already falling: after 1953 there was a rapid decline in the barter terms of trade for Nigerian agricultural produce on world markets.[61]

This continued deterioration in the terms of trade facing farmers had a marked effect on the career patterns and aspirations of young men. It was shown in Chapter 8 that Ngwa youths in the 1920s and 1930s often sought their fortunes outside the sphere of food and palm production, which was tightly controlled by their seniors; but many later returned with their profits to settle down as farmers in middle age. Similarly, Sara Berry found in the early 1970s that many of the Yoruba cocoa farmers whom she interviewed had previously been traders.[62] An earlier survey of Yoruba cocoa farmers, in 1951–3, had shown that many carried on trade as an ancillary to farming, again with many similarities to the Ngwa pattern.[63] However, from the 1950s both Igbo and Yoruba men began to develop new means of seeking their fortunes, which led to different career patterns later in life.

In a survey of Ijesha men made in 1974, J. D. Y. Peel found that about 75 per cent had travelled at some time in their lives. Of those who were young men and travelling in the 1920s, 80 per cent were working as *osomaalo* traders, making retail sales of cloth on credit to farmers throughout Yorubaland. This pattern is very similar to that of the Ngwa bicycle traders, retailing salt, meat and imported goods during the inter-war period. Peel estimates that it began to break down in the 1940s and 1950s, when migrants moved towards Ibadan and towards other kinds of trade; and when large numbers of boys began attending school. By the time of Peel's survey, 85 per cent of all the interviewees who had been born in the 1950s had some education; 32 per cent were employed as clerks, and 38 per cent were still receiving education, financed partly by their fathers' savings from cocoa and partly by the use of government revenue.[64]

In Eastern Nigeria too, the educational system expanded rapidly after the Second World War. In 1931 there had been 753 schools in Owerri Province, with 41,258 pupils. By 1965, the province could boast 389,425 pupils enrolled in primary schools, and 17,922 in secondary schools. These figures represent 2 per cent and 18 per cent, respectively, of the province's total population in each year; an unknown number of pupils were being educated elsewhere.[65] Unfortunately, the statistics do not include details on the age or sex of pupils, but, as was noted in Chapter 6, it is commonplace knowledge in the Ngwa region that the schools initially catered for boys, with girls beginning to gain access to them only in the 1960s.

Like their Ijesha counterparts, school-leavers in the Ngwa and neighbouring regions travelled forth in search of clerical or public service work, joining their kin who had earlier travelled to other parts of Nigeria as tin miners, railway workers, import traders, carpenters and car repairers.[66] This kind of career pattern could lead a man to return to his village as a teacher or local politician; but more often it led to the establishment of a permanent urban home, cemented by the migration of at least one wife and children to the town. Salaried urban men today often maintain a village house to which they return for public holidays and major family celebrations, but this is quite different to the maintenance of yam farming as the ultimate goal of a successful career. Aspirations may shift again if austerity measures reduce the prospects of salaried city jobs; but in 1980 the contrast between the recalled aspirations of elder Ngwa men, and the career patterns of their juniors, seemed marked and ineradicable.[67]

Within Ngwa village society, another major contrast emerges between the political structures of the period after 1950 and those of the 1920s and 1930s. Changes began to appear in the 1940s, when charges of corruption led to a further overhaul of the Native Court system. In 1945–6 the number of Ngwa Group Courts was reduced from twenty-two to nine, and the 'massed bench' of elders in each was replaced by a smaller group of eminent men, chosen either by their fellows, or in disputed cases by the divisional officer. It was hoped that some of the elders left off the court rolls would begin settling cases more cheaply at home: the informal judicial system was still seen to be useful and valid.[68] However, a direct challenge was soon posed to this principle by Mr Marcus Ubani – whose name suggests that he may have had good personal reasons for challenging the authority of 'traditional' elders.

In 1946 Mr Ubani was selected to be the first member for Owerri Province in the new Eastern House of Assembly. At the time, he was the president of Ngwa Clan Council, where he was leading a movement to remove court members from this and lesser councils, and to prevent them from hearing cases at home. An opposing faction soon grew up under the leadership of Josiah Wachukwu, who came from a well-established northern Ngwa trading family and was the leader the Nsulu Group Council.[69] In 1948 he convened an emergency meeting of the Ngwa clan – not the council – which passed a resolution deposing Ubani and nominating Wachukwu in his place. This proved too much for the administration to bear, and in 1949 the Ngwa Native Authority system was altered yet again. The unofficial Ngwa clan meetings, hitherto held monthly, were banned; court members were excluded from the Clan Council; the Clan Council itself was reduced in size, and secret ballots were introduced for its members' annual elections. A period of intense competition for the Council Presidency ensued, with Wachukwu and Ubani being elected by turns.[70]

A series of changes introduced in Eastern Nigeria during the 1950s confirmed these local trends of modernisation, and of increased official restrictions on alternative forms of political and judicial assembly. In 1953, a new system of local government was introduced, modelled on the British system and designed to attract educated men into village politics. Four District Councils were established for the new Aba-Ngwa County, to which members were elected by a ballot of all tax-payers.[71] The new District Councils soon began pressing for an extension of the authority of the courts. For example, in 1955 the Eastern Nigerian Committee on Bride Price recommended that all marriages should be registered and that divorce should be granted only by the courts. The committee noted that the three Ngwa Rural District Councils had already drawn up such regulations.[72]

One curious feature of the 1950s reforms was that the ideal of chieftaincy was revived and, after a long controversy, endorsed by the creation of an Eastern House of Chiefs. Opponents of this action had argued that it would effectively revive the warrant chief system in a politicised form, since the chiefs would be selected from among the many village-group leaders of Eastern Nigeria and recognised by the regional government.[73] G. I. Jones, who was asked to investigate the status of chiefs and natural rulers in the region, concluded that the position of local chiefs was indeed different from that of 'chiefs' as recognised within the system of indirect rule. Eastern Nigerian chiefs were essentially ceremonial and religious figures who headed village-group hierarchies of seniority but played little active role in politics. Natural rulers, on the other hand, were charismatic and wealthy men who wielded considerable power.[74]

The administrative system which emerged from the 1950s reforms gave considerable scope to 'natural rulers' who wished to increase their power. Within the Ngwa region, the two great rivals, Wachukwu and Ubani, soon emerged at the head of a new hierarchy based on wealth, education and access to state resources; a hierarchy which overlapped with and eclipsed

131

those of lineage-based seniority and *Okonko*-based wealth and power. Josiah Wachukwu was highly successful at the local level: he retained the chairmanship of the county council from 1953 to 1958, and then became chairman of the Northern Ngwa District Council. In 1960 he was chosen to be a First-Class Chief, and was the first representative of the Ngwa region to hold this status in the Eastern House of Chiefs. Meanwhile, Marcus Ubani had gained the seat for Aba Central in the Lagos House of Representatives, where he served from 1959 to 1964. He then succeeded to Wachukwu's eminent position in the Eastern House of Chiefs.[75]

Josiah Wachukwu died in 1962, but he left a potentially powerful successor in his son, Jaja. Jaja Wachukwu had been one of the first Ngwa youths to study abroad. He obtained a degree in law from Trinity College, Dublin, in the early 1940s, and rapidly became a leading local lawyer and politician, even taking the opposite side to his father in the dispute over the Pioneer oil mill in 1948. By 1949 he was well known as a nationalist politician at Aba. Together with his fellow lawyer, Mr Ubani-Ukoma, he was elected to the Ngwa Clan Council in 1949, and to the Eastern House of Representatives (for the N.C.N.C.) in 1951. In 1954 he was elected to the Lagos House of Assembly, and held a number of federal ministerial posts over the following decade, including Speaker of the House of Representatives and Minister of Economic Development.[76]

Like many other Igbos, Jaja Wachukwu found a promising Federal career cut short by the events of 1966 and the Civil War. He returned home to Aba, where he took a leading role in local government until the closing months of the war. In June 1969 he was arrested, and Aba province put under martial law, for flagging in support for Ojukwu and the war effort.[77] However, by the time I visited his Nbawsi home in 1980 he was once more a prominent local citizen, whose interests ranged well beyond the Ngwa region itself. The war undoubtedly scarred his life, as it did that of many other Ngwas to the extent that few of those I lived among wished to recall it or discuss it. However, by 1980 it was clear that many individuals, and the region itself, had returned to prosperity.

Some individuals also rose to prosperity and eminence during the war. In 1980–1, the political system in the Ngwa region appeared to foster individual eminence just as effectively as had the system constructed in the 1950s. However, new people had risen to power. Within Ngwa-Ukwu village group, the most powerful individual was undoubtedly Chief Ben Enweremadu, who was well known and well liked by many dignitaries in the Imo State capital, Owerri. Chief Enweremadu had a magnificent compound, with electricity and running water, and was hoping to set up a soft-drinks factory in the village. He had also contributed substantially to the new Ngwa-Ukwu Secondary Technical School. While clearly belonging to a generation for whom wealth and access to the state are the keys to status, Chief Enweremadu retains a respect for 'tradition'. On 26 December 1980 he presided over the Ngwa-Ukwu Cultural Festival, essentially a public feast at which the chief himself dispatched a goat to the applause of the spectators. Special T-shirts had been produced for the occasion, neatly symbolising the blend of present and past.

For less eminent members of Ngwa society, the Civil War may well have left more scars. Great suffering was experienced in the northern Ngwa region, which formed part of the Biafran 'siege economy' during the period between May 1968 and December 1969. Port Harcourt fell to Federal forces in May 1968; Aba, in September; and Umuahia, in late April 1969. The population of the Ngwa and other Igbo regions had already increased before the war, with the return of one and a half million Igbos from other parts of Nigeria. With each city that fell, more refugees fled into the rural Biafran heartland, increasing the pressure on local land resources.[78] It has been shown above that this pressure was already severe in the northern Ngwa region before the war: the region was hardly equipped to bear a sudden refugee influx.

During 1968–9, these problems were compounded by the effective Federal blockade of Biafra. Enugu, Onitsha, Calabar and Port Harcourt had all been captured by May 1968, and Biafra's original land frontier with Cameroun had been cut off. It has been emphasised throughout this book that trade for the Ngwa and neighbouring peoples did not simply bring beads, cloth and other imported luxuries; it also brought vitally important supplies of iron, salt and proteins, like stockfish and northern Nigerian cattle, without which their very survival was threatened. In late 1967, when the Federal blockade began to be effective, starvation assaulted Biafra. Kwashiorkor, the disease most closely associated with protein deficiency, became rampant: airlifts could relieve, but not halt the famine.[79]

The intense suffering caused by the Civil War clearly made a lasting impression on farmers' minds. In 1980 I was struck by the frequency with which interviewees would date economic changes like the reduction of fallow periods, or the beginning of inflation, to the Civil War. For those living near Aba, the war brought direct destruction of their yam fields or businesses; while for those in the Ngwa-Ukwu village group, it was a time of hardship which has come to symbolise the shift from an economy with abundant land and good prices to the more difficult circumstances of the 1980s. In one respect, the transition was not simply symbolic but real: the war marked the emergence of cassava as a staple foodstuff, finally displacing the yam, which is now cultivated only on a small scale in the northern Ngwa region. *Gari* became and has remained the most popular form of cooked cassava among villagers.[80]

Since the war, Southern Igbo farmers have been experimenting with new cropping patterns in an attempt to relieve the pressure which high population density continues to exert on their land. In 1974–5 Johannes Lagemann conducted a detailed study of agriculture in three Southern Igbo villages, including Umuokile, which lies to the north-west of Ngwa-Ukwu and which had a somewhat higher 1963 population density of about 1,000 per square mile.[81] The farming techniques and cropping patterns described by Lagemann were very similar to those described by Mbagwu, with the major exception that in Umuokile cassava had become overwhelmingly important on the main fallowed fields, where it was intercropped with small quantities of cocoyam, maize, yam and groundnuts. The main yam crop was obtained from heavily fertilised compound farms.[82]

In 1965 Mbagwu had observed that compound farms, fertilised with household refuse, provided an ideal environment for high quality yams, vegetable crops, bananas and plantains.[83] Ten years later, Lagemann observed that compound farms were becoming increasingly important to householders as population density grew. They remained small, at most a quarter of an acre per household, but were continuously cultivated and provided high yields. Meanwhile, yields on the fallowed fields may also have been increased as farmers reduced field sizes and increased the length of fallows. Lagemann found that the average area of fallowed farmland cultivated annually by each household in Umuokile was only two acres, roughly half the amount cultivated by northern Ngwa households in 1965. But the fallow period was twice as long, at nearly four years.[84]

Despite these measures, Lagemann argued that 'soil mining' was occurring in Umuokile. The four-year fallow period was not long enough to restore soil fertility, and yields in Umuokile were markedly lower than in the village of Okwe, to the south-east of Umuahia, where the fallow period was between five and six years.[85] The long-term outlook for the farming economy appeared bleak. The use of compound farms had alleviated the problems posed by population pressure, but farmers lacked the funds necessary to purchase artificial fertiliser and other inputs which could raise the yields on short-fallowed fields further away from their compounds. In Umuokile, the average household income from farming in 1974–5 was 321 Naira, of which only 4 per cent was spent on hired labour and purchased inputs. The main sources of income differentiation within the three villages surveyed by Lagemann were trading and off-farm employment, with educational attainment being the key to success in the latter sphere. Given the importance of off-farm earnings, it is not surprising that farmers were still choosing to invest any surplus funds available in trade and in school fees, rather than in farming. The one exception to this rule was the *gari*-grating machine, which continued to grow in popularity.[86]

By the mid 1970s small-scale farmers were beginning to come back into fashion as targets of development planning schemes; Lagemann's survey is a good example of the renewed concern for matching Western technical skills with the needs of indigenous farmers. At the International Institute of Tropical Agriculture, and elsewhere, researchers began to explore the intricacies of local farming systems; and in 1973, the World Bank launched a new programme of support for development schemes aimed at the rural poor. Meanwhile, the Federal government assumed control over the Marketing Boards and increased producer prices substantially in 1974.[87]

By the time I arrived in Okpuala-Ngwa, the World Bank had been operating a Smallholder Oil Palm Project in the region for about three years. This belonged to the same tradition as the small-scale grove improvement schemes of the 1930s, which had been succeeded by an Oil Palm Rehabilitation Scheme in the 1960s.[88] The World Bank scheme, like the 1960s scheme, supplied farmers with improved palm seedlings, fertiliser and the advice of extension workers, together with a cash subsidy designed to cover the labour and land costs of making fresh palm plantations. The seedlings used provided an impressive contrast with 'wild' varieties, bearing fruit with a high oil content which could be harvested only four years after planting, without the need to use ladders or climb tall trees. At last it seemed that Nigeria had gained an equivalent of the South-East Asian Deli palm.

The new palms had attractions for local farmers in the 1960s, both because of their yields and because they were not subject to the rules of communal harvesting, which still restricted the dates on which compound palms could be harvested.[89] However, by the 1980s these rules no longer seemed to be closely enforced and many farmers were extremely pessimistic about the future of the oil palm industry itself. After the price rises of 1974, palm produce prices both on the internal and the export market had remained fixed at a time of rapid inflation in other sectors.[90] Many of the farmers involved in the World Bank scheme were keen to invest their subsidies in urban housing or in poultry farms, rather than in paid labour for the continued care and harvesting of their palms.

In 1980–1 even the harvesting of some World Bank farmers' trees was made difficult by shortages of labour. The association of men with palm fruit harvesting continued to be strong, even though it was no longer necessary to climb the new trees. Yet very few young men remained in the villages, other than teachers, local administrators and extension workers. Hired male labour was extremely expensive and was rarely used. While strains on female labour placed limits on the expansion of the Ngwa oil palm industry in its heyday, the absence of male labour inhibits its revival today. Meanwhile, the 'female' sector of Ngwa agriculture, the cassava industry and associated crop-growing and vegetable-gathering activities, receives little attention from governments and planners. Several wealthy men in Okpuala-Ngwa own *gari* graters, which women pay fees for using; there are no schemes for making similar machines available at subsidised rates to female household heads or co-operatives. Finally, the fallow period has shrunk once more to two years or even one; the problem of soil exhaustion and falling yields now demands urgent attention, but is not receiving it.

During the past thirty years, the Ngwa economy has undergone revolutionary changes. The adjustments which accompanied the rise of the oil palm industry before the First World War seem minor by comparison. Since 1955, population pressure has made it increasingly difficult for farmers to supply their own needs for starchy foodstuffs, thus intensifying a dependence on trade which had its origins in the local shortage of iron, salt and proteins. But it has become increasingly difficult for farmers to gain income from trading farm produce alone. As the oil palm industry has declined, so young men have increasingly moved outside the rural sector altogether. With the rise of education and state employment, many have gained jobs which no longer reflect a temporary urban stage of their lives, but which reflect aspirations for a permanent urban career. As more women have gained education over the past twenty years, they have come to share these aspirations: very few of the teenage girls I knew in Okpuala-Ngwa wanted to spend their lives in the village. In the 1970s and early 1980s the agricultural economy was impoverished and largely female: as at the time of Lagemann's survey, many of the luxuries visible were financed by remittances and off-farm income.

One gleam of hope for the rural economy lay in the fact that many wealthy Owerri families maintained a foothold in their home villages, constructing durable brick-and-zinc villas with electricity and water. The compound where I lived had its own standpipe, provided by a wealthy Lagos-based family within it. In the current phase of austerity and official retrenchment, perhaps more families will return to invest in the rural economy, in a greater variety of ways than planners can hope to do. However, such investments are unlikely to spread beyond housing to production, unless prices for food and palm kernels begin to rise rapidly again. The decline of agriculture has proceeded so far that it may take another revolution to reverse it.

11

Conclusion

This book has its origins in a desire to shed light on the problems of poverty and agrarian change in contemporary Africa. In the course of writing it, a further aim developed: that of reconstructing Ngwa economic history in a way that reflects the perceptions and experiences both of farmers and of officials. While the latter aim dictated the structure of the main narrative chapters, the desire to explore the wider implications of the Ngwa experience remained, and will be reflected in the analysis below. The Ngwa case study will be shown to have two major implications. Firstly, it demonstrates that the current 'food crisis' cannot be explained in all cases as the outcome of 'underdevelopment'. In the Ngwa case, the limitations and ultimate failure of export-led rural development require analysis of a different kind from that needed to explain the current decline in soil fertility and food production. Secondly, the regional comparisons made in this study show that the impact upon farmers of falling cash incomes and food supply problems can vary regionally, socially and over time; similar variations can be found in farmers' strategies for dealing with these problems. An appreciation of the origins of different strategies is essential for all who wish to imitate or modify them.

Within dependency and vent-for-surplus theory, changes within the export sector are held to set the pace of changes outside it. Within Ngwa economic history, the expansion of export production certainly preceded the onset of serious shortages of staple foods. For both these reasons, this concluding survey will begin with an exploration of export sector history and will then examine the causes of recent changes in the Ngwa domestic economy. In each case, local environmental, demographic and social differences will be shown to have influenced the pattern of change in the Ngwa and neighbouring regions.

Local social tensions and resource constraints played an especially important role in export sector history before the 1940s. During the nineteenth century and the early colonial period, foreign firms and colonial officials rarely intervened directly in village-level economic life. In Chapter 3 it has been shown that however ambitious their economic aspirations were, colonial officials were prevented from implementing interventionist policies by their lack of local knowledge and of funds. They were able to keep the peace and to stimulate cash crop production through transport innovations. However, they failed to suppress the institutions of pawning and domestic slavery and they were unable to determine the ways in which innovations like cash currency and the colonial courts were used by African farmers and traders. If anything, the creation of a dual cash–manilla currency system initially favoured the African middlemen as against the European traders, and the difficulties experienced in enforcing contracts through the courts provided another check on the growth of European commercial power. European firms penetrated inland along the railway route, but usually employed Africans as their local agents.

In the late 1920s European firms and officials began to gain more power at the local level, as indicated by the implementation of direct taxation and produce inspection, and the shift in trading credit terms to favour the Europeans. The formation of the United Africa Company in 1929 represented a significant consolidation of British traders' monopoly power. However, Ngwa and Ibibio farmers retained their ability to shift between the domestic and export sectors. They never became the helpless victims of monopoly power, and they mounted vigorous protests which succeeded in limiting the intrusions of colonial agricultural officers into their region. The Women's War of 1929 seriously alarmed officials, although they interpreted it in their own terms as being primarily a commentary on local administrative structures, rather than a sign of economic discontent.

The assumption made by dependency theorists writing on Africa, that farmers entered and remained in the export sector under colonial duress, is clearly inaccurate in the case of eastern Nigeria. Vent-for-surplus theory, with its emphasis on rising world market prices and colonial transport innovations, provides a more convincing explanation of the origins and continued expansion of the oil palm export industry in this region. However, after the First World War this explanation begins to wear thin in view of the substantial and long-term decline in the barter terms of trade facing Nigerian palm producers. The evidence provided in Chapters 7 to 10 suggests that Ngwa and neighbouring palm producers began looking for other lucrative occupations in the 1920s, but that most of the opportunities then available were related either to the import–export trade, or to the growth of state employment in construction schemes and clerical work. Palm production remained the only viable agricultural export industry; even farmers who had many other occupations remained ultimately dependent on this industry for their cash income. The further expansion of palm production during the 1920s to 1960s is clearly related to the 'dependency trap' of regional specialisation. While prices fell, production rose as farmers struggled to maintain their real incomes.

During the long period of export expansion, the Ngwa and neighbouring economies experienced varying kinds of strain on labour and natural resources. This experience of strain finds no echo in vent-for-surplus theory, while in dependency theory it is assumed that all strains are resolved by the diversion of resources from the domestic economy to the export sector. In eastern Nigeria, labour migration to the sparsely populated Ahoada region of the Niger Delta and food imports to the Ibibio region would seem to confirm the dependency view, but these were not the only strategies by which strains on labour supplies were resolved. A labour-saving method of processing palm oil was developed in the Niger Delta, and this was later adopted by the Ngwa, who imported neither food nor labour as their own palm processing industry expanded. This pattern of labour-saving innovation attracted no favourable comment in official sources or later studies of the oil palm industry, partly because it involved no mechanisation. The contemporary South-East Asian pattern of mechanisation accompanied by quality improvements impressed officials, but found no echo in eastern Nigerian initiatives.

After the 1920s, farmers in eastern Nigeria showed an interest in the hand presses introduced by colonial agricultural officers, and since 1950 many have invested in cassava-grating machinery on their own initiative. However, in general this evidence supports the vent-for-surplus and dependency view that a very limited degree of capital-using innovation has been associated with the expansion of agricultural export production. Furthermore, the evidence provided above on real income trends in eastern Nigeria after the First World War supports the 'dependency' view that poverty arising from poor terms of trade has been a major impediment to capital-using innovation. The decline in Ngwa farmers' cash incomes began well before the 1940s, when the Nigerian government began to intervene decisively in rural economies through the imposition of Marketing Board price controls and the funding of relatively ambitious development projects.

However, it has been argued in this study that poverty is not the only explanation for the absence of capital-using innovation in the expanding oil palm industry. It was shown in Chapters 7 and 10 that senior and wealthy men were engaged throughout the colonial period in a series of power struggles which absorbed much of their energy. The means by which control could be acquired over palms, labour and land were frequently disputed; but ultimately, control rested in the hands of those who could claim seniority in lineage terms. This reduced the ease with which wealth could be translated into useful combinations of agriculturally productive assets or passed on intact to an under-age heir. By the 1920s, trade and education were emerging as the two major means by which wealth could be used to reproduce itself, and through which junior men could seek their initial fortunes.

By the 1940s, many Ngwa men had begun seeking their fortunes outside the oil palm industry, and capital was being invested away from the land. Meanwhile, women remained closely identified with food production and with domestic responsibilities. In Chapters 2 and 6 it has been shown that this aspect of local gender roles, originating within Ngwa culture, had been strongly reinforced by the local experience of Christianity. The expansion of the palm kernel export industry after 1870, and the adoption of cassava after 1914, gave women increased autonomy within the household economy. However, their use of cash to buy extra food and some clothing for their children left them with few opportunities to acquire wealth. Thus, those who remained most closely tied to the land and to food production had very few surplus resources to invest in it. Significantly, the machines for grating cassava which I saw in the Ngwa region in 1980–1 were all owned by men, although women were their main users.

After the 1940s, the oil palm industry entered a decisive phase of decline. The preference of farmers for investing outside the industry was reinforced by the heavy taxes imposed through the Marketing Boards, and the funds invested by the government in the industry were devoted to mill-and-plantation schemes which proved uneconomic. Meanwhile, the dramatic expansion of urban employment during the 1950s and 1960s confirmed the preference of junior men for seeking their fortunes outside the rural economy. Mineral oil revenues sustained the expansion of the state and industrial sectors in eastern Nigeria until the early 1980s, so that for a time it seemed that the limitations of a regional economy based on palm produce exports had been transcended. However, as the oil boom fades, these limitations may well reappear. In addition to the limitations of world demand, which have been demonstrated in this study with reference to the 1920s and 1930s, eastern Nigerian palm producers in the 1980s need to come to terms with strong competition from South-East Asia. As indicated in Chapter 5, this competition is founded not only on the well-publicised efficiency and low labour costs of South-East Asian mills, but also on the exceptional ecological advantages of the region by comparison with eastern Nigeria.

Despite the apparent prosperity of the Ngwa and neighbouring regions in the early 1980s, their long-term prospects as agricultural exporters looked bleak. Yet I would choose to describe the process of change which brought them to this pass, not as 'the development of underdevelopment', but rather as 'development diverted'. Considerable financial gains were made from the palm produce trade, at the cost of a great increase in female and to a lesser extent male workloads. However, as local struggles over power, income and employment developed during the colonial period, funds were invested in ways that favoured the development of trade and administration, rather than agriculture. Meanwhile, the development of rival agricultural industries elsewhere, and the long-term limitations of the world market for palm produce, made the development of alternative cash crops or industries imperative. The oil boom disguised but did not solve the problem.

This view of 'development diverted' is substantially different from those provided by dependency and vent-for-surplus theorists, both of whom seek to explain the absence of a certain kind of development, rather than the appearance of alternatives. It is too early to say whether the eastern Nigerian pattern exists widely elsewhere in tropical Africa: we need more local histories of regions which were heavily involved in export production. However, there are preliminary indications of a similar pattern of investment and mobility among men in Ghana and western Nigeria.[1]

While the export sector went through its phases of boom and decline, the domestic economy was changing according to a logic of its own. These two main sectors overlapped at several points, in a complex relationship which can by no means be described as export sector domination. In this way the theoretical implications of this study diverge once again from those of vent-for-surplus theory, which holds that in the case of palm production the domestic economy was unaffected by export sector pressures; and from those of dependency theory, which holds that the export sector drained the domestic economy of essential resources.

The oil palm industry in itself provides a point of contact between the domestic economy and the export sectors, since palm oil could be used as a local foodstuff or as an item of regional trade along the Cross River, as well as being exported. The early use of palm oil revenues to finance imports of iron and salt provided a further point of contact. Iron could be used to make hoes, while refined Manchester salt satisfied a common dietary taste in a way which could not be achieved using local resources. In Chapter 2, further evidence was provided to show that during the nineteenth century, the oil palm export industry developed in accordance with a long-established trend of diversification, by which Ngwa and neighbouring farmers drew on a wide range of agricultural and other activities to provide an ever-increasing range of craft goods and foodstuffs. In the twentieth century, the adoption of cassava continued this trend.

Within dependency theory, further increases in food imports to African countries during the twentieth century are held to be symptomatic of the diversion of resources to cash crop production or other non-food uses. Rising food imports thus indicate the growing dimensions of the continental 'food crisis'.[2] This view has an element of truth. However, rising imports of salt in the nineteenth century, and stockfish in the twentieth, allowed farmers to diversify their diet and raise their standard of living. This evidence implies that theorists should make a clear distinction between food imports which result from changing tastes and represent additions to the local diet, and food imports which are growing because farmers cannot meet the demand for their locally grown substitutes. While foreign exchange shortages may induce governments to regard the first type of food import growth as crisis-inducing, only the second type of import growth may be symptomatic of agrarian decline.

There are marked regional differences in the timing of the second type of import growth within south-eastern Nigeria. In the Ibibio region, yam imports from the upper Cross River had already begun to grow before the colonial period; but the Ngwa region remained self-sufficient in starchy staples until at least the 1950s. Both regions were heavily involved in the Atlantic palm oil trade before the colonial period. The most obvious difference between them was one of population density: successive census enquiries made during the early colonial period revealed the population density of the agricultural Ibibio region to be roughly double that of the Ngwa region. The causes of the relative population densities of the early colonial period will probably never be known, but their association with the regional economic contrasts of the period is clear. High population densities were associated with increasingly specialised palm production and food imports in the Ibibio region; and with the migration of slaves and free labourers from the Ibibio and Owerri regions to the sparsely populated regions of the Niger Delta and the upper Cross River. In the Niger Delta, migrants were used initially in the transportation and from the 1910s in the production of palm oil and kernels; in the upper Cross River, they worked in the yam fields.

The Ngwa region remained outside these currents of food trade and labour migration throughout the colonial period. After 1950, the northern Ngwa region began to experience severe population pressure, and local fallow periods fell beyond the level at which soil fertility could be renewed without the use of manure or artificial fertilisers. By this time the oil palm industry, which had never competed with yams or other food crops for land, was entering its final period of decline. Cassava was becoming important as a cash crop to supply demand from the growing towns, but only those farmers with access to extra land could grow a surplus. Changes in the commercial sector after 1950 thus reinforced the pressure placed by population growth upon Ngwa natural resources. By contrast, the growth of the oil palm industry over the previous 150 years had provided Ibibio and Owerri farmers with an outlet for their energies which made no fresh demands on local land supplies. In the Ngwa region, the growth of the oil palm industry posed no threat to the balanced relationship which farmers had established with their environment; such a threat has only been posed since the 1950s.

The oil palm industry may well have been exceptional in the low demands which it made on local natural resources, because it was primarily a processing rather than strictly agricultural industry. However, the Ngwa case raises issues of more general importance for West African agrarian history. It demonstrates the impact of population pressure upon a typically diversified and flexible West African farming system, which farmers have created over centuries in response to the challenges and opportunities provided by the local environment. The rapid growth of population after the Second World War threatened the survival of this system. It became necessary to make innovations of a new kind, designed to control and modify the local environment in order to increase the productivity of land. In Chapter 10 it was shown that Ngwa and neighbouring farmers have already begun to do this on their compound farms. However, they will need funds if they are to do so effectively on a larger scale.

Meanwhile, for some men wage labour continues to provide a viable alternative to food farming. However, the urban basis of much wage labour today means that the alternative has become much sharper than it was in the inter-war period. Urbanisation is clearly associated with growing food imports, partly because the convenience foods which suit urban consumers are often imported. But as population pressure restricts the production of food surpluses in some regions, and the movement of men off the land limits the expansion of yam farming in others, the second type of food import – that which covers a local deficit – is clearly growing too.[3] While eastern Nigeria cannot be said to be experiencing a 'food crisis' analogous to that of the drought-stricken Sahel, there are undoubtedly growing problems of food supply within the region.

The problems both of the eastern Nigerian oil palm industry and of the region's food producers are urgent and complex. However, to end on such a gloomy note would be to deny the spirit of the Ngwa farmers who allowed me to share their lives briefly in 1980–1. They are energetic, enterprising, and often look more to the future than to that past which I was always asking them to recall. Flexibility and diversification have been the hallmarks of their economy in the past, and they may well find ingenious and inventive solutions to the problems of the present. I would like to end by calling upon planners and governments to listen to their views of their problems, and to support them in their search for solutions.

Statistical appendix

Table 1 *Palm oil prices, Liverpool, 1879–1930* (£ s.d. per ton)

		Range	Annual average
May	1879	£32	
	1880	£31 5s.0d. to £32	
	1886		£20
December	1888	£23 to £24	
	1892	£19 15s.0d. to £24 15s.0d.	
	1893	£22 15s.0d. to £27 5s.0d.	
May	1894	£21 12s.6d.	
	1894	£20 5s.0d. to £23 15s.0d.	
	1895	£19 to £24 4s.0d.	
April	1900	£24 15s.0d. to £26 10s.0d.	
	1905	£23 to £27 10s.0d.	
	1906	£26 to £30 5s.0d.	
	1907	£27 5s.0d. to £33 10s.0d.	£30 1s.0d.
	1908	£23 16s.6d. to £27 12s.6d.	£25 8s.6d.
	1909	£24 15s.0d. to £31	£26 10s.0d.
	1910		£33 5s.0d.
July	1911	£30 5s.0d. to £30 10s.0d.	
	1911	£29 5s.0d. to £30 17s.6d.	£31 15s.0d. *or* £31 0s.10d.
	1912	£27 10s.0d. to £30 12s.6d.	£29 18s.0d. *or* £28 17s.6d.
	1913	£30 10s.0d. to £31	£32 15s.0d. *or* £31
	1914	£28 10s.0d. to £30 10s.0d.	£29 8s.4d.
	1915	£27 7s.6d. to £41	£31 3s.4d.
	1916	£33 to £45	£37 17s.6d.
	1917	£45 7s.6d. to (controlled price) £48	£46 16s.8d.
	1918	£48	£48
	1919	£48 till April; £79 to £86 10s.0d. May–December	£71 9s.2d.
	1920	£88 (March); £42 10s.0d. (December)	£66 12s.6d.
	1921	January–October; £31 10s.0d. to £40 5s.0d.	£34 14s.9d.
	1922	£31 2s.0d. to £40 5s.0d.	
	1923	£34 12s.6d. to £38	
	1924	£37 to £44	
	1925	£39 to £41 10s.0d.	
	1926	£35 to £38 7s.6d.	
	1927	£30 10s.0d. to £35 2s.6d.	
	1928	£33 2s.6d. to £38	
	1929	£36 (March) to £31 15s.0d. (December)	
	1930	£28 2s.6d. (March) to £20 10s.0d. (December)	

Table 2 *Palm kernel prices, Liverpool, 1888–1930* (£ s.d. per ton)

		Range	Annual average
December	1888	£10 5s.0d. to £10 15s.0d.	
	1892	£10 11s.3d. to £11 12s.6d.	
	1893	£11 1s.3d. to £12 15s.0d.	
	1894	£9 12s.6d. to £11.17s.6d.	
	1895	£9 5s.0d. to £10	
April	1900	£11 17s.6d.	
	1905	£13 to £13 15s.0d.	
	1906	£14 to £16 10s.0d.	
	1907	£13 12s.6d. to £19 10s.6d:	£16 15s.0d.
	1908	£12 12s.6d. to £14 2s.3d.	£13 11s.0d.
	1909	£14 5s.0d. to £18	£15 6s.6d.
	1910		£19
July	1911	£18 13s.9d. to £18 15s.0d.	
	1911	£16 12s.6d. to £20 10s.0d.	£18 6s.0d. *or* £18 11s.1d.
	1912	£18 17s.6d. to £21 2s.6d.	£19 15s.0d. *or* £19 16s.8d.
	1913	£21 18s.9d. to £24 10s.0d.	£23 5s.0d. *or* £23 6s.0½d.
	1914	£23 8s.9d. (January) to £17 2s.6d. (October)	£19 13s.11½d.
	1915	£13 16s.3d. to £19 12s.6d.	£15 5s.0d. *or* £16 19s.7d.
	1916	£18 15s.4d. to £26 10s.10d.	£22 8s.9d.
	1917	£24 15s.0d. to £26	£25 11s.0½d.
	1918	£26 (controlled price)	£26
	1919	£26 to March;	
		£39 12s.6d. to £43 12s.6d.	£36 0s.3¾d.
	1920	£45 15s.0d. (March)	
		to £28 2s.6d. (December)	£37 15s.6¼d.
	1921	January–October: £18 10s.0d. to £22 3s.0d.	£20 9s.1¾d.
	1922	£18 17s.0d. (March) to £16 10s.0d. (September)	
	1923	£18 15s.0d. to £20 8s.9d.	
	1924	£20 7s.6d. to £22 15s.0d.	
	1925	£20 5s.0d. to £21 15s.0d.	
	1926	£21 5s.0d. (June) to £19 (December)	
	1927	£19 10s.0d. to £20 16s.3d.	
	1928	£20 5s.0d. to £20 15s.0d.	
	1929	£18 16s.3d. (March) to £17 2s.6d. (December)	
	1930	£14 12s.6d. (March) to £10 17s.6d. (December)	

Sources for Tables 1 and 2
Oil prices, May 1879 and May 1894: Liverpool Chamber of Commerce, Manchester Ship Canal Special Committee, *Report on the Trade of Liverpool* (Liverpool, 1894), table D, p. 20.
   Oil prices, 1880–6: Watts to Holt, 1 January 1880 and 15 October 1886, John Holt Papers, R.H., Mss. Afr. s. 1525, Box 19, file 3.
   Oil and kernel prices, December 1888: Consul H. H. Johnston, 'Report on the Oil Rivers Protectorate', 1 December 1888, F.O. 84/1882, f. 220.
   Oil and kernel prices, 1892–5: John Holt, *Diary of Produce Sales*, Liverpool, 1892–5, John Holt Papers, Liverpool Record Office, 380 HOL I, file 6/6.
   Oil and kernel prices, 1900: Welsh to Holt, 10 and 13 April 1900, John Holt Papers, R.H., Mss. Afr. s. 1525, Box 19, file 4.
   Price ranges, 1905–9: Southern Nigeria: *Trade Reports* (*T.R.*) compiled by C. A. Birtwistle, Commercial Intelligence Officer: *T.R.*, 1906, C.O. 592/3, p. 10; *T.R.*, 1907, C.O. 592/3, p. 94; *T.R.*, 1908, C.O. 592/5, p. 105; *T.R.*, 1909, C.O. 592/7, p. 378. Also Egerton to Crewe, 23 August 1908, C.O. 520/64.
   Price ranges, 1911–30: Empire Marketing Board Publication no. 54, *Survey of Vegetable Oilseeds and Oils*, vol. I, *Oil Palm Products* (H.M.S.O., 1932), pp. 114 and 116. Also, palm kernels, 1912–16: telegram, Lugard to Long, 3 February 1917: attached letter, Long to Devonport, 10 February 1917, C.O. 554/33. These figures are very similar to the E.M.B. ones.
   Annual average prices, 1907–13 (left-hand column on both tables): *Southern Nigeria Report*, 1908, Colonial Reports (Annual) no. 630, p. 8; *S.N.R.*, 1909, C.R.A. no. 665, p. 8; *S.N.R.*, 1910, C.R.A. no. 695, p. 8; *S.N.R.*, 1912, C.R.A. no. 782, p. 9; *S.N.R.*, 1913, C.R.A. no. 825, p. 11.
   Annual average prices, 1911–21 (right-hand column on both tables): *Report of the Committee on Trade and Taxation for British West Africa* (P.P. 1922, XVI, Cmd 1600), pp. 39–40.

Table 3 *Lagos prices, palm oil and palm kernels; with U.K. wholesale price and Nigerian import price indices*, 1911–48

	Nigeria: Lagos prices				Nigeria:	U.K.:
	Palm oil (£/ton index 1913=100)		Palm kernels (£/ton index 1913=100)		Import price index (1913=100)	Wholesale price index (1913=100)
1911	24.0	100.0	14.6	79.3	95.1	93.9
1912	21.8	90.8	15.2	82.6	99.8	98.6
1913	24.0	100.0	18.4	100.0	100.0	100.0
1914	22.6	94.2	14.4	78.3	101.9	100.6
1915	18.3	76.3	10.2	55.4	131.2	123.5
1916	17.3	72.1	9.9	53.8	154.9	160.1
1917	21.9	91.3	13.8	75.0	186.8	208.6
1918	21.3	88.8	14.4	78.3	259.9	230.1
1919	43.9	182.9	23.6	128.3	307.9	254.5
1920	42.3	176.3	25.9	140.8	468.0	316.6
1921	17.7	73.8	11.7	63.6	416.4	197.2
1922	21.7	90.4	11.0	59.8	302.8	158.8
1923	23.6	98.3	12.9	70.1	281.0	158.9
1924	25.8	107.5	14.8	80.4	299.5	166.2
1925	26.1	108.8	15.2	82.6	301.3	159.1
1926	24.3	101.3	14.1	76.6	289.0	148.1
1927	22.5	93.8	14.3	77.7	257.9	141.6
1928	24.2	100.8	15.4	83.7	256.1	140.3
1929	23.7	98.8	13.4	72.8	253.1	136.5
1930	16.0	66.7	9.2	50.0	220.3	119.5
1931	6.3	26.3	9.2	50.0	181.1	104.2
1932	9.6	40.0	7.2	39.1	168.0	101.6
1933	7.0	29.2	4.9	26.6	159.5	100.9
1934	5.0	20.8	3.6	19.6	143.0	104.1
1935	11.4	47.5	16.7	90.8	150.9	105.5
1936	10.6	44.2	6.4	34.8	152.9	111.9
1937	13.4	55.8	9.2	50.0	173.2	128.8
1938	6.4	26.7	5.5	29.9	164.6	120.2
1939	5.8	24.2	5.2	28.3	161.9	121.8
1940	5.9	24.6	5.1	27.7	213.1	161.9
1941	6.0	25.0	4.6	25.0	227.2	180.8
1942	6.2	25.8	4.7	25.5	274.0	188.9
1943	9.4	39.2	5.7	31.0	351.5	192.9
1944	10.1	42.1	7.8	42.4	388.0	196.9
1945	12.3	51.3	8.7	47.3	371.6	200.3
1946	13.1	54.6	9.2	50.0	404.8	207.6
1947	15.3	63.8	10.7	58.2	475.8	227.2
1948	35.3	147.1	21.0	114.1	479.9	259.9

Sources: T. B. Birnberg and S. A. Resnick, *Colonial Development: an Econometric Study* (New Haven, 1975), table A.35 (Paasche Import Price Index); Helleiner, *Peasant Agriculture*, tables II-B-2 and II-B-3; B. R. Mitchell, *Abstract of British Historical Statistics* (Cambridge, 1962), pp. 476–7, and Mitchell and H. G. Jones, *Second Abstract of British Historical Statistics* (Cambridge, 1971), pp. 188–9, on U.K. wholesale prices (Board of Trade indices).

Table 4 *Barter terms of trade for Nigerian cocoa, groundnuts and palm produce, 1911–48* (index: 1913=100)

	Cocoa	Groundnuts	Palm kernels	Palm oil
1911	88.9		83.4	105.1
1912	86.4	66.8	82.7	91.0
1913	100.0	100.0	100.0	100.0
1914	78.5	155.4	76.8	92.4
1915	60.3	57.2	42.3	58.1
1916	33.5	48.4	34.7	46.5
1917	21.5	78.5	40.1	48.8
1918	17.7	66.0	30.1	34.1
1919	53.2	72.5	41.7	59.4
1920	9.6	83.0	30.1	37.7
1921	11.9	35.6	15.3	17.7
1922	19.1	55.0	19.7	29.9
1923	13.3	73.0	25.0	35.0
1924	22.9	68.5	26.9	35.9
1925	22.1	74.1	27.4	36.1
1926	42.3	62.3	26.5	35.0
1927	45.4	77.5	30.1	36.4
1928	33.0	84.0	32.7	39.4
1929	30.8	72.4	28.8	39.0
1930	19.2	67.3	22.7	30.3
1931	21.8	45.1	27.6	14.5
1932	24.4	67.5	23.3	23.8
1933	19.9	59.6	16.7	18.3
1934	22.8	31.5	13.7	14.6
1935	24.7	77.3	23.0	31.5
1936	34.3	85.0	30.9	28.9
1937	37.3	61.6	28.9	32.2
1938	20.0	31.4	18.2	16.2
1939	24.1	57.6	17.5	14.9
1940	15.1	42.2	13.0	11.5
1941	15.2	39.6	11.0	11.0
1942	10.9	39.5	9.3	9.4
1943	8.5	42.7	8.8	11.1
1944	13.6	51.5	10.9	10.8
1945	17.0	53.8	12.7	13.8
1946	28.4	65.9	12.4	13.5
1947	30.2	56.0	12.2	13.4
1948	57.5	66.7	23.8	30.6

Sources: As Table 3, and Helleiner, *Peasant Agriculture*, table II-B-4; S. S. Berry, *Cocoa, Custom and Socio-Economic Change in Rural Western Nigeria* (Oxford, 1975), appendix III, table 3.

Table 5 *Volumes of cocoa, groundnuts and palm produce exported from Nigeria, 1900–48*

	Cocoa exports (tons per annum)	Cocoa export volumes (index 1913=100)	Groundnut exports (tons per annum)	Groundnut export volumes (index 1913=100)	Palm kernel exports (tons per annum)	Palm kernel export volumes (index 1913=100)	Palm oil exports (tons per annum)	Palm oil export volumes (index 1913=100)
1900	202	5.58	599	3.11	85,624	49.01	45,508	54.77
1901	206	5.69	210	1.09	114,046	65.27	56,766	68.32
1902	307	8.48	322	1.67	132,556	75.87	64,167	77.23
1903	281	7.76	468	2.43	131,898	75.49	54,257	65.30
1904	531	14.66	777	4.03	129,818	74.30	57,946	69.74
1905	470	12.98	790	4.10	108,822	62.28	50,562	60.85
1906	723	19.97	1,661	8.61	113,347	64.87	57,250	68.90
1907	933	25.77	1,936	10.04	133,630	76.48	65,480	78.81
1908	1,366	37.72	1,654	8.58	136,558	78.16	70,460	84.80
1909	2,241	61.89	1,615	8.37	159,046	91.03	82,143	98.86
1910	2,932	80.97	995	5.16	172,997	99.01	83,870	100.94
1911	4,401	121.54	1,179	6.11	176,390	100.96	77,181	92.89
1912	3,390	93.62	2,518	13.05	184,625	105.67	76,994	92.66
1913	3,621	100.00	19,288	100.00	174,719	100.00	83,089	100.00
1914	4,939	136.40	16,997	88.12	162,451	92.98	72,499	87.25
1915	9,105	251.45	8,910	46.19	153,319	87.75	72,994	87.85
1916	8,956	247.33	50,368	261.14	161,580	92.48	67,537	81.28
1917	15,422	425.90	50,334	260.96	185,998	106.46	74,619	89.81
1918	10,219	282.21	57,554	298.39	205,167	117.43	86,425	104.01
1919	25,711	710.05	39,334	203.93	216,913	124.15	100,967	121.52
1920	17,155	473.76	45,409	235.43	207,010	118.48	84,856	102.13
1921	17,944	495.55	50,979	264.30	153,354	87.77	52,771	63.51
1922	31,271	863.60	23,890	123.86	178,723	102.29	87,609	105.44

Table 5 (*cont.*)

1923	32,821	906.41	22,887	118.66	223,172	127.73	99,439	119.68
1924	37,205	1027.48	78,266	405.78	252,847	144.72	127,083	152.95
1925	44,705	1234.60	127,226	659.61	272,925	156.21	128,113	154.19
1926	39,099	1079.78	126,799	657.40	249,100	142.57	113,267	136.32
1927	39,210	1082.85	90,773	470.62	257,206	147.21	113,240	136.29
1928	49,163	1357.72	103,161	534.85	246,638	141.16	127,111	152.98
1929	55,236	1525.43	147,379	764.10	251,477	143.93	131,845	158.68
1930	52,331	1445.21	146,371	758.87	260,022	148.82	135,801	163.44
1931	52,806	1458.33	159,739	828.18	254,454	145.64	118,179	142.23
1932	71,039	1961.86	188,123	975.34	309,061	176.89	116,060	139.68
1933	60,737	1677.35	204,606	1060.79	259,945	148.78	128,696	154.89
1934	77,982	2153.60	244,886	1269.63	289,447	165.66	112,773	135.73
1935	88,143	2434.22	183,993	953.92	312,746	179.00	142,628	171.66
1936	80,553	2224.61	218,389	1132.25	386,145	221.01	162,778	195.91
1937	103,216	2850.48	325,929	1689.80	337,749	193.31	145,718	175.38
1938	97,104	2681.69	180,136	933.93	312,048	178.60	110,243	132.68
1939	113,841	3143.91	147,263	763.50	299,943	171.67	126,042	151.70
1940	89,737	2478.24	169,480	878.68	235,521	134.80	132,723	159.74
1941	104,681	2890.94	247,176	1281.50	378,124	216.42	127,778	153.78
1942	59,937	1655.26	194,190	1006.79	344,596	197.23	151,287	182.08
1943	87,487	2416.10	142,152	737.00	331,292	189.61	135,268	162.80
1944	70,051	1934.58	156,194	809.80	313,530	179.45	124,829	150.24
1945	77,004	2126.59	176,242	913.74	292,588	167.46	114,199	137.44
1946	100,186	2766.80	285,668	1481.07	277,242	158.68	100,885	121.42
1947	110,793	3059.73	255,866	1326.56	316,376	181.08	125,954	151.59
1948	91,449	2525.52	245,155	1271.02	327,174	187.26	139,204	167.54

Table 6 *Volumes of palm oil and palm kernels exported from eastern, western and central Nigeria, 1906–48*

	E. Nigeria palm kernel exports (tons per annum)	E. Nigeria palm kernel export volumes (index 1913=100)	W. and C. Nigeria palm kernel exports (tons per annum)	W. and C. Nigeria palm kernel export volumes (index 1913=100)	E. Nigeria palm oil exports (tons per annum)	E. Nigeria palm oil export volumes (index 1913=100)	W. and C. Nigeria palm oil exports (tons per annum)	W. and C. Nigeria palm oil export volumes (index 1913=100)
1906	39,572	70.4	73,775	62.3	32,780	73.9	24,470	63.1
1907	46,794	83.3	86,836	73.3	38,890	87.7	26,590	68.6
1908	47,103	83.8	89,455	75.5	37,030	83.5	33,430	86.3
1909	50,674	90.2	108,372	91.4	40,393	91.1	41,750	107.7
1910	51,930	92.4	121,067	102.2	43,846	98.9	40,024	103.3
1911	51,954	92.4	124,436	105.0	42,645	96.2	34,536	89.1
1912	52,789	93.9	131,836	111.2	39,852	89.9	37,142	95.8
1913	56,207	100.0	118,512	100.0	44,336	100.0	38,753	100.0
1914	52,292	93.0	110,159	93.0	39,820	89.8	32,679	84.3
1915	49,103	87.4	104,216	87.9	36,341	82.0	36,653	94.6
1916	48,721	86.7	112,859	95.2	34,864	78.6	32,673	84.3
1917	Only figures available		palm kernels 185,998		palm oil 74,619			
1918	Total exports, Nigeria		205,167		86,425			
1919	tons per annum		216,913		100,967			
1920	65,186	116.0	141,824	119.7	54,266	122.4	30,590	78.9
1921	49,384	87.9	103,970	87.7	35,626	80.4	17,145	44.2
1922	59,914	106.6	118,809	100.3	54,359	122.6	33,250	85.8
1923	71,086	126.5	152,086	128.3	59,620	134.5	39,819	102.8
1924	84,122	149.7	168,725	142.4	75,619	170.6	51,464	132.8
1925	93,814	166.9	179,111	151.1	77,906	175.7	50,207	129.6
1926	83,429	148.4	165,671	139.8	65,059	146.7	48,208	124.4
1927	92,741	165.0	164,465	138.8	67,189	151.5	46,051	118.8
1928	84,690	150.7	161,948	136.7	77,613	175.1	49,498	127.7
1929	97,310	173.1	154,167	130.1	84,970	191.7	46,875	121.0

Table 6 (*cont.*)

1930	95,786	170.4	164,236	138.6	85,397	192.6	50,404	130.1
1931	93,713	166.7	160,741	135.6	75,007	169.2	43,172	111.4
1932	116,577	207.4	192,484	162.4	77,737	175.3	38,323	98.9
1933	107,000	190.4	152,945	129.1	90,170	203.4	38,526	99.4
1934	122,129	217.3	167,318	141.2	89,222	201.2	23,551	60.8
1935	112,565	200.3	200,181	168.9	95,863	216.2	46,765	120.7
1936	137,093	243.9	249,052	210.1	109,590	247.2	53,188	137.2
1937	135,066	240.3	202,683	171.0	106,033	239.2	39,685	102.4
1938	131,963	234.8	180,085	152.0	88,968	200.7	21,275	54.9
1939	131,326	233.6	168,617	142.3	96,644	218.0	29,398	75.9
1940	95,865	170.6	139,656	117.8	102,630	231.5	30,093	77.7
1941	176,883	314.7	201,241	169.8	95,415	215.2	32,363	83.5
1942	141,566	251.9	203,030	171.3	103,688	233.9	47,599	122.8
1943	144,238	256.6	187,054	157.8	90,377	203.8	44,891	115.8
1944	138,955	247.2	174,575	147.3	92,508	208.7	32,321	83.4
1945	135,776	241.6	156,812	132.3	87,138	196.5	27,061	69.8
1946	112,077	199.4	165,165	139.4	76,524	172.6	24,361	62.9
1947	128,060	227.8	188,316	158.9	90,992	205.2	34,962	90.2
1948	151,383	269.3	175,790	148.3	105,865	238.8	33,075	85.3

Sources for Tables 5 and 6

On cocoa and groundnuts: G. K. Helleiner, *Peasant Agriculture, Government, and Economic Growth in Nigeria* (Homewood, Illinois, 1966), table IV-A-8.

On palm produce: *A.R.E.P.*, 1906–9, C.O. 592/3, C.O. 592/5 and C.O. 592/7; *T.R.*, 1906, C.O. 592/3; *T.R.*, 1909, C.O. 592/7; *T.R.*, 1910 and *A.R.F.D.*, 1910, C.O. 592/9; *Trade Statistical Abstract*, 1911, C.O. 592/15; *A.R.C.D.*, 1913–30, C.O. 657 series, files 3, 6, 7, 9, 12, 14, 17, 20, 22, 24 and 27; *T.R.*, 1931–48, C.O. 657 series, files 30, 34, 36, 38, 40–1, 46–7, 54–6, 66, 68 and 70.

The sources listed for palm produce contain export figures for each port of shipment; the ports of Eastern Nigeria were Calabar, Opobo, Bonny, Port Harcourt, Degema, Brass, Akassa and (from 1924) Victoria, in the Cameroons. Those for Western and Central Nigeria include exports from Lagos, Koko, Sapele, Warri and Burutu (Forcados).

The total figure obtained by adding exports from all listed ports diverges slightly from the national figures provided by official statisticians, because the trade became increasingly concentrated during the colonial period and ports like Bonny, Brass and Akassa were no longer listed separately after their annual shipments dropped to a few thousand tons.

The original figures were recorded in varying weights and measures before the First World War; all figures have been converted into tons at the rates of 280 gallons of palm oil and 20 cwt of palm kernels per ton, as used by contemporary officials (*T.R.*, 1909, C.O. 592/9, pp. 12–13).

Table 7 *Palm oil exports from selected ports of eastern Nigeria, 1903–48* (tons per annum)

	Calabar	Opobo	Port Harcourt	Degema	E. Nigeria (total)
1903		12,186			
1904		13,521			
1905		10,329			
1906	8,910	13,970		4,580	
1907	10,600	17,300		5,560	
1908	10,029	16,665		5,422	
1909		17,468			
1910	14,789	16,578		6,137	
1911	13,986	17,604		5,414	42,645
1912	12,633	17,199		4,461	39,852
1913	13,133	20,783		5,042	44,336
1914	11,652	19,202		5,890	39,820
1915	9,926	17,313		4,838	36,341
1916	10,399	13,962		5,744	34,864
1917		24,000			
1918		21,056			
1919	12,000	19,000	13,000		
1920	8,568	17,102	18,835	8,368	54,266
1921	4,707	15,311	9,950	5,089	35,626
1922	9,930	15,946	18,656	7,679	54,359
1923	10,028	16,707	20,958	10,539	59,620
1924	14,296	20,242	25,803	13,070	75,619
1925	16,567	19,259	28,287	11,828	77,906
1926	14,269	15,866	21,311	11,679	65,059
1927	14,492	15,654	22,194	13,186	67,189
1928	18,994	15,957	23,085	16,073	77,613
1929	20,205	21,122	26,827	14,229	84,970
1930	21,609	19,867	26,404	14,950	85,397
1931	16,956	18,209	22,370	15,144	75,007
1932	20,799	14,471	24,619	15,221	77,737
1933	24,031	19,072	26,800	17,883	90,170
1934	18,652	28,848	20,730	19,514	89,222
1935	22,809	28,629	21,009	21,685	95,863
1936	27,013	32,297	28,872	19,760	109,590
1937	25,206	27,008	33,675	17,958	106,033
1938	26,437	21,952	26,673	12,319	88,968
1939	26,648	21,497	29,548	17,681	96,644
1940	26,868	31,534	24,621	19,607	102,630
1941	28,425	18,933	31,134	16,922	95,415
1942	30,850	9,062	41,628	22,148	103,688
1943	30,873	0	42,452	17,052	90,377
1944	32,396	2,635	34,083	23,395	92,508
1945	34,127	0	31,417	21,594	87,138
1946	27,672	0	31,481	17,371	76,524
1947	33,042	0	41,052	16,898	90,992
1948	41,293	0	42,006	22,566	105,865

Sources: As Table 6, and for Opobo 1903–9: *T.R.*, 1909, C.O. 592/7; for Opobo 1917–18, *Opobo Collector of Customs' Annual Report*, 1917, Calprof 5/7/987, file C 1238/17; Cal.Prov. A.R., 1918, Calprof 5/9/80, file C 100/19.

Table 8 *Palm kernel exports from selected ports of eastern Nigeria,*
1903–48 (tons per annum)

	Calabar	Opobo	Port Harcourt	Degema	E. Nigeria (total)
1903		9,786			
1904		10,841			
1905		11,032			
1906	14,440	12,548		5,633	39,572
1907	17,606	14,339		6,466	46,794
1908	17,427	14,754		5,821	47,103
1909		17,945			
1910	19,949	17,434		6,023	51,930
1911	20,225	18,645		5,005	51,954
1912	21,142	17,075		6,195	52,789
1913	23,954	16,472		7,854	56,207
1914	21,576	17,086		7,709	52,292
1915	19,244	16,838		6,676	49,103
1916	18,164	14,320		7,557	48,721
1917		20,000			
1918		17,387			
1919	25,000	12,000	11,000		
1920	23,119	15,344	15,206	9,992	65,186
1921	17,058	13,906	10,952	6,922	49,384
1922	19,245	15,565	12,655	9,446	59,914
1923	24,294	12,952	18,037	11,950	71,086
1924	28,734	14,037	19,993	17,600	84,122
1925	31,616	15,052	24,129	18,980	93,814
1926	31,643	11,760	19,116	16,052	83,429
1927	33,714	12,036	21,116	19,357	92,741
1928	36,457	14,910	16,983	18,725	84,690
1929	37,603	16,816	16,035	20,312	97,310
1930	36,515	15,541	18,560	18,513	95,786
1931	35,382	14,795	20,276	17,709	93,713
1932	41,031	17,751	31,810	19,865	116,577
1933	40,263	17,704	24,154	21,347	107,000
1934	44,884	21,420	25,819	28,722	122,129
1935	37,898	20,738	21,196	30,539	112,565
1936	52,112	22,743	28,207	31,650	137,093
1937	52,434	18,231	32,184	30,364	135,066
1938	52,997	19,946	24,790	32,803	131,963
1939	48,913	15,264	28,524	32,506	131,326
1940	35,179	9,304	21,653	29,474	95,865
1941	68,361	11,340	65,295	31,163	176,883
1942	48,836	1,956	83,145	7,371	141,566
1943	51,319	0	92,835	0	144,238
1944	49,061	0	87,520	1,284	138,955
1945	48,188	0	84,231	2,432	135,776
1946	42,783	0	60,948	7,645	112,077
1947	38,099	0	78,597	10,453	128,060
1948	60,007	0	73,664	17,063	151,383

Sources: As Table 6, and for Opobo 1903–9: *T.R.*, 1909, C.O. 592/7; for Opobo 1917–18, *Opobo Collector of Customs' Annual Report*, 1917, Calprof 5/7/987, file C 1238/17; Cal.Prov. A.R., 1918, Calprof 5/9/80, file C 100/19.

Appendix

Table 9 *Total quantities of palm produce, copra, coconut oil, groundnuts and cocoa entering world trade, 1909–13 and 1926–30* (Five-year averages: thousands of tons per annum)

	Palm oil	Palm kernels	Copra	Coconut oil	Groundnuts	Cocoa
1909–13	122	317	551	not known	586	226
1926–30	224	546	1,064	208*	1,401	493

* exports from copra-producing countries

Sources: Empire Marketing Board, nos. 54 and 61, *Survey of Vegetable Oilseeds and Oils*, vol. I: *Oil Palm Products* (H.M.S.O., 1932), pp. 117 and 123; vol. II: *Coconut Palm Products* (H.M.S.O., 1932), pp. 174–5 and 186; Imperial Economic Committee, Intelligence Branch, I.E.C./S/2, *Survey of Vegetable Oilseeds and Oils*, vol. III: *Ground Nut Products* (H.M.S.O., 1934), pp. 220–1; D. H. Urquhart, *Cocoa* (3rd impression, 1956), p. 174.

Table 10 *Income terms of trade for Nigerian cocoa, groundnuts and palm producers, 1911–48* (index: 1913=100)

	Cocoa: Nigeria	Groundnuts: Nigeria	Palm kernels: E. Nigeria	Palm kernels: W. and C. Nigeria	Palm oil: E. Nigeria	Palm oil: W. and C. Nigeria
1911	108.1	6.0	77.1	87.6	101.1	93.7
1912	80.8	10.9	77.7	92.0	81.8	87.2
1913	100.0	100.0	100.0	100.0	100.0	100.0
1914	107.1	100.4	71.5	71.4	83.0	77.9
1915	151.6	31.4	36.9	37.2	47.7	55.0
1916	82.9	174.8	30.1	33.1	36.6	39.2
1917	91.8	217.2	n.a.	n.a.	n.a.	n.a.
1918	49.9	202.3	n.a.	n.a.	n.a.	n.a.
1919	378.0	129.7	n.a.	n.a.	n.a.	n.a.
1920	45.6	136.8	34.9	36.0	46.1	29.7
1921	58.8	152.6	13.4	13.4	14.2	7.8
1922	165.2	90.8	21.0	19.8	36.6	25.6
1923	120.1	82.0	31.6	32.0	47.1	36.0
1924	235.1	278.8	40.2	38.2	61.2	47.7
1925	272.3	454.1	45.8	41.4	63.4	46.8
1926	457.0	463.3	39.4	37.1	51.4	43.6
1927	491.3	361.2	49.7	41.8	55.1	43.2
1928	448.5	412.6	49.3	44.7	68.9	50.3
1929	469.7	556.7	49.8	37.4	74.8	47.2
1930	277.5	569.7	38.7	31.5	58.3	39.4
1931	318.4	476.7	46.0	37.4	24.5	16.1
1932	477.9	637.5	48.3	37.8	41.8	23.5
1933	333.6	739.4	31.8	21.5	37.2	18.2
1934	491.6	743.3	29.7	19.3	29.3	8.9
1935	600.7	792.5	46.2	38.9	68.1	38.0
1936	762.4	1063.8	75.4	65.0	71.4	39.6
1937	1062.9	1337.9	69.4	49.4	77.1	33.0
1938	535.5	454.0	42.6	27.6	32.5	8.9
1939	758.7	369.8	40.8	24.8	32.5	11.3
1940	374.3	395.8	22.2	15.3	26.7	9.0
1941	438.8	538.3	34.6	18.7	23.7	9.2
1942	180.6	352.1	23.5	16.0	22.1	11.6
1943	205.4	239.8	22.6	13.9	22.7	12.9
1944	263.6	296.5	27.0	16.1	22.6	9.0
1945	361.8	414.6	30.7	16.8	27.1	9.6
1946	785.7	801.3	24.6	17.2	23.3	8.5
1947	924.0	768.3	27.9	19.4	27.5	12.1
1948	1452.2	847.8	64.1	35.3	74.0	26.4

Sources: As for Tables 4, 5 and 6.

Table 11 *Population densities, Southern Nigeria, 1911–63* (persons per square mile)

	1911	1921	1931	1953	1963
Northern Ngwa			345		
Western Ngwa			272		
Southern Ngwa			201		
Ngwa (average)			260		614
Eastern Nigeria: by Division					
Aba	191	174	214	413	
Afikpo	157		237	340	486
Bende	335		276	389	481
Eket	104		210	327	1090
Ikot-Ekpene	437	437	496	641	957
Okigwi	135	423	570	754	506
Owerri	369	596	527	517	616
Abakaliki	225	148	134	257	332
Ahoada	141		117	143	
Obubra	100	28	77	90	262
Ogoja	95	72	79	75	132
Central and western Nigeria: by Province					
Warri		44	74	92	
Benin		48	57	106	
Ondo		48	56	116	
Oyo		30	37	81	
Ibadan		169	208	365	
Ijebu		75	125	142	
Abeokuta		74	102	148	

Sources: 1911: Report on the Southern Nigeria Census, 1911, C.O. 592/9, f. 634.

1921: P. A. Talbot, *The Peoples of Southern Nigeria*, vol. ɪᴠ, *Linguistics and Statistics* (1926), table 4.

1931: *Census of Nigeria*, 1931: vol. ɪ, *Nigeria*, by S. M. Jacob (Crown Agents, 1933), pp. 97–9.

1953: Nigeria: Department of Statistics, *Population Census of Nigeria, 1952–53* (Lagos, n.d.), p. 3; Eastern Nigeria, *Statistical Digest, 1966* (4th edn, Enugu, 1967), p. 2.

1963: East-Central State of Nigeria, *Statistical Digest, 1971* (Enugu, 1974), p. 3; South-Eastern State of Nigeria, *Statistical Digest, 1968–70* (Calabar, 1971), p. 1.

Ngwa people: Supplementary Intelligence Reports on the Ngwa, by J. G. C. Allen, nos. ɪ and ɪɪ (1933), CSO 26/29033, vol. ɪ; no. ɪɪɪ (1934), CSO 26/29033, vol. ɪɪ.

The figures are for Divisions and Provinces as defined in 1921, with the exception of Ibadan (1950s definition used). The original figures have been adjusted to take account of boundary changes where necessary. The 1931 Census for Eastern Nigeria was held to be inaccurate at the time, and the figures given here for 1931 represent a 'scaling up' of the 1921 figures along the lines suggested by Mr Jacob (p. 23).

Table 12 *Opobo prices, palm oil, 1914–29* (£ s.d. per ton)

1914	£21 10s.9d. to £24 6s.0d.	*or*	£18 to £22 10s.0d.
1915	£13 17s.0d. to £15 7s.8d.		
1916	£16 18s.6d. to £18 9s.3d.	*or*	£13 10s.0d.
1917	£18 9s.3d. to £20		
1918	£20 to £21 10s.9d.		
1919	£23 1s.6d. (February)		
1920	£73 17s.0d. (January–April)		
	£58 9s.0d. (April–October)		
	£15 7s.0d. (December)		
1921	£9 4s.6d. to £25 7s.6d.	*or*	£11 4s.0d. to £26 8s.0d.
1922			£13 to £23 5s.0d.
1923			£20 10s.6d. to £27 4s.0d.
1924	Over £30		
1925			
1926	£23 8s.6d.		
1927	£21 4s.3d.	*or*	£19 4s.0d. to £24
1928	£24 2s.3d.	*or*	£25
1929	£21 15s.3d.	*or*	£20 5s.8d.

Table 13 *Opobo prices, palm kernels, 1914–29* (£ s.d. per ton)

1914	£16 1s.6d.	or	£11 to £20 15s.0d.
1915	£11 5s.0d.		
1916	£8 0s.9d.	or	£7 2s.6d.
1917	£9 12s.10d.		
1918	£13 13s.0d.		
1919	£14 1s.4d. (February)		
1920	£30 (January–October)		
	£20 (December)		
1921	£9 5s.0d. to £13 10s.0d.	or	£11 to £17 10s.0d.
1922			£11 5s.0d. to £13 17s.0d.
1923			£12 to £15 17s.2d.
1924	£17 11s.5d. and over		
1925			
1926	£13 17s.6d.		
1927	£13 10s.0d.	or	£13 14s.3d. to £16 5s.0d.
1928	£15	or	£16 12s.0d.
1929	£11 16s.3d.	or	£12 16s.0d.

Sources for Tables 12 and 13
1914–19 (left-hand column): D.O., Opobo, to R.C.P., 15 February 1919, Calprof 4/7/48, file C
Conf. 18/18 (oil prices given per puncheon, and kernel prices per measure – converted to prices
per ton using the following equivalents: 1 puncheon=13 cwt and 1 measure=28 bushels; 1
ton=20 cwt of oil; and 1 ton=45 bushels of kernels. These measurements, in the case of
kernels, are taken from the documents by Biffen and Henderson, cited below).
1914 and 1921–3 (right-hand column): *A.R.C.D.*, 1923, C.O. 657/9, para. 6. 1916 (right-hand
column): Report by Biffen, 17 April 1916, in Cookey to C.S.G., 29 May 1916, CSO 19/3, file N
3531/1915.
1920: A.R., Opobo Dist., 1920, Calprof 5/11/359, file C 429/21.
1921: Statistical supplement to A.R., Opobo Div., 1921, Calprof 5/12/48, file C 53/22.
1924: A.R., Opobo Div., 1924, Calprof 5/15/65, file C 69/1925.
1926–9 (left-hand column): Henderson (U.A.C., Aba) to R.O.P., 7 January 1930, Umprof
1/5/2, file C 53/1929 vol. I, part 2, ff. 55–6; reprinted in the *Report of the Aba Commission*,
1930, C.O. 583/176/1002/1930, annexure I, para. 217.
1927 (right-hand column): A.R., Opobo Div., 1927, Calprof 5/18/38, file G 45/28, appendix A.
1928–9 (right-hand column): A.R., Opobo Div., 1929, Calprof 5/20/39, file C 65/30, para. 117.

Table 14 *Aba and Umuahia prices, palm oil, 1916–29* (£ s.d. per ton)

1916	£14			
1921	£10 18s.0d. to £14			
1924	£24 5s.0d. to £28	*or*	£25 5s.0d.	*or* £28
1925	£20 9s.6d. to £26 5s.6d.			*or* £25
1926	£24 2s.0d.			*or* £25
1927	£21			*or* £23

1928   Umuahia: November–December   Aba: £24
         £24 10s.0d.   average
         £24 6s.6d.   'mixed' oil
         £25 4s.0d.   'edible' oil

1929   Umuahia: May   Aba: April–June
         £20 13s.0d.   average   £20 5s.0d.   average
         £18 12s.0d.   'mixed' oil
         £21 7s.0d.   'edible' oil

        Umuahia: October   Aba: October–December
         £19 4s.0d.   average   £19 12s.6d.   average
         £18   'mixed' oil
         £20 2s.6d.   'edible' oil

1929   Umuahia: December
         £19 19s.0d.   average
         £19 1s.6d.   'mixed' oil
         £20 16s.6d.   'edible' oil

Table 15 *Aba and Umuahia prices, palm kernels, 1916–29* (£ s.d. per ton)

1916	£3 17s.6d.				
1921	£9 13s.0d.				
1924	£12 10s.0d. to £16 16s.0d.	*or*	£15 9s.0d.	*or*	£14 10s.0d.
1925	£13 16s.0d. to £17 10s.9d.			*or*	£15 10s.0d.
1926	£14 5s.0d.			*or*	£14 5s.0d.
1927	£13 2s.0d. Umahia: £12		Aba: £13		

1928   Umahia: November   Aba: £14 10s.0d.
            £13 2s.6d.

1929   Umahia: May   Aba: April–June
            £10 4s.4d.   £10 17s.6d.
        Umahia: October   Aba: October–December
            £10 2s.6d.   £10 6s.3d.
        Umahia: December
            £10

Sources for Tables 14 and 15
1916: Report by Biffen, 17 April 1916, in Cookey to C.S.G., 29 May 1916, CSO 19/3, file N3531/1915.
1921: D.O., Aba to R.O.P., 4 March 1921, Rivprof 8/9/209, file OW 245/21A.
1924–7, left-hand column: A.R., Aba Div., 1924, Abadist 1/28/14, p. 22; A.R., Aba Div., 1925, Abadist 1/11/34, file 40/19, p. 8; A.R., Aba Div., 1926, Abadist 1/28/18, p. 8; A.R., Aba Div., 1927, Abadist 1/28/20, p. 7. These figures relate to Aba Division (excluding Umuahia) and, for palm oil, are given in the original for puncheons or casks, rather than tons. The terms 'puncheon' and 'cask' were used interchangeably to denote a unit of 180 gallons (1 ton=approx. 280 gallons of palm oil.)
1924, middle column: average of monthly returns supplied by D.O., Aba to R.O.P., 1924, in Abadist 1/16/48, file 83/1924.
1927, middle column (kernels only): Ass. Rep., Bende Div., 1927, CSO 26/20646, p. 19.
1924–9, right-hand column: A.R., Aba Div., 1929, Rivprof 8/17/372, file OW 483/1929, p. 16: these figures are given in tons for both oil and kernels, and exclude Umahia.
1928–9, left-hand column: R.O.P. to S.S.P., 19 December 1929, and E. G. Wright (Chairman, Umuahia Agents) to Capt. J. N. Hill, D.O., Bende, 2 January 1930, Umprof 1/5/1, file C 53/1929, vol. I, part 1. These figures are given for 4-gallon tins of oil and for bushels of palm kernels (280 gallons and 45 bushels=1 ton). The figures for 1924–9 (right-hand column) and 1925–9 (left-hand column) generally differ from the earlier figures in that they represent official factory prices, in contrast to the 'guesstimates' of D.O.s as to the prevalent prices offered by large-scale middlemen.

Notes

All books cited in the notes and bibliography were published in London, and the edition referred to is the first, unless otherwise stated.

1. Introduction

1 For overviews, see A. G. Hopkins, *An Economic History of West Africa* (1973); K. Hart, *The Political Economy of West African Agriculture* (Cambridge, 1982); J. Iliffe, *The Emergence of African Capitalism* (1983).

2 For a good example, and an excellent guide to the genre, see M. Watts, *Silent Violence: Food, Famine and Peasantry in Northern Nigeria* (Berkeley, 1983).

3 On 'vent-for-surplus', see H. Myint, *The Economics of the Developing Countries* (4th edn, 1973); on 'dependency', W. Rodney, *How Europe Underdeveloped Africa* (1973).

4 For example, P. A. Talbot, *The Peoples of Southern Nigeria: a Sketch of their History, Ethnology and Languages*, 4 vols. (1926); D. Forde and R. Scott, *The Native Economies of Nigeria*: vol. I, *The Economics of a Tropical Dependency*, edited by M. Perham (1946).

5 Among others, Meillassoux *et al.*, as in D. Seddon, editor, *Relations of Production: Marxist Approaches to Economic Anthropology* (1978).

6 Outline and details for Map 1 drawn from G. E. K. Ofomata, editor, *Nigeria in Maps: Eastern States* (Benin City, 1975). The major histories are K. O. Dike, *Trade and Politics in the Niger Delta, 1830–1885* (Oxford, 1956); G. I. Jones, *The Trading States of the Oil Rivers* (1963); A. J. H. Latham, *Old Calabar, 1600–1891: the Impact of the International Economy upon a Traditional Society* (Oxford, 1973); B. N. Ukegbu, 'Production in the Nigerian Oil Palm Industry, 1900–1954' (unpublished Ph.D. thesis, University of London (external), 1974); E. J. Usoro, *The Nigerian Oil Palm Industry: Government Policy and Export Production, 1906–1965* (Ibadan, 1974); D. Northrup, *Trade without Rulers: Pre-Colonial Economic Development in South-Eastern Nigeria* (Oxford, 1978); W. I. Ofonagoro, *Trade and Imperialism in Southern Nigeria, 1881–1929* (New York, London and Lagos, 1979); A. I. Nwabughuogu, 'Political Change, Social Response and Economic Development: the Dynamics of Change in Eastern Nigeria, 1930–1950' (unpublished Ph.D. thesis, Dalhousie University, 1981).

7 The problems of sources for the nineteenth century are discussed in Chapter 2.

8 Sources as in Statistical appendix, Table 11; see also Map 5, Chapter 2.

9 T. C. Mbagwu, 'The Oil Palm Economy in Ngwaland (Eastern Nigeria)' (unpublished Ph.D. thesis, University of Ibadan, 1970); J. E. N. Nwaguru, *Aba and British Rule: the Evolution and Administrative Developments of the Old Aba Division of Igboland, 1896–1960* (Enugu, 1973); J. N. Oriji, 'A History of the Ngwa People: Social and Economic

161

Developments in an Igbo Clan, from the Thirteenth to the Twentieth Centuries' (unpublished Ph.D. thesis, The State University of New Jersey, New Brunswick, 1977).

10 Map 2 source: I. W. O. Johnson (now I. W. Jimonu), 'A Study of Local Community of Ngwauku-Ofoasato' (unpublished B.A. dissertation, Institute of Education, University of Ibadan, 1965).

11 See Chapter 9.

12 Official policy debates and achievements are well surveyed in A. McPhee, *The Economic Revolution in British West Africa* (1926) and W. K. Hancock, *A Survey of British Commonwealth Affairs*, vol. II, part 2 (1942).

13 A. Smith, *An Inquiry into the Nature and Causes of the Wealth of Nations* (Cannan edn, New York, 1937; 1st edn, 1776), book I, ch. I; book III, chs. I and IV; book IV, ch. I.

14 *Ibid.*, book I, ch. XI; book III, ch. II; book IV, ch. IX; quotation from p. 629, where Smith is discussing the views of the French physiocrats.

15 *Ibid.*, book IV, ch. I, esp. p. 415.

16 H. Myint, 'The "Classical Theory" of International Trade and the Underdeveloped Countries', *Economic Journal*, 68, 2 (1958), referring to Mill, p. 322.

17 Smith, *Wealth of Nations*, book I, ch. XI.

18 J. Goody, *Technology, Tradition and the State in Africa* (1971); *Production and Reproduction: a Comparative Study of the Domestic Domain* (Cambridge, 1976); E. Boserup, *The Conditions of Agricultural Growth: the Economics of Agrarian Change under Population Pressure* (1965).

19 See also Hopkins, *Economic History*, pp. 32–9; J. Levi and M. Havinden, *Economics of African Agriculture* (1982), pp. 8–9.

20 P. Richards, 'Ecological Change and the Politics of African Land Use', and M. Watts, '"Good Try, Mr Paul": Populism and the Politics of African Land Use', *African Studies Review*, 26, 2 (1983), pp. 1–83.

21 In this tradition, see B. Warren, *Imperialism: Pioneer of Capitalism* (1980).

22 Myint, 'Classical Theory', pp. 317–37; *Economics of the Developing Countries*, chs. 3, 8 and 9.

23 P. A. Baran, *The Political Economy of Growth* (1973; 1st edn, 1957); A. G. Frank, *Capitalism and Underdevelopment in Latin America: Historical Studies of Chile and Brazil* (1971; 1st edn, New York, 1967).

24 A. Emmanuel, *Unequal Exchange: a Study of the Imperialism of Trade* (1972; 1st edn, Paris, 1969).

25 *Ibid.*, appendices I–V; G. Kay, *Development and Underdevelopment: a Marxist Analysis* (1975), pp. 107–19.

26 A. G. Frank, *Dependent Accumulation and Underdevelopment* (1978), ch. 5; S. Amin, 'Underdevelopment and Dependence in Black Africa – Origins and Contemporary Forms', *Journal of Modern African Studies*, 10, 4 (1972), pp. 518–24; Rodney, *How Europe Underdeveloped Africa*, ch. 5, esp. p. 175.

27 Frank, *Dependent Accumulation*, pp. 101–2; Smith, *Wealth of Nations*, book IV, ch. VII, part III, esp. pp. 570–1.

28 Amin, *Unequal Development: an Essay on the Social Formations of Peripheral Capitalism* (1976; 1st edn, Paris, 1973), ch. 4, esp. p. 204.

29 Earlier studies are summarised by Hopkins, *Economic History*, pp. 216–36; the flavour of the dependency debate is well caught in J. S. Hogendorn, 'The "Vent-for-Surplus" Model and African Cash Agriculture to 1914', *Savanna*, 5, 1 (1976), pp. 15–28 and debate with W. M. Freund and R. W. Shenton, *Savanna*, 6, 2 (1977), pp. 191–9.

30 K. Marx, *Pre-Capitalist Economic Foundations*, edited by E. J. Hobsbawm (1964), pp. 71–80.

31 C. Meillassoux, '"The Economy" in Agricultural Self-Sustaining Societies: a Preliminary Analysis', first published 1960, translation in Seddon, ed., *Relations of Production*, pp.

127–57; *Maidens, Meal and Money: Capitalism and the Domestic Community* (Cambridge, 1981; 1st edn, Paris, 1975); E. Terray, *Marxism and 'Primitive' Societies* (1972; 1st edn, Paris, 1969); P. P. Rey, 'The Lineage Mode of Production', *Critique of Anthropology*, no. 3 (1975), pp. 27–79; Rey, 'Class Contradiction in Lineage Societies', *ibid.*, 4, 13–14 (1979), pp. 41–60.

32 Meillassoux, 'Self-Sustaining Societies', p. 139; *Maidens*, chs. 2 and 3.

33 Terray, *'Primitive' Societies*, pp. 95–186.

34 Rey, 'Lineage Mode', *passim*.

35 E. Boserup, *Woman's Role in Economic Development* (1970), chs. 1 and 2; M. Molyneux, 'Androcentrism in Marxist Anthropology', and B. Bradby, 'Male Rationality in Economics', *Critique of Anthropology*, 3, 9–10 (1977), pp. 55–81 and 131–8.

36 Rey, 'Class Contradiction', pp. 57–60.

37 See, for example, T. Shanin, 'The Nature and Logic of the Peasant Economy', *Journal of Peasant Studies*, 1, 1 (1973), pp. 63–80, and *ibid.*, 1, 2 (1974), pp. 186–206; K. Post, '"Peasantization" and Rural Political Movements in Western Africa', *Archives Euro-péennes de Sociologie*, 13 (1972), pp. 223–54; M. A. Klein, ed., *Peasants in Africa* (1980).

38 A. V. Chayanov, *The Theory of Peasant Economy*, edited by Thorner *et al.* (Homewood, Illinois, 1966; 1st edn, Moscow, 1925); W. Kula, *An Economic Theory of the Feudal System: Towards a Model of the Polish Economy, 1500–1800* (1976; 1st edn, 1962).

39 Polly Hill's work on rural inequality is also stimulating from this point of view; for example, *Rural Hausa: a Village and a Setting* (Cambridge, 1972).

40 Hart, *Political Economy*, chs. 2, 3 and 5.

41 P. Hill, *The Migrant Cocoa-Farmers of Southern Ghana* (1963); Hopkins, *Economic History*, pp. 216–22; J. S. Hogendorn, *Nigerian Groundnut Exports: Origins and Early Development* (Zaria and Ibadan, 1978); Iliffe, *African Capitalism*, pp. 24–9.

42 A. Mabogunje, *Regional Mobility and Resource Development in West Africa* (1972); S. S. Berry, *Cocoa, Custom and Change in Rural Western Nigeria* (Oxford, 1975), ch. 5; P. David, *Les Navetanes: histoire des migrants saisonniers de l'Arachide en Senegambie des origines à nos jours* (Dakar, 1980).

43 Hopkins, *Economic History*, pp. 244–6; Berry, *Cocoa, Custom and Change*, pp. 169–71; J. Guyer, *Family and Farm in Southern Cameroon* (Boston, 1984), pp. 51–5.

44 Ukegbu, 'Production in the Nigerian Oil Palm Industry', pp. 61–89 and 140–66; Usoro, *Nigerian Oil Palm Industry*, pp. 46–7.

45 See notes 6 and 12.

46 See Chapters 4 and 6.

47 J. Heyer, P. Roberts and G. Williams, eds., *Rural Development in Tropical Africa* (New York, 1981), esp. ch. 2.

48 K. R. M. Anthony, W. O. Jones, B. F. Johnston and V. C. Uchendu, *Agricultural Change in Tropical Africa* (Ithaca and London, 1978), pp. 20–4.

49 H. Ruthenberg, *Farming Systems in the Tropics* (3rd edn, Oxford, 1980; 1st edn, 1971), pp. 9–13 and 28–9; J. Lagemann, *Traditional African Farming Systems in Eastern Nigeria: an Analysis of Reaction to Increasing Population Pressure* (Munich, 1977), pp. 5–18; Lagemann's findings are compared with those of anthropologists and geographers in Chapter 10, below.

50 Boserup, *The Conditions of Agricultural Growth*, pp. 23–7; see also her *Population and Technology* (Oxford, 1981).

51 E. le Roy Ladurie, *Times of Feast, Times of Famine: a History of Climate Since the Year 1000* (New York, 1971; 1st edn, Paris, 1967).

52 J. E. G. Sutton, 'Irrigation and Soil-Conservation in African Agricultural History', *J.A.H.*, 25, 1 (1984).

53 Richards, 'Ecological Change', pp. 22–41; Watts, *Silent Violence*, pp. 392–441; M. Chastanet, 'Les Crises de subsistances dans les villages Soninke du cercle de Bakel, de 1858 à 1945', *Cahiers d'Etudes Africaines*, 23, 1–2 (1983), pp. 5–36.

54 Hopkins, *Economic History*, pp. 58–60; debate on 'ecologically-based trade' in *Cahiers d'Etudes Africaines*, 20, 1–2 (1980).
55 On the climate of Eastern Nigeria, see R. K. Udo, *Geographical Regions of Nigeria* (1970), pp. 66–7.
56 See Chapter 10.
57 On the last point, see Richards, 'Ecological Change', pp. 22–41.
58 See Chapter 2.
59 Hopkins, *Economic History*, p. 31.
60 Oriji, 'History of the Ngwa People'; 1930s Intelligence Reports, as listed in Bibliography.
61 See, for example, J. C. Miller, ed., *The African Past Speaks: Essays on Oral Tradition and History* (Archon, Folkestone, and Hamden, Connecticut, 1980), editor's Introduction.
62 Oriji, 'History of the Ngwa People', appendix I.

2. Ecology, society and economic change to 1891

1 A. G. Leonard, 'Notes of a Journey to Bende', *Journal of the Manchester Geographical Society*, 14 (1898), pp. 190–207.
2 Int. Rep., Ngwa Clan, by J. Jackson, 1931, and Supplementary Int. Reps., Ngwa Clan, Nos. I, II and III, by J. G. C. Allen, 1933, CSO 26/29033, vols. I and II; J. N. Oriji, 'A History of the Ngwa People: Social and Economic Developments in an Igbo Clan from the Thirteenth to the Twentieth Centuries' (unpublished Ph.D. thesis, The State University of New Jersey, New Brunswick, 1977).
3 J. R. Harlan, J. M. J. de Wet and A. B. L. Stemler, eds., *Origins of African Plant Domestication* (The Hague and Paris, 1976), articles by T. Shaw and D. R. Harris; D. Forde and R. Scott, *The Native Economies of Nigeria*: vol. I, *The Economics of a Tropical Dependency*, edited by M. Perham (1946), ch. II; R. K. Udo, *Geographical Regions of Nigeria* (1970).
4 A. J. H. Latham, *Old Calabar, 1600–1891: the Impact of the International Economy on a Traditional Society* (Oxford, 1973); D. Northrup, *Trade without Rulers: Pre-Colonial Economic Development in South-Eastern Nigeria* (Oxford, 1978); B. N. Ukegbu, 'Production in the Nigerian Oil Palm Industry, 1900–1954' (unpublished Ph.D. thesis, University of London (external), 1974).
5 M. A. Onwuejeogwu, 'The Dawn of Igbo Civilization in the Igbo Culture Area', *Odinani* (the Journal of the Odinani Museum, Nri, Anambra State), 1, 1 (1972), pp. 23–50.
6 Allen, 'First Report on the Ngwa', CSO 26/29033, vol. I, p. 14; Oriji, 'History of the Ngwa', pp. 40–8.
7 Map 3 sources: G. E. K. Ofomata, ed., *Nigeria in Maps: Eastern States* (Benin City, 1975); Udo, *Geographical Regions*, pp. 66–7; T. C. Mbagwu, 'The Oil Palm Economy in Ngwaland (Eastern Nigeria)' (unpublished Ph.D. thesis, University of Ibadan, 1970), p. 25.
8 Map 4 is drawn from Oriji, 'History of the Ngwa', pp. 50–87 and 130–6; the northern village-groups are as mapped by Allen, 'First Report on the Ngwa', CSO 26/29033, vol. I. Oriji favours the earlier, and Allen the later, date for the first migrations.
9 Map 5 sources: maps accompanying Intelligence Reports, as listed in Bibliography. The reports detail the cultural features of each ethnic group.
10 Dundas to MacGregor, 28 May 1917, Abadist 1/10/25, file 25/18; Ewing to Dundas, 17 March 1920, and Ashley to Falk, 27 September 1920, Abadist 1/12/35, file 35/1920; Firth to Jackson, 25 April 1927, Abadist 1/19/12, file 60/1927; A.R., Aba Div., 1924, Abadist 1/28/14, p. 7; A.R., Aba Div., 1925, Abadist 1/11/34, file 40/19, p. 1; Quarterly Reports, Aba Div., April–June and July–September 1923, Abadist 1/15/32, file 41/1923.
11 Sources as note 8.
12 D. R. Harris, 'Traditional Systems of Plant Food Production and the Origins of Agriculture in West Africa', in Harlan *et al.*, eds., *Origins*, pp. 329–33.

164

13 J. S. Harris, 'Ibo Papers, 1938–9', 4: Ozuitem Yam Types (unpublished Mss.), R.H. Mss. Afr. s. 1505 (8); see also E. Isichei, *A History of Nigeria* (1983), pp. 22–5.

14 Harris, 'Ibo Papers', 2: Ozuitem Food Crops.

15 C. W. S. Hartley, *The Oil Palm (Elaeis Guineensis Jacq.)* (1977; 1st edn, 1967), pp. 4–7 and 77–8.

16 Northrup, *Trade Without Rulers*, p. 13.

17 *Ibid.*, pp. 65–83.

18 T. Shaw, 'Early Crops in Africa: a Review of the Evidence', in Harlan *et al.*, eds., *Origins*, pp. 130–2; W. B. Morgan, 'The Influence of European Contacts on the Landscape of Southern Nigeria', *Geographical Journal*, 125, 1 (1959), pp. 48–64.

19 Northrup, *Trade Without Rulers*, pp. 102–3 and 168; Isichei, *History of Nigeria*, p. 44.

20 Harris, 'Traditional Systems', pp. 329–33.

21 Isichei, *History of Nigeria*, p. 32; Harcourt, report enclosed in Moor to Salisbury, 6 May 1896, F.O. 2/101; Leonard, 'Notes of a Journey to Bende', p. 200.

22 Figure 1 sources: interview no. 4; Harris, 'Ibo Papers', 2: Ozuitem Food Crops; C. D. Forde, 'Land and Labour in a Cross River Village, Southern Nigeria', *Geographical Journal*, 5, 90 (1937), pp. 29 and 40–1.

23 Mbagwu, 'Oil Palm Economy', pp. 105–8; W. B. Morgan, 'Farming Practice, Settlement Pattern and Population Density in South-Eastern Nigeria', *Geographical Journal*, 121, 3 (1955), p. 330; J. Guyer, 'Naturalism in Models of African Production', *Man*, N.S. 19, 3 (1984), pp. 371–88.

24 J. S. Harris, 'Papers on the Economic Aspect of Life among the Ozuitem Ibo: II: Sexual Division of Labour among the Ozuitem Ibo', *Africa*, 14, 1 (1943), pp. 14–19; G. T. Basden, *Among the Ibos of Nigeria* (1966; 1st edn, 1921), pp. 88–93.

25 As note 24, and Basden, *Niger Ibos* (1966; 1st edn, 1938), pp. 195–6.

26 H. Baumann, 'The Division of Work According to Sex in African Hoe Culture', *Africa*, 1, 3 (1928), pp. 289–319; E. Boserup, *Woman's Role in Economic Development* (1970), pp. 16–24; J. K. Brown, 'A Note on the Division of Labour by Sex', *American Anthropologist*, 72 (1970), pp. 1073–8.

27 C. C. Robertson and M. A. Klein, eds., *Women and Slavery in Africa* (Madison, 1983).

28 Northrup, *Trade Without Rulers*, p. 78.

29 Oriji, 'History of the Ngwa', pp. 50–63 and 130–6; Allen, 'First Report on the Ngwa', CSO 26/29033, vol. I, pp. 9–10 and 25–6.

30 M. M. Green, *Igbo Village Affairs* (1964; 1st edn, 1947), pp. 41–2 and 175; S. Leith-Ross, *African Women* (1965; 1st edn, 1939), pp. 90 and 143; C. K. Meek, *Law and Authority in a Nigerian Tribe* (1950; 1st edn, 1937), pp. 202–3; L. T. Chubb, *Ibo Land Tenure* (Ibadan, 1961; 1st edn, 1947), pp. 12–22 and 47–51; interviews nos. 4, 13, 18 and 20.

31 A. Martin, *The Oil Palm Economy of the Ibibio Farmer* (Ibadan, 1956), pp. 14–15; Basden, *Among the Ibos*, pp. 53, 90–3 and 194–7.

32 C. Meillassoux, *Maidens, Meal and Money* (Cambridge, 1981), pp. 28–9; K. Gough, 'The Origin of the Family', in R. Reiter, ed., *Toward an Anthropology of Women* (New York, 1975), pp. 70–1.

33 Personal observation and informal interviews, 1980–1; C. Ifeka-Moller, 'Female Militancy and Colonial Revolt: the Women's War of 1929, Eastern Nigeria' in S. Ardener, ed., *Perceiving Women* (1975), p. 135; I. Andreski, *Old Wives' Tales: Life-Stories from Ibibioland* (1970), pp. 52–3.

34 Meek, *Law and Authority*, pp. 259–66; Green, *Igbo Village Affairs*, part II; J. S. Harris, 'Papers on the Economic Aspect of Life Among the Ozuitem Ibo: I: Economic Activities of Ozuitem Children', *Africa*, 14, 1 (1943), pp. 13–14; and evidence from the following Ngwa divorce cases: *Wahunwuo* v. *Ujuakuonu and Nwakwa*, Cases 302 and 303 of 1930, in Civil Judgement Book, 1930, Ahiaba N.C. 3/1/1; Petition by Ihedacho Njoku Adighku, 18 May 1932, Abadist 1/26/141, file 180; Petition by Nannediya, 8 September 1934, Abadist 1/7/83,

file OW 1564 (xIV); Petitions in connection with Ntegha N.C. Case 111/34, *Nwaosuagwu* v. *David Onwumelu*, Abadist 1/7/351, file OW 2538.

35 Interviews nos. 1, 3, 8, 10, 17 and 20.

36 Meek, *Law and Authority*, p. 267.

37 E. M. Falk, 'Nigeria Papers, 1910–1933: Notes on the Customs and Superstitions of the Population of the Aba Division', (unpublished Mss., 24 December 1920), R.H. Mss. Afr. s. 1000 (1), p. 31; Morgan, 'Farming Practice', pp. 320–3.

38 Allen, 'First Report on the Ngwa', CSO 26/29033, vol. I, pp. 9–10 and 25–6; Green, *Igbo Village Affairs*, pp. 14–20; Harris, 'Economics of Sixteen Ibo Individuals', pp. 302–35; Meek, *Law and Authority*, pp. 98–100.

39 As note 38, and Meek, *Law and Authority*, pp. 106–9.

40 Oriji, 'History of the Ngwa', pp. 50–3 and 130–6; Allen, 'First Report on the Ngwa', CSO 26/29033, vol. I, pp. 14–19.

41 H. S. Burrough, 'Report on Land Tenure in Aba District', 31 October 1912, enclosure in Lugard to Harcourt, 19 February 1913, C.O. 520/122.

42 Allen, 'First Report on the Ngwa', CSO 26/29033, vol. I, pp. 9–10 and 23–5.

43 *Ibid.*, pp. 29–44; Oriji, 'History of the Ngwa', pp. 101–29.

44 Allen, 'First Report on the Ngwa', CSO 26/29033, vol. I, pp. 39–40.

45 Interviews nos. 11 and 20.

46 Allen, 'First Report on the Ngwa', CSO 26/29033, vol. I, pp. 69–75.

47 Northrup, *Trade Without Rulers*, p. 120; Oriji, 'History of the Ngwa', pp. 154–68.

48 Oriji, 'History of the Ngwa', pp. 189–206.

49 Chubb, *Ibo Land Tenure*, pp. 12–22 and 47–51; G. I. Jones, 'Ibo Land Tenure', *Africa*, 19, 4 (1949), pp. 309–23.

50 Northrup, *Trade Without Rulers*, p. 21; Basden, *Among the Ibos*, p. 30; Basden, *Niger Ibos*, pp. 306–8.

51 Int. Rep., Ediene and Itak Clans, 1932, CSO 26/27615, pp. 13–16 and 25; Int. Rep., Okun and Afaha Clans, 1931, CSO 26/26506, pp. 6–8, 50–9 and 63; Int. Rep., Ukana Group, 1931, CSO 26/27604, pp. 21–6; Allen, 'First Report on the Ngwa', CSO 26/29033, vol. I, p. 32.

52 Interviews nos. 1, 9, 10, 11, 14, and 15.

53 Latham, *Old Calabar*, pp. 5–7; Northrup, *Trade Without Rulers*, pp. 217–19.

54 Northrup, *Trade Without Rulers*, pp. 149–64 and 177–81.

55 A. McPhee, *The Economic Revolution in British West Africa* (1926), pp. 30–1; W. E. Minchinton, *The British Tinplate Industry: a History* (1957), pp. 27 and 55.

56 Latham, *Old Calabar*, pp. 55–7, 86–7 and appendix I; Northrup, *Trade Without Rulers*, p. 183; Latham, 'Price Fluctuations in the Early Palm Oil Trade', *J.A.H.*, 19, 2 (1978), p. 215.

57 Oriji, 'History of the Ngwa', pp. 239–40; Northrup, *Trade Without Rulers*, pp. 183 and 192; 'Report on Forestry and Agriculture in the Eastern Province, Oct.–Dec. 1907', Calprof 14/3/127, file E 182/08, p. 2; interview no. 23.

58 Northrup himself has suggested this: 'The Compatibility of the Slave and Palm Oil Trades in the Bight of Biafra', *J.A.H.*, 17, 3 (1976), p. 361.

59 Map 6 is drawn from the map enclosed in Allen, 'First Report on the Ngwa', CSO 26/29033, vol. I; also, Ass. Rep., Aba NC area, 1927, CSO 26/20610, p. 16; B. W. Hodder and U. I. Ukwu, *Markets in West Africa* (Ibadan, 1969), pp. 128–9; interview no. 7.

60 Interviews nos. 1, 7 and 23.

61 C. A. Birtwistle (Commercial Intelligence Officer), 'Report on Cross River Trade', in Egerton to Lyttelton, 6 June 1905, C.O. 520/31.

62 Interviews nos. 1, 9, 10 and 23; *Minutes of Evidence Taken by the Committee of Inquiry into the Liquor Trade in Southern Nigeria* (P.P. 1909, LX, Cd 4907), pp. 55, 99, 301, 319, 386 and 421; G. I. Jones, 'Native and Trade Currencies in Southern Nigeria During the Eighteenth and Nineteenth Centuries', *Africa*, 28, 1 (1958), pp. 43–54.

63 Latham, *Old Calabar*, p. 24; Northrup, *Trade Without Rulers*, pp. 164–71.

64 Latham, *Old Calabar*, pp. 73–5; Northrup, *Trade Without Rulers*, pp. 208–14; C. W. Newbury, 'Prices and Profitability in Early Nineteenth-Century West African Trade', in C. Meillassoux, ed., *The Development of Indigenous Trade and Markets in West Africa* (Oxford, 1971), p. 93.
65 Newbury, 'Prices and Profitability', p. 94; Latham, 'Price Fluctuations', pp. 213–14.
66 A. G. Hopkins, *An Economic History of West Africa* (1973), p. 125.
67 On this form of adaptation, see Hopkins, *ibid.*, p. 143; Latham, *Old Calabar*, pp. 91–6 on food plantations; and literature summarised by P. Manning, *Slavery, Colonialism and Economic Growth in Dahomey, 1640–1960* (Cambridge, 1982), pp. 50–6.
68 Ukegbu, 'Production in the Nigerian Oil Palm Industry', pp. 30–6 and 42–4; see also Allen, 'First Report on the Ngwa', CSO 26/29033, vol. I, pp. 33–4.
69 See note 11; and Allen, 'Third Report on the Ngwa', CSO 26/29033, vol. II, pp. 6–8; though this interpretation is disputed by Oriji, 'History of the Ngwa', pp. 88–96.
70 'Extract of a Report by the Director of Agriculture on the Agricultural Possibilities of the Lands adjoining the Eastern Railway, to be Printed in the Trade Supplement, 10 Aug. 1917', CSO 19/5, file N 2037/1917.
71 Ukegbu, 'Production in the Nigerian Oil Palm Industry', pp. 25–7; H. N. Thompson, 'Notes on the Oil Palm', *Southern Nigeria Government Gazette*, 5 February 1908, C.O. 591/5, p. iii; J. H. J. Farquhar, *The Oil Palm and its Varieties*, edited and revised by H. N. Thompson (Crown Agents, 1913), pp. 13–14.
72 Hartley, *The Oil Palm*, pp. 4 and 7.
73 *A.R.E.P.*, 1907, C.O. 592/3, p. 32.
74 Oriji, 'A Re-Assessment of the Organisation and Benefits of the Slave and Palm Produce Trade Among the Ngwa-Igbo', *Canadian Journal of African Studies*, 16, 3 (1982), pp. 539–40; Allen, 'First Report on the Ngwa', CSO 26/29033, vol. I, p. 70.
75 Granville, 'Report on the Ozoakoli Slave Market', 10 June 1902, in Morrissey to High Commissioner, Old Calabar, 12 June 1902, Calprof 10/3, vol. III; Northrup, 'Nineteenth-Century Patterns of Slavery and Economic Growth in South-Eastern Nigeria', *International Journal of African Historical Studies*, 12, 1 (1979), pp. 1–16.
76 Ukegbu, 'Production in the Nigerian Oil Palm Industry', pp. 30–4.
77 'Lagos Palm Oil', *Kew Bulletin*, 262 (1892), pp. 206–7; Farquhar, *The Oil Palm*, pp. 25–6.
78 'Lagos Palm Oil', p. 205; Thompson, 'Notes on the Oil Palm', *Southern Nigeria Government Gazette*, 5 February 1908, C.O. 591/5, p. ii; Farquhar, *The Oil Palm*, p. 1; Basden, *Niger Ibos*, pp. 402–3; the method was demonstrated to me by Friday Nwankpa of Ahiaba-Okpuala, 13 December 1980.
79 Farquhar, *The Oil Palm*, p. 24; J. E. Gray, 'Native Methods of Preparing Palm Oil', *First Annual Bulletin of the Agricultural Department, Nigeria* (Lagos, 1922), pp. 30–2; A. C. Barnes, 'The Extraction of Oil Palm Products', *Proceedings of the First West African Agricultural Conference* (Lagos, 1927), pp. 40–1; method as demonstrated at Ahiaba-Okpuala by Joseph and Josephine Nwogu, 24 November 1980; Benjamin Nwosu and others, 28 November 1980; Beatrice Ebere Chigbundu and others, 17 December 1980; Regina Nwaoma Osuji and others, 20 December 1980; and at Amiri (near Omoba) by Rita Moses and others, 5 February 1981.
80 'Report on the Cultivation of Oil Palms', 1908, Calprof 14/3/807, file E 2760/8; Farquhar, *The Oil Palm*, pp. 24–6 and 42.
81 See Map 7, and Statistical appendix, Table 11.
82 'Lagos Palm Oil', pp. 203–5; Farquhar, *The Oil Palm*, p. 20; Mbagwu, 'Oil Palm Economy', p. 90; see also J. Tosh, 'The Cash-Crop Revolution in Tropical Africa: an Agricultural Reappraisal', *African Affairs*, 79 (1980), pp. 79–94.
83 Interviews nos. 11 and 20.
84 Interviews nos. 1, 3, 9, 10, 11, 13, 18, and 20; Ukegbu, 'Production in the Nigerian Oil Palm Industry', pp. 30–4.

85 Oriji, 'Slave and Palm-Produce Trade', p. 537; Leonard, 'Notes of a Journey to Bende', pp. 191–7.
86 Oriji, 'History of the Ngwa', p. 205; Allen, 'First Report on the Ngwa', CSO 26/29033, vol. I, pp. 76–8; Allen to D.O. Aba, 17 July 1933, Abadist 1/26/278, file 529.

3. The Ngwa and colonial rule, 1891–1914

1 J. C. Anene, *Southern Nigeria in Transition, 1885–1906* (Cambridge, 1966), pp. 29–47, 59–60 and 113–14.
2 *Ibid.*, pp. 222–35; A. Osuntokun, *Nigeria in the First World War* (1979), ch. 4.
3 P. J. Cain and A. G. Hopkins, 'The Political Economy of British Expansion Overseas, 1750–1914', *Economic History Review*, 2nd ser. 33, 4 (1980), pp. 484–6.
4 J. D. Hargreaves, *West Africa Partitioned*, vol. I: *The Loaded Pause, 1885–1889* (1974), pp. 37–49.
5 R. V. Kubicek, *The Administration of Imperialism: Joseph Chamberlain at the Colonial Office* (Durham, N.C., 1969), ch. 4; A. Smith, 'An Analysis of Imperial Aid and Colonial Borrowings, 1880–1914', unpublished I.C.S. Seminar Paper, 'British Tropical Dependencies' series, paper no. 3, 1951/2; D. Meredith, 'The British Government and Colonial Economic Policy, 1919–1939', *Economic History Review*, 2nd ser. 28 (1975), pp. 484–99.
6 *Report on the Administration of the Niger Coast Protectorate, August 1891 to August 1894*, by Sir Claude MacDonald (P.P. 1895, LXXI, C 7596), pp. 3–15; *Translations of Protocols and General Act of the Slave Trade Conference Held at Brussels, 1889–90* (P.P. 1890, L, C 6049–1), pp. 34–5 and 188–9.
7 *Report on the Niger Coast Protectorate, 1891–4* (C 7596), p. 16.
8 Blue Book, Niger Coast Protectorate, 1896–7, C.O. 464/1, ff. 81 and 95–7.
9 Blue Book, Protectorate of Southern Nigeria, 1900, C.O. 473/1, ff. 127–52, 157 and 163. The new Protectorate included Forcados and Akassa, formerly within the territories of the Royal Niger Company.
10 *S.N.R.*, 1910 (P.P. 1911, LI, Cd 5467–31), pp. 4–7.
11 *Report on the Niger Coast Protectorate, 1891–4* (C. 7596), pp. 33–43; MacDonald to F.O., 13 September 1894, F.O. 2/64; Moor to Salisbury, 14 June 1896, F.O. 2/101; Moor to Salisbury, 29 December 1896, F.O. 2/102; Leonard, 'Notes of a Journey to Bende', *Journal of the Manchester Geographical Society*, 14 (1898), p. 191.
12 See, for example, Moor to Salisbury, 14 June 1896, and Gallwey to Salisbury, 24 September 1896, F.O. 2/101; Moor to Salisbury, 17 May 1898, and Gallwey to Salisbury, 2 June 1898, F.O. 2/179.
13 See, for example, Anene, *Southern Nigeria*, pp. 222–32.
14 These were reported in annual despatches to the Colonial Office, for example Probyn to Chamberlain, 10 August 1903, C.O. 520/20, and Egerton to Crewe, 11 September 1909, C.O. 520/81.
15 Final Report on the Aro Expedition: Moor to Chamberlain, 17 April 1902, C.O. 520/13; Egerton to Lyttelton, 16 July 1905, C.O. 520/31.
16 Interviews listed in Bibliography; on the Aro Expedition and the Anang, see Moor to Chamberlain, 4, 15, 19 and 28 February 1902, C.O. 520/13; Egerton to Lyttelton, 11 April 1904, C.O. 520/24; Egerton to Lyttelton, 22 July 1905, C.O. 520/31; Egerton to Elgin, 13 May 1907, C.O. 520/45; Egerton to Crewe, 11 September 1909, C.O. 520/81.
17 M. Chanock, *Law, Custom and Social Order: the Colonial Experience in Malawi and Zambia* (Cambridge, 1985), chs. 5 and 6.
18 On the destruction of Jujus, see Egerton to Lyttelton, 16 July 1904, C.O. 520/25; Egerton to Crewe, 28 August 1909, C.O. 520/80; F. Hives and G. Lumley, *Ju-Ju and Justice in Nigeria* (1930); on the *dibias*, see I. Andreski, *Old Wives' Tales* (1970), pp. 75–80; C. K. Meek, *Law and Authority in a Nigerian Tribe* (1950; 1st edn, 1937), pp. 82–7; S.

Leith-Ross, *African Women* (1965; 1st edn, 1939), pp. 117–20; M. M. Green, *Igbo Village Affairs* (1964; 1st edn, 1947), pp. 53–8.

19 The power of *Okonko* came to public notice only after the establishment of Christianity in the Ngwa region during the First World War; see Chapters 5 and 6, below.

20 Chanock, *Law, Custom and Social Order*, pp. 16–21.

21 J. Iliffe, *A Modern History of Tanganyika* (Cambridge, 1979), p. 117.

22 A. H. M. Kirk-Greene, 'The Thin White Line: the Size of the British Colonial Service in Africa', *African Affairs*, 79 (1980), pp. 25–44; Bende Dist. Rep., April–June 1911, Rivprof 3/5/104, file E 3031/11; Egerton to Lyttelton, 9 June 1904, C.O. 520/25; Egerton to Lyttelton, 16 July 1905, C.O. 520/31.

23 Probyn to Chamberlain, 10 August 1903, C.O. 520/20; Ow. Prov. Rep., January–March 1914, Rivprof 8/2/179, File OW 273/14, p. 2.

24 A. E. Afigbo, *The Warrant Chiefs: Indirect Rule in South-Eastern Nigeria, 1891–1929* (1972), pp. 60–77; for a Central African parallel, see Chanock, *Law, Custom and Social Order*, pp. 103–11.

25 Afigbo, *Warrant Chiefs*, pp. 76–7 and 108–12.

26 Correspondence, January–February 1914, Umprof 3/1/1, File OW (Conf.) 1/1914.

27 Interview no. 17.

28 Afigbo, *Warrant Chiefs*, pp. 60–77.

29 Correspondence in Umprof 3/1/1, File OW (Conf.) 1/1914; Ow. Prov. Rep., January–March 1914, Rivprof 8/2/179, File OW 273/14, p. 2.

30 Ass. Rep., Bende Div., 1927, Abadist 1/5/16, File OW 342/27, p. 8.

31 Chanock, *Law, Custom and Social Order*, pp. 106–11.

32 Annual District Reports: on Ikot Ekpene, for 1911, in Calprof 14/7/59, file 'D' E 72/12; Abak, 1910, Calprof 14/6/96, file 'I' E 125/11; Abak, 1911, Calprof 14/7/57, file 'G' E 72/12; Aba, 1909, Calprof 14/4/950, file 'A' E 3793/9; Aba, 1910, Rivprof 3/4/61, file E 2189/10; Bende, 1911, Rivprof 3/5/104, file E 3031/11.

33 Moor to Chamberlain, 9 September 1899, C.O. 444/2; Moor to Chamberlain, 24 November 1901, C.O. 520/10; *S.N.R.*, 1902 (P.P. 1904, LVII, Cd 1768–10), pp. 4–5.

34 *Report on the Niger Coast Protectorate, 1891–4* (C 7596), pp. 19–33; *Report on the Niger Coast Protectorate, 1894–5* (P.P. 1895, LXXI, C 7916), pp. 1–4.

35 Moor to Chamberlain, 15 March 1902, C.O. 879/69; H. N. Thompson, 'History of the Forestry Department, Nigeria', *Farm and Forest*, 9 (1948), pp. 11–19.

36 Dudgeon to C.O., 22 May 1906, C.O. 879/88, f. 187.

37 Report on the Forest Administration of Southern Nigeria, Eastern Province, 1907, C.O. 592/3, f. 241; H. N. Thompson, 'Notes on the Oil Palm (Elaeis Guineensis)', 28 December 1907, in *Southern Nigeria Government Gazette*, 5 February, 1908, C.O. 591/5.

38 'Further Correspondence Relating to Botanical and Forestry Matters in British West Africa, 27 May 1907 – 24 Nov. 1909', C.O. Confidential Print, African (West) No. 912 (1910), C.O. 879/99; 'Investigations in Connection with the African Palm Oil Industry', *Bull.Imp.Inst.*, 7 (1909), pp. 357–94; Egerton to Elgin, 30 April 1907, C.O. 520/45; Thorburn to Elgin, 28 June 1907, C.O. 520/47; Egerton to Crewe, 7 July 1908, C.O. 520/62; Thorburn to Crewe, 20 May 1909, C.O. 879/99.

39 J. H. J. Farquhar, *The Oil Palm and its Varieties*, edited and revised by H. N. Thompson (Crown Agents, 1913) pp. 23–4 and 38.

40 Correspondence, 1918–27, in Calprof 5/8/430, file C 497/18; *Report of the Committee upon the System of Produce Inspection in Nigeria, 1931* (Nigeria: Sessional Paper no. 1 of 1932), C.O. 657/35.

41 1932 *Report*, C.O. 657/35, pp. 3–4; MacDonald to F.O., 26 November 1894, F.O. 2/64; MacDonald to F.O., 6 February 1896, and Moor to F.O., 9 April 1896, F.O. 2/100; Probyn to C.O., 9 May 1903, C.O. 520/19; *T.R.*, 1906, C.O. 592/3, p. 20.

42 Lugard to Harcourt, 21 January 1915, C.O. 583/30; Pollen to R.C.P., 15 June 1918, Calprof 5/8/430, file C 497/18.

43 S. Miers, *Britain and the Ending of the Slave Trade* (1975), pp. 174–89; *Brussels Protocols. . .1889–90* (C 6049–1).

44 Moor to F.O., 19 March 1894, F.O. 2/63; Moor to Chamberlain, 18 April 1902, C.O. 520/14; *A.R.E.P.*, 1907, C.O. 592/3, p. 23.

45 *Report of the Committee of Inquiry into the Liquor Trade in Southern Nigeria* (P.P. 1909, LX, Cd 4906); *N.R.*, 1916, C.R.A. No. 946, p. 39.

46 Anene, *Southern Nigeria*, pp. 304–8; T. N. Tamuno, *The Evolution of the Nigerian State* (1972), pp. 317–37; W. I. Ofonagoro, 'An Aspect of British Colonial Policy in Southern Nigeria: the Problem of Forced Labour and Slavery, 1895–1928', in B. I. Obichere, ed., *Studies in Southern Nigerian History* (1982), pp. 236–9.

47 Tamuno, *Evolution of the Nigerian State*, pp. 328–37; Report by Major J. W. Garden summarised in Miller to C.S.G., 14 June 1934, CSO 26/28994. In Malawi and Zambia, colonial policies were similarly weak regarding existing slaves, and slave status proved similarly durable: Chanock, *Law, Custom and Social Order*, pp. 167–70.

48 A. G. Hopkins, 'The Currency Revolution in South-Western Nigeria in the Late Nineteenth Century', *J.H.S.N.*, 3 (1966), pp. 471–83; G. I. Jones, 'Native and Trade Currencies in Southern Nigeria during the Eighteenth and Nineteenth Centuries', *Africa*, 28, 1 (1958), pp. 43–54; 'Report of the West African Currency Committee', C.O. Confidential Print African (West) no. 616 (1900), C.O. 879/62.

49 Report by Birtwistle in Lugard to Harcourt, 23 June 1913, C.O. 520/125.

50 *S.N.R.*, 1899–1900 (P.P. 1901, XLV, Cd 431–7), p. 6; 'The Manilla Problem', *U.A.C. Statistical and Economic Review*, 3 (1949), p. 54; Ofonagoro, *Trade and Imperialism*, p. 288.

51 Egerton to Harcourt, 20 September 1911, C.O. 520/106; Lugard to Harcourt, 23 June 1913, C.O. 520/15.

52 'The Manilla Problem: Post-Scriptum', *U.A.C. Statistical and Economic Review*, 4 (1949), pp. 59–60.

53 Ashley to S.S.P., 10 July 1925, and Ingles to S.S.P., 13 August 1925, CSO 26/15184, vol. I; interviews nos. 1, 9, 10, 22 and 23.

54 Moor to D.C.s, 31 March 1902, Calprof 9/2, vol. I; A.R. Aba Dist., 1909, Calprof 14/4/950, file 'A' E 3793/9; Aba. Dist. Rep., January–June 1918, Rivprof 8/6/377, file OW 388/18.

55 Report by Birtwistle in Lugard to Harcourt, 23 June 1913, C.O. 520/125; Report by Lovering in Hives to Maxwell, 21 November 1917, Rivprof 8/5/584, file OW 577/17.

56 *S.N.R.*, 1908 (P.P. 1910, LXIV, Cd 4964–4), p. 32; *A.R.M.D.*, 1912, C.O. 592/16, ff. 171–2.

57 Probyn to Chamberlain, 1 August 1903, C.O. 520/20; *A.R.M.D.*, 1909, C.O. 592/7, f. 714; *A.R.M.D.*, 1913, C.O. 657/3, pp. 29–30.

58 *A.R.M.D.*, 1924, C.O. 657/12, p. 23; *A.R.M.D.*, 1927, C.O. 657/20, p. 32.

59 Moor to Chamberlain, 6 June 1902, C.O. 520/14; Egerton to Elgin, 30 June 1905, C.O. 520/31; Egerton to Elgin, 26 February and 14 June 1907, C.O. 520/43.

60 *Report by Sir F. D. Lugard on the Amalgamation of Northern and Southern Nigeria, and Administration, 1912–1919* (P.P. 1919, XXXVI, Cmd 468), p. 49; *N.R.A.R.*, 1916 (Ebute Metta, 1917), p. 110.

61 *N.R.A.R.*, 1926–7, C.O. 657/17, p. 34.

62 Lugard, *Report on Amalgamation* (Cmd 468), pp. 46–8.

4. The expansion of the oil palm industry, 1884–1914

1 A. J. H. Latham, *Old Calabar, 1600–1891* (Oxford, 1973), p. 69.

2 See Statistical appendix, Table 1.

3 Latham, *Old Calabar*, pp. 67–8.

4 C. Wilson, *The History of Unilever: a Study in Economic Growth and Social Change*, vol. I (1954), pp. 28–31.
5 See Statistical appendix, Table 2.
6 C. Newbury, 'On the Margins of Empire: the Trade of Western Africa, 1875–1890' (unpublished paper, Berlin Conference, February 1985), p. 10.
7 *Blue Books, Niger Coast Protectorate, 1896–7 to 1899–1900*, C.O. 464/1 to C.O. 464/4.
8 Newbury, 'Margins of Empire', pp. 8–9.
9 R. Dumett, 'The Rubber Trade of the Gold Coast and Asante in the Nineteenth Century', *J.A.H.*, 12, 1 (1971), pp. 79–101; K. Arhin, 'The Economic and Social Significance of Rubber Production and Exchange on the Gold and Ivory Coasts, 1880–1900', *Cahiers d'Etudes Africaines*, 20, 1–2 (1980), pp. 49–62; A. G. Hopkins, 'Innovation in a Colonial Context: African Origins of the Nigerian Cocoa-Farming Industry, 1880–1920', in C. Dewey and A. G. Hopkins, eds., *The Imperial Impact* (1978) pp. 83–96; Sara Berry, *Cocoa, Custom and Socio-Economic Change in Rural Western Nigeria* (Oxford, 1975), ch. II.
10 *Blue Book, Niger Coast Protectorate, 1896–7*, C.O. 464/1, ff. 96–7; Berry, *Cocoa, Custom and Change*, p. 23; Dumett, 'Rubber Trade', p. 94.
11 Dumett, 'Rubber Trade', pp. 86–8; J. M. Dalziel, *The Useful Plants of West Tropical Africa* (Crown Agents, 1937), pp. 371–5.
12 Berry, *Cocoa, Custom and Change*, p. 6; J. I. Guyer, *Family and Farm in Southern Cameroon* (Boston, 1984), pp. 11, 20 and 51; *Census of Nigeria, 1931*: vol. III, *Census of the Southern Provinces* (Crown Agents, 1932), p. 21; see also Statistical appendix, Table 11.
13 The western Nigerian cocoa belt falls within the rainfall region of 40–60 inches per annum: R. K. Udo, *Geographical Regions of Nigeria* (1970), p. 2; see also F. R. Irvine, *West African Crops* (3rd edn, 1969), p. 5.
14 Forestry and Agriculture Reports, Eastern Province, October–December 1907, Calprof 14/3/128, file E 182/08, pp. 2–3.
15 Reports from D.C., Aba, 3 March 1912; D.C., Abakaliki, 29 December 1912; and D.C., Afikpo, 10 January 1913; Calprof 14/7/2503, file E 4227/1912.
16 'Investigations in Connection with the African Palm Oil Industry', *Bull.Imp.Inst.*, 7, 4 (1909), p. 379.
17 Hartley, *The Oil Palm*, p. 8.
18 Personal observation and interviews nos. 3, 6, 9, 11, 13 and 14.
19 Interviews, as note 18.
20 As note 18; also, M. M. Green, *Land Tenure in an Ibo Village in South-Eastern Nigeria* (1941), pp. 6–23 and 33–5; J. S. Harris, 'Economics of Sixteen Ibo Individuals', pp. 321–30.
21 Harris, 'Economics of Sixteen Ibo Individuals'; C. K. Meek, *Law and Authority in a Nigerian Tribe: a Study in Indirect Rule* (1950; 1st edn, 1937), pp. 265–76 and 314–19; M. M. Green, *Igbo Village Affairs* (1964; 1st edn, 1947), p. 36.
22 *Blue Books, Niger Coast Protectorate, 1896–7 to 1899–1900*, C.O. 464/1 to C.O. 464/4, ff. 89–112.
23 T. P. Hughes, 'Technological Momentum in History: Hydrogenation in Germany, 1898–1933', *Past and Present*, 44 (1969), pp. 106–32; J. H. van Stuyvenberg, ed., *Margarine: an Economic, Social and Scientific History, 1869–1969* (Liverpool, 1969), p. 16; Wilson, *The History of Unilever*, vol. I, pp. 118–20; vol. II, pp. 122–3.
24 See Statistical appendix, Tables 1 and 2.
25 *T.R.*, 1910, C.O. 592/9, p. 12; Table enclosed in Long to Davenport, 10 February 1917, draft letter attached to telegram, Lugard to Long, 3 February 1917, C.O. 554/33.
26 Burrough, 'Commercial Notes on Aba District', June 1912, Rivprof 3/5/104, file E 3031/11; Ag. D.O., Owerri, to Maxwell, 22 January 1916, Rivprof 8/3/420, file OW 590/15; F. K. Ekechi, 'Aspects of Palm Oil Trade at Oguta (Eastern Nigeria), 1900–1950', *African Economic History*, 10 (1981), pp. 40–6.

27 Burrough, 'Commercial Notes', 1912, Rivprof 3/5/104, file E 3031/11; Report on Forestry and Agriculture in the Eastern Provinces, October–December 1907, Calprof 14/3/128, file E 182/08; Ag. D.O., Aba, to Maxwell, 18 December 1915, Rivprof 8/3/420, file OW 590/15.

28 Interviews nos. 1 and 23.

29 Interviews nos. 1, 7, 11 and 15.

30 Burrough, 'Commercial Notes', 1912, Rivprof 3/5/104, file E 3031/11; Ag. D.O., Owerri, to Maxwell, 22 January 1916, Rivprof 8/3/420, file OW 590/15; Report by Biffen, 17 April 1916, in Cookey to C.S.G., 29 May 1916, CSO 19/3, file N 3531/1915.

31 Aba Div. Rep., January–March 1916, Rivprof 8/4/181, file OW 236/16 'A'.

32 Contrast the cocoa and groundnut industries: literature cited in Introduction, notes 29 and 40–3.

33 A.R. Aba Dist., 1909, Calprof 14/4/950, file 'A' E 3793/9; Minute on Opobo Squatters at Aba, by the Chief Commissioner of Lands, 22 November 1929, Rivprof 8/11/109, file OW 128/23, vol. ii.

34 Interviews nos. 1 and 7; Burrough, 'Commercial Notes', 1912, Rivprof 3/5/104, file E 3031/11; Report on Forestry and Agriculture, 1907, Calprof 14/3/128, file E 182/08.

35 Interviews nos. 1 and 7; I. W. O. Johnson (now I. W. Jimonu), 'A Study of Local Community of Ngwauku-Ofoasato' (unpublished B.A. dissertation, Institute of Education, University of Ibadan, April 1965), pp. 50–1.

36 See Chapter 3.

37 Moor to D.C.s, E. Div. and Cross River Div., 31 March 1902, Calprof 9/2, vol. i; Report by Birtwistle in Lugard to Harcourt, 23 June 1913, C.O. 520/125, paras. 3–4.

38 Report by Biffen, 17 April 1916, in Cookey to C.S.G., 29 May 1916, CSO 19/3, file N 3531/1915; A.R., Bende Dist., 1910, Rivprof 3/4/60; Burrough, 'Commercial Notes', 1912, Rivprof 3/5/104, file E 3031/11.

39 Burrough, 'Commercial Notes', 1912, Rivprof 3/5/104, file E 3031/11.

40 Interview no. 1.

41 Bende Dist. Rep., January–June 1911, Rivprof 3/5/104, file E 3031/11; Ag. D.O., Owerri, to Maxwell, 22 January 1916, and Ag. D.O., Aba, to Maxwell, 18 December 1915, Rivprof 8/3/420, file OW 590/15.

42 *Blue Book, Protectorate of Southern Nigeria*, 1900, C.O. 473/1, f. 135; Helleiner, *Peasant Agriculture*, tables iv-A-1 and iv-A-10, pp. 492 and 514.

43 Contrast the picture presented in Chapter 2.

44 Basden, *Among the Ibos*, p. 194; Harris, 'Economics of Sixteen Ibo Individuals', pp. 326–7.

45 See Statistical appendix, Tables 5, 6, 7 and 8.

46 *Ibid.*, Tables 7 and 8.

47 *Ibid.*, Tables 1, 2, 7 and 8. Liverpool prices have been used in this paragraph, because prices for Opobo are not known and prices at Lagos followed similar trends to those in Liverpool (see Table 3).

48 *Lagos: Report for 1903* (P.P. 1905, lii, Cd 2238–4), p. 21.

49 See Statistical appendix, Table 6; calculations made using a conversion rate of 280 gallons per ton of oil.

50 Egerton minute, 20 June 1905, on Report by Birtwistle, enclosed in Egerton to Lyttelton, 24 June 1905, C.O. 520/31.

51 See Statistical appendix, Table 7, for oil exported from Opobo; all other figures are calculated from the sources to Table 9.

52 See Statistical appendix, Tables 7 and 8.

53 *Ibid.*, Table 8.

54 On the overlapping hinterlands of Opobo and Calabar: Farquhar to P.S.E.P., 18 March 1910, CSO 15/1/8, file B 4113/09; Bende Dist. Rep., January–June 1911, Rivprof 3/5/104, file E 3031/11; A.R., Abak Dist., 1911, Calprof 14/7/57, file Ref. 'G' E 72/12.

55 Report by Birtwistle, 20 May 1905, in Egerton to Lyttelton, 24 June 1905, C.O. 520/31; Report by Biffen, 17 April 1916, in Cookey to C.S.G., 29 May 1916, CSO 19/3, file N 3531/1915; Aba Div. Rep., January–March 1916, Rivprof 8/4/181, file OW 236/16 'A'.

56 Aba Div. Rep., January–March 1916, Rivprof 8/4/181, file OW 236/16 'A'; Report by Biffen, 17 April 1916, in Cookey to C.S.G., 29 May 1916, CSO 19/3, file N 3531/1915.

57 Burrough, 'Commercial Notes', June 1912, Rivprof 3/5/104, file E 3031/11.

58 *Ibid.*; and Aba Div. Rep., July–September 1914, Rivprof 8/2/552, file OW 773/14.

59 See Statistical appendix, Tables 7 and 8.

60 These changes occurred after the Second World War; see Chapter 10.

61 On population, see Statistical appendix, Table 11.

62 *Ibid.*, though it should be noted that estimates vary for the Ngwa area. In 1927, tax assessors estimated that Ayaba Native Court Area (including the Ngwa-Ukwu village-group) had a population of 307 persons per square mile; and in 1931, the estimated population of the whole Ngwa area was 235 per square mile. Ass. Rep., Bende Div., 1927, CSO 26/20646, pp. 13 and 18; Int. Rep., Ngwa Clan, by J. Jackson, 1931, CSO 26/29033, vol. I, p. 3.

63 Ag. D.C., Ahoada to P.S.E.P., 13 October 1908, Calprof 14/3/807; Aba Div. Rep., January–March 1916, Rivprof 8/4/181, file OW 236/16 'A'.

64 Dudgeon, 'Third Report on Nigerian Agriculture', 13 June 1908, in Egerton to Crewe, 7 July 1908, C.O. 520/62.

65 See Statistical appendix, Table 8.

66 On production methods in the Ngwa area in the early twentieth century: D.C., Aba to P.S.E.P., 6 October 1908, Calprof 14/3/807, file E 2760/8; J. H. J. Farquhar, *The Oil Palm and Its Varieties*, edited and revised by H. N. Thompson (Crown Agents, 1913), pp. 24 and 42–3.

5. The end of the boom

1 See Statistical appendix, Table 4 for figures to 1948; from 1948, G. K. Helleiner, *Peasant Agriculture, Government and Economic Growth in Nigeria* (Homewood, Illinois, 1966), tables II-B-2 and II-B-3.

2 See Chapter 10.

3 Lugard to Harcourt, 20 October 1914, C.O. 583/19; *West Africa: Committee on Edible and Oil-Producing Nuts and Seeds: Report* (P.P. 1916, IV, Cd 8247), p. 5.

4 Long to Devonport, 10 February 1917, letter attached to telegram, Lugard to Long, 3 February 1917, C.O. 554/33.

5 See Statistical appendix, Table 1.

6 A. Osuntokun, *Nigeria in the First World War* (1979), pp. 30–1; *Edible Nuts and Seeds Committee: Report* (Cd 8247), pp. 4 and 20–1.

7 See Statistical appendix, Table 2; 'Control of Oleaginous Produce after the War', C.O. Confidential Print, Miscellaneous no. 339, 1918, C.O. 885/26; Wilson, *The History of Unilever: a Study in Economic Growth and Social Change*, vol. I, pp. 218–21 and 227–33.

8 *Report of a Committee on Trade and Taxation for British West Africa* (P.P. 1922, XVI, Cmd 1600), pp. 39–40; memo by Harding on Clifford to Milner, tel., 27 January 1919, C.O. 554/41.

9 *Edible Nuts and Seeds Committee: Report* (Cd 8247), pp. 22–4.

10 *Report on Trade and Taxation* (Cmd 1600), pp. 59–60.

11 Boyle to Long, 20 December 1918, C.O. 554/37; Harding on Clifford to Milner, tel., 27 January 1919, C.O. 554/41.

12 P. N. Davies, *The Trade Makers: Elder Dempster in West Africa, 1852–1972* (1973), pp. 192–3; *Edible Nuts and Seeds Committee: Minutes of Evidence* (P.P. 1916, IV, Cd 8248), pp. 209–11; memo by Harding on Clifford to Milner, tel., 27 January 1919, C.O. 554/41.

13 A.R. Collector of Customs, Calabar, 1917, Calprof 5/7/987, file C 1238/17; Report by Fraser (Af. Assn) in Lugard to Long, 18 April 1918, CSO 19/5, file N 2114/1917.

14 See Statistical appendix, Tables 1 and 3; F. Pedler, *The Lion and the Unicorn in Africa: a History of the Origins of the United Africa Company, 1787–1931* (1974), pp. 146–50 and 225–6.

15 *Report on Trade and Taxation* (Cmd 1600), p. 12; Boyle to Milner, 21 January and 28 March 1919, C.O. 554/41.

16 *Report by Sir F. D. Lugard on the Amalgamation of Northern and Southern Nigeria, and Administration, 1912–1919* (P.P. 1919, xxxvi, Cmd 468), p. 46.

17 Lugard to Harcourt, 10 August 1914, C.O. 583/17; Lugard to Long, 28 February 1918, C.O. 583/65; Osuntokun, *Nigeria in the First World War*, pp. 126–32.

18 *Report on Trade and Taxation* (Cmd 1600), p. 7.

19 Lugard, *Report on Amalgamation* (Cmd 468), p. 46.

20 *Report on Trade and Taxation* (Cmd 1600), pp. 9–13 and 24.

21 *Ibid.*, pp. 31–2.

22 See Statistical appendix, Table 3.

23 *Report on Trade and Taxation* (Cmd 1600), pp. 11–12.

24 Lugard, *Report on Amalgamation* (Cmd 468), p. 46.

25 *A.R.F.D.*, 1916 and 1917, C.O. 657/5; Lugard to Long, 23 April 1918, C.O. 583/66.

26 See Statistical appendix, Table 4.

27 E. J. Usoro, *The Nigerian Oil Palm Industry: Government Policy and Export Production, 1906–1965* (Ibadan, 1974), p. 75.

28 Evidence of Sir George Watson, Mr C. C. Knowles, and Sir Alfred Mansfield, *West Africa: Minutes of Evidence Taken Before the Committee on Trade and Taxation* (Crown Agents, 1921), pp. 41–2, 49 and 95; on oil yields, 'Control of Oleaginous Produce After the War', C.O. Confidential Print, Miscellaneous no. 339, 1918, C.O. 885/26, p. 3.

29 K. Snodgrass, *Copra and Coconut Oil* (Stanford, 1928), p. 127; Empire Marketing Board no. 61, *Survey of Oilseeds and Vegetable Oils*: vol. ii, *Coconut Palm Products* (H.M.S.O., 1932), pp. 174–5.

30 As note 29, and Food and Agricultural Organization of the United Nations, *F.A.O. Commodity Series Bulletin No. 13, Fats and Oils* (1949), pp. 46–7.

31 *F.A.O. Commodity Series Bulletin No. 13, Fats and Oils*; see Statistical appendix, Table 4.

32 'Control of Oleaginous Produce', C.O. 885/26.

33 Snodgrass, *Copra*, pp. 15–21; E.M.B. no. 61, *Coconut Palm Products*, pp. 10–13, 29–32 and 42.

34 For examples of this attitude, see 'Investigations in Connection with the African Palm Oil Industry', *Bull.Imp.Inst.*, 7 (1909), p. 391; Usoro, *Nigerian Oil Palm Industry*, pp. 35–6.

35 S. M. Martin, 'Gender and Innovation', *J.A.H.* 25, 4 (1984), pp. 411–27; S. S. Berry, 'The Food Crisis and Agrarian Change in Africa', *African Studies Review*, 27, 2 (1984), pp. 89–97.

36 W. K. Hancock, *A Survey of British Commonwealth Affairs*, vol. ii, part 2 (1942), pp. 188–200; see also Wilson, *History of Unilever*, vol. i, pp. 159–67; *West Africa: Correspondence Respecting the Grant of Exclusive Rights for the Extraction of Oil from Palm Fruits* (P.P. 1912–13, lix, Cd 6561); 'West African Lands Committee: Draft Report' (completed 1915), C.O. Confidential Print, African (West) no. 1046, 1917, C.O. 879/117, pp. 75–89 and 105–22.

37 D. Meredith, 'Government and the Decline of the Nigerian Oil-Palm Export Industry, 1919–1939', *J.A.H.*, 25, 3 (1984), pp. 311–29; Usoro, *Nigerian Oil Palm Industry*, ch. 7.

38 L. Valensi, *Fellahs tunisiens: l'économie rurale et la vie des campagnes aux 18e. et 19e. siècles* (Paris, 1977), p. 165; T. K. Derry and M. Williams, *A Short History of Technology, from the Earliest Times to A.D. 1900* (Oxford, 1970), pp. 59–60.

39 'The African Oil Palm Industry – iii, Machinery', *Bull.Imp.Inst.*, 15 (1917), pp. 57–78; *Edible Nuts and Seeds Committee: Minutes of Evidence* (P.P. 1916, iv, Cd 8248), pp. 37–9, 70–1 and 93–9.

40 D. K. Fieldhouse, *Unilever Overseas: the Anatomy of a Multinational, 1895–1965* (London and Stanford, 1978), pp. 507–9.

41 Memoranda by Harding and Strachey on Oil Palm Committee to Thomas, 21 March 1924, C.O. 554/63.

42 *Edible Nuts and Seeds Committee: Minutes of Evidence* (Cd. 8248), pp. 93 and 99; 'African Palm Oil Industry', p. 364; 'Machinery for Use in the Palm Oil Industry', *Bull.Imp.Inst.*, 24 (1926), pp. 224–7.

43 P. Creutzberg, ed., *Changing Economy in Indonesia*, vol. I (Amsterdam, 1975), pp. 95–8; Lim Chong-Yah, *Economic Development of Modern Malaya* (1967), p. 337.

44 Report on a conference with the Association of West African Merchants in Clifford to Devonshire, 20 December 1923, C.O. 554/58; 'Correspondence (Sep. 20, 1924 – April 16, 1932) Relating to the Palm Oil Industry', C.O. Confidential Print, African (West), no. 1113, C.O. 879/122.

45 Report and Minutes of Meetings of Oil Palm Committee, Committee to Thomas, 21 March 1924, C.O. 554/63: Report published as Colonial no. 10, *West Africa: Palm Oil and Palm Kernels* (H.M.S.O., 1925); Waters to Amery, 15 January 1927, C.O. 583/146/75/1927; G. G. Auchinleck and H. B. Waters, 'The Oil-Palm Plantation Industry in Sumatra and Malaya', *Proceedings of the First West African Agricultural Conference* (Lagos, 1927), pp. 30–7.

46 J. E. Gray, 'Native Methods of Preparing Palm Oil', *First Agric.Dept.Bull.* (1922), pp. 29–50.

47 Faulkner, 'Palm Oil "Central" Factories: their Commercial and Economical Possibilities', *First Agric.Dept.Bull.* (1922), pp. 18–28; memo. by Faulkner in Clifford to Churchill, 20 June 1922, C.O. 583/110.

48 Clifford to Amery, 31 December 1924, C.O. 583/128.

49 Cal. Prov. Rep., January 1920–March 1921, CSO 26/50324, p. 18.

50 A.R., Abak Dist., 1923, Calprof 5/14/50, file C 56/24; memo. by Faulkner in Clifford to Churchill, 20 June 1922, C.O. 583/110.

51 Minute by Harding on Clifford to Churchill, 20 June 1922, C.O. 583/110; Clifford to Devonshire, 25 October 1923, C.O. 583/120; Clifford to Amery, 31 December 1924, C.O. 583/128.

52 A.R. Abak Dist., 1923, Calprof 5/14/50, file C 56/24, p. 9.

53 Hyslop Bell to Amery, 21 March 1927, and Smart to Flood, 20 May 1927, C.O. 583/146/75/1927; B. Bunting, C. D. V. Georgi and J. N. Milsum, *The Oil Palm in Malaya* (Kuala Lumpur, 1934), pp. 125–8, 136, 162–3 and 235–9; E. Leplae, *Le Palmier à huile en Afrique: son exploitation au Congo Belge et en Extrême-Orient* (Brussels, 1939), pp. 31, 79 and 87.

54 Cameron to Passfield, 11 September 1931, 'Correspondence on the Palm Oil Industry, 1924–1932', C.O. 879/122, p. 131.

55 Memo. by Faulkner in Thomson to Amery, 15 January 1926, and telegram, Amery to Thomson, 30 April 1926, *ibid.*, pp. 44–6 and 57.

56 Minutes of Meeting, Joint W.Afr. Committee, London, Liverpool and Manchester Chambers of Commerce, 27 September 1927, *ibid.*, pp. 95–7; Minutes of Conference with Assn W.Afr. Merchants, 27 October 1925, in Cowan to Ormsby-Gore, 10 June 1926, C.O. 554/68.

57 Report enclosed in Thomson to Amery, 10 March 1927, 'Correspondence on the Palm Oil Industry, 1924–1932', C.O. 879/122, pp. 72–5.

58 Hartley, *The Oil Palm*, pp. 4 and 7.

59 Bunting *et al.*, *The Oil Palm in Malaya*, pp. 1, 38–9 and 52; Leplae, *Le Palmier à huile*, pp. 23–7; Auchinleck and Waters, 'Oil-Palm Plantation Industry', pp. 30–7.

60 *A.R.A.D.*, 1926 (*sic*), C.O. 657/17, p. 9.

61 Hancock, *Survey*, pp. 198–200 and 236; see also A. G. Hopkins, *An Economic History of West Africa* (1973), p. 213; memoranda by Harding and Strachey on Oil Palm Committee to Thomas, 21 March 1924, C.O. 554/63.

62 Egerton to Crewe, 19 August, 1908, C.O. 520/64; *A.R.A.D.*, 1929, C.O. 657/24, p. 16.
63 *A.R.A.D.*, 1927, C.O. 657/20, pp. 7–8.
64 A. F. B. Bridges, 'Report of Oil Palm Survey, Ibo, Ibibio and Cross River Areas' (unpublished Mss., June 1938), R.H. Mss. Afr. s. 697 (1), p. 30.
65 *A.R.A.D.*, 1936, C.O. 657/41, pp. 26–7; *A.R.A.D.*, 1938, C.O. 657/46, p. 19.
66 *A.R.A.D.*, 1940, C.O. 657/54, p. 4; *A.R.A.D.*, 1941, C.O. 657/54, p. 6; *A.R.A.D.*, 1943, C.O. 657/55, p. 19.
67 R. A. Bull, 'A Preliminary List of the Oil Palm Diseases Encountered in West Africa', *Journal of the West African Institute for Oil Palm Research*, 2 (September 1954), pp. 53–93.
68 *A.R.A.D.*, 1939, C.O. 657/47, p. 22.
69 *A.R.A.D.*, 1940, C.O. 657/54, p. 4; *A.R.A.D.*, 1943, C.O. 657/55, p. 21.
70 On these two policies, see also Usoro, *Nigerian Oil Palm Industry*, pp. 43–6.
71 *Gold Coast Botanical and Agricultural Department Report, 1903*, C.O. 98/13, pp. 7–8; report of Birtwistle's trial in Boyle to Bonar Law, 12 August 1915, C.O. 554/24.
72 Evidence of Birtwistle, *Edible Nuts and Seeds Committee: Minutes of Evidence* (Cd. 8248), p. 30.
73 *A.R.A.D.*, 1923, C.O. 657/9, pp. 5–6.
74 *A.R.A.D.*, 1924, C.O. 657/12; *A.R.A.D.*, 1925, C.O. 657/14; A. C. Barnes, 'The Extraction of Oil Palm Products', *Proceedings of the First West African Agricultural Conference* (Lagos, 1927), pp. 38–51.
75 *A.R.A.D.*, 1925, C.O. 657/14, pp. 10–11.
76 *A.R.A.D.*, 1926, C.O. 657/17, p. 10; *A.R.A.D.*, 1928, C.O. 657/22, p. 11.
77 This point will be explored for Ngwa society in Chapters 7, 8 and 9.
78 *A.R.A.D.*, 1927, C.O. 657/20, p. 7.
79 *A.R.A.D.*, 1928, C.O. 657/22, p. 11.
80 F. E. Buckley, 'The Native Oil Palm Industry and Oil Palm Extension Work in Owerri and Calabar Provinces', *Third West African Agricultural Conference: Papers* (Lagos, 1938), pp. 214–15.
81 *A.R.A.D.*, 1936, C.O. 657/41, p. 32.
82 *A.R.A.D.*, 1940, C.O. 657/54, p. 4; *A.R.A.D.*, 1943, C.O. 657/55, pp. 20–1.

6. Cassava and Christianity

1 Aba Div. Rep., July–September 1914, Rivprof 8/2/552, file OW 773/14; Aba Dist. Rep., January–March 1915, Rivprof 16/1/28; Aba Div. Rep., January–March 1916, Rivprof 8/4/181, file OW 236/16 'A'; Monthly Returns of Palm Produce Exported, January–April 1914 and 1915, CSO 19, file N 444/1915.
2 See Statistical appendix, Table 8.
3 A. Osuntokun, *Nigeria in the First World War* (1979), ch. 4; on Owerri Province, Lugard to Harcourt, 28 October 1914, C.O. 583/19; Lugard to Harcourt, 27 February 1915, C.O. 583/31; Lugard to Bonar Law, 24 June and 3 July 1915, C.O. 583/34; Boyle to Bonar Law, 4 November 1915, C.O. 583/38.
4 Walker to Maxwell, 18 November 1914, Umprof 4/1/1, file OW 26/1915.
5 Lugard to Bonar Law, 23 June 1915, C.O. 583/34; Report on Railway Work, Bende Div., July–September 1914, Rivprof 8/2/552, file OW 773/14; Lugard to Long, 6 February 1917, C.O. 583/55.
6 Alternatively, the burning of 'oracles'. Interviews nos. 1, 11, 17 and 18. On the confrontation between Braide and the colonial administration, see G. O. M. Tasie, *Christian Missionary Enterprise in the Niger Delta, 1864–1918* (Leiden, 1978), ch. v.
7 C. Ifeka-Moller, 'White Power: Social-Structural Factors in Conversion to Christianity, Eastern Nigeria, 1921–1966', *Canadian Journal of African Studies*, 8, 1 (1974), pp. 62–5; F. K. Ekechi, *Missionary Enterprise and Rivalry in Igboland, 1857–1914* (1971).

8 Ifeka-Moller, 'White Power', pp. 65–6; Ekechi, *Missionary Enterprise*, pp. 145–55.

9 R. Horton and J. D. Y. Peel, 'Conversion and Confusion: a Rejoinder on Christianity in Eastern Nigeria', *Canadian Journal of African Studies*, 10, 3 (1976), pp. 482–4 and 491; E. Ilogu, *Christianity and Ibo Culture* (Leiden, 1974), pp. 34–43; P. A. Talbot, *The Peoples of Southern Nigeria*, vol. II (1926), pp. 40–54. On the regional division of missionary labour in Eastern Nigeria: C.M.S., 'Minutes of Niger Executive Committee, July 1913', C.M.S. Archives, Birmingham, file G3 A3/P5, f. 465; F. W. Dodds, 'Ibo Openings', Methodist Missionary Archives, S.O.A.S., London, M.M.S. Box 567.

10 For a similar comment on the appeal of Aladura churches, see Horton and Peel, 'Conversion and Confusion', p. 496; also H. W. Turner, *History of an African Independent Church*, vol. I: *The Church of the Lord (Aladura)* (Oxford, 1967), pp. 6–16; J. D. Y. Peel, *Aladura: a Religious Movement Among the Yoruba* (1968), pp. 57–91 and ch. 4.

11 Tasie, *Christian Missionary Enterprise*, chs. III–IV; see also J. B. Webster, *The African Churches Among the Yoruba, 1888–1922* (Oxford, 1964).

12 *Minutes of Proceedings of the Second Session of the Niger Delta Pastorate Church Board, held at Bonny, March 10–14, 1914* (volume held in C.M.S. Library, 157 Waterloo Road, London); Tasie, *Christian Missionary Enterprise*, pp. 134 and 168–9.

13 G. O. M. Tasie, 'Christian Awakening in West Africa, 1914–1918: a Study in the Significance of Native Agency', *West African Religion*, 16 (1975), pp. 45–60; O. U. Kalu, 'Waves from the Rivers: the Spread of the Garrick Braide Movement in Igboland, 1914–1934', *J.H.S.N.*, 8, 4 (1977), pp. 95–100; interviews nos. 1, 8, 17, 18 and 22.

14 Tasie, *Christian Missionary Enterprise*, pp. 166–79.

15 *Ibid.*, pp. 176–84.

16 G. M. Haliburton, *The Prophet Harris: a Study of an African Prophet and his Mass-Movement in the Ivory Coast and the Gold Coast, 1913–1915* (1971), esp. chs. 7–9; see also S. S. Walker, *The Religious Revolution in the Ivory Coast* (1983).

17 Aba Div. Rep., January–March 1916, Rivprof 8/4/181, file OW 236/16 'A'; Aba Div. Rep., April–June 1916, Rivprof 8/4/343, file OW 382/1916.

18 Dodds, 'Ibo Openings', p. 10.

19 H. G. Brewer, 'Invasion for God: the Story of Methodism in Eastern Nigeria, 1893–1943', M.M.S. Archives, Box 567.

20 Talbot, *Peoples of Southern Nigeria*, vol. IV, pp. 105 and 123.

21 W. O. Jones, *Manioc in Africa* (Stanford, 1959), pp. 4, 23 and 74; S. A. Agboola, 'The Introduction and Spread of Cassava in Western Nigeria', *Nigerian Journal of Economic and Social Studies*, 10 (1968), pp. 369–85.

22 Interviews nos. 11, 13 and 18; Report on the Agricultural Possibilities of the Lands Adjoining the Eastern Railway, 1917, CSO 19/5, file N 2037/1917; D.O., Aba to R.O.P., 11 June 1928, and D.O. Bende to R.O.P., 21 June 1928, Rivprof 8/15/390, file OW 482/27.

23 Interview no. 13.

24 D. C. Ohadike, 'The Influenza Pandemic of 1918–1919 and the Spread of Cassava Cultivation on the Lower Niger: a Study in Historical Linkages', *J.A.H.*, 22, 3 (1981), pp. 379–91.

25 A.R., Cal. Prov., 1918, Calprof 5/9/80, file C 100/19, paras. 2–3; K. D. Patterson, 'The Demographic Impact of the 1918–1919 Influenza Pandemic in Sub-Saharan Africa: a Preliminary Assessment', *African Historical Demography*, vol. II (Centre of African Studies, Edinburgh, 1981), pp. 410–20.

26 D. Birmingham and P. M. Martin, eds., *History of Central Africa*, vol. I (1983), pp. 69–70; J. Gahama, *Le Burundi sous administration Belge* (Paris, 1983), pp. 171–9.

27 Agboola, 'Introduction of Cassava', pp. 378–85.

28 Jones, *Manioc*, pp. 16–19 and 184; D.O., Aba to R.O.P., 11 June 1928, and D.O., Bende to R.O.P., 21 June 1928, Rivprof 8/15/390, file OW 482/27; see also L. C. Uzozie, 'Patterns of Crop Combination in the Three Eastern States of Nigeria', *Journal of Tropical*

Geography, 33 (1971), pp. 62–72; and J. S. Harris, 'Some Aspects of the Economics of Sixteen Ibo Individuals', p. 322.

29 Interview no. 18.

30 Interviews nos. 3, 6, 18 and 20; see also P. V. Ottenberg, 'The Changing Economic Position of Women Among the Afikpo Ibo', in W. R. Bascom and M. J. Herskovits, eds., *Continuity and Change in African Cultures* (Chicago, 1959), p. 215.

31 Harris, 'Economics', notes 2, 12, 16 and 29; Ottenberg, 'Changing Economic Position', pp. 208–17 and 'Marriage Relationships in the Double Descent System of the Afikpo Ibo of South-Eastern Nigeria' (unpublished Ph.D. thesis, Northwestern University, 1958), pp. 31, 118–20 and 217–18; R. L. Harris, *The Political Organization of the Mbembe, Nigeria* (1965), p. 9.

32 Ass. Rep., Aba N.C. area, 1927, CSO 26/20610, p. 13; Ass. Rep., Bende Div., 1927, CSO 26/20646, p. 9.

33 Interviews nos. 3 and 18.

34 See Chapter 10.

35 Brooks to Sinclair, 1 March 1918, Calprof 5/8/227, file C 274/18; A.R., Ikot Ekpene Div., 1921, Calprof 5/12/121, file C 133/1922; Allen to D.O., Aba, 17 July 1933, Abadist 1/26/278, file 529. See also A. E. Afigbo, 'Revolution and Reaction in Eastern Nigeria, 1900–1929', *J.H.S.N.*, 3, 3 (1966), pp. 548–9; O. U. Kalu, 'Missionaries, Colonial Government and Secret Societies in South-Eastern Igboland, 1920–1950', *J.H.S.N.*, 9, 1 (1977), p. 86.

36 A.R., Ow. Div., 1920, Rivprof 8/9/147, file OW 170/21; A.R., Ow. Prov., January 1920–March 1921, Rivprof 8/9/551, file OW 655/21; A.R., Ow. Prov., 1921, CSO 26/03928.

37 See Statistical appendix, Tables 12 and 13; A.R., Cal Prov., 1920–1, CSO 26/50324; D.O., Bende to R.O.P., 26 February 1921, Rivprof 8/9/209, file OW 245/21 A; N.C. Clerks, Aba and Owerrinta to D.O., Aba, 25 and 28 February 1921, Abadist 1/13/55, file 69/21.

38 See Statistical appendix, Table 10; R.O.P. to S.S.P., 8 March 1921, Rivprof 8/9/209, file OW 245/21 A; A.R., Aba Dist., 1921, Abadist 1/13/99.

39 Native Authority v. *Obi* and seventeen others, case heard at Bende N.C., 25 January 1921; R.O.P. to D.O., Bende, 22 February 1921; and petition by Chief Wogu and others, Oloko N.C., against Rev. O. Ockiya, N.D.P., Rivprof 8/8/433, file OW 557/20.

40 Bishop Gelsthorpe to Deputy Resident i/c, Aba Div., 28 June 1933, Abadist 1/26/278, file 529; Kalu, 'Missionaries, Government and Secret Societies', p. 84.

41 On Anglican attitudes and practice, see D. C. Okeke, 'Policy and Practice of the Church Missionary Society in Igboland, 1857–1929' (unpublished Ph.D. thesis, Aberdeen University, 1977); Ilogu, *Christianity and Ibo Culture*; and Tasie, *Christian Missionary Enterprise*. On the Catholics: R. A. Ozigboh, 'A Christian Mission in the Era of Colonialism: a Study of the Catholic Missionary Enterprise in South-Eastern Nigeria, 1885–1939' (unpublished Ph.D. thesis, University of Birmingham, 1980). Oral information is used in G. D. Johnston, 'A Project in Local Church Histories', *West African Religion*, 4 (1965), pp. 8–13.

42 Interviews nos. 11, 15 and 20; Iris Andreski, *Old Wives' Tales: Life Stories from Ibibioland* (1970), p. 38; G. T. Basden, *Niger Ibos* (1966; 1st edn, 1938), ch. xv; C. K. Meek, *Law and Authority in a Nigerian Tribe: a Study in Indirect Rule* (1950; 1st edn, 1937), p. 271.

43 Interviews nos. 15, 17 and 20; Meek, *Law and Authority*, p. 272; the phrase 'singlet-mindedness' is taken from Sylvia Leith-Ross, *African Women: a Study of the Ibo of Nigeria* (1965; 1st edn, 1939), pp. 131–2.

44 Ilogu, *Christianity and Ibo Culture*, p. 47; interviews, Regina Nwaoma Osuji, aged twenty-seven, of Omoba, and Catherine Obioma Chigbundu, aged sixteen, of Ahiaba-Okpuala, 14 December 1980, while attending the kitchen ceremony of our neighbour, Mrs Chinyere Nwosu, who attends the African Church.

45 Meek, *Law and Authority*, pp. 82–7; Ilogu, *Christianity and Ibo Culture*, pp. 72–5; Leith-Ross, *African Women*, pp. 118–26, 159–62, 292 and 305; personal observation, 1980–1.

46 C.M.S. Historical Record, 1922–3, pp. 25–6 and 1927–8, p. 42; *Advance: Missionary Organ of the Primitive Methodist Church*, February 1923, pp. 38–9 and November 1926, pp. 204–5.

47 Aba N.C. Area, Ass. Rep., 1927, CSO 26/20610, pp. 5–6; Harris, 'Economics', pp. 305–19 and notes 8 and 23.

48 J. B. Webster, 'The Bible and the Plough', *J.H.S.N.*, 2, 4 (1963), pp. 418–34; S. S. Berry, 'Christianity and the Rise of Cocoa Growing in Ibadan and Ondo', *J.H.S.N.*, 4, 3 (1968), pp. 439–51.

7. Authority, justice and property rights

1 See Statistical appendix, Tables 3 and 4.

2 See Chapter 5.

3 T. O. Elias, *Nigerian Land Law and Custom* (1951), pp. 43–55.

4 Correspondence in files CSO 16/15, C 380/1913; CSO 16/18, C 22/16.

5 'Lands Committee Report', C.O. 879/117, pp. 90–1.

6 Lugard to Harcourt, 30 April 1915, C.O. 583/22; *Report by Sir F. D. Lugard on the Amalgamation of Northern and Southern Nigeria, and Administration, 1912–1919* (P.P. 1919, xxxvi, Cmd 468), p. 71.

7 Women of Calabar: Petition, 21 September 1916, in Lugard to Long, 12 February 1917, C.O. 583/56.

8 *A.R.F.A.*, 1922, C.O. 657/7, p. 3; *A.R.F.A.*, 1923, C.O. 657/9, pp. 4–5; *A.R.F.A.*, 1924, C.O. 657/12, pp. 6–7; *A.R.F.A.*, 1925, C.O. 657/14, pp. 5 and 10; *A.R.F.A.*, 1926, C.O. 657/17, pp. 4 and 10.

9 A.R., Ow. Prov., 1924, CSO 26/11930, vol. ii, p. 6; A.R., Bende Div., 1927, Rivprof 8/15/390, file OW 482/27, p. 12.

10 File on 'Imo River Reserve', Abadist 1/7/1359, file OW 7075.

11 See Chapter 3.

12 O. Adewoye, *The Judicial System in Southern Nigeria, 1854–1954: Law and Justice in a Dependency* (1977), pp. 139–40; Lugard, *Report on Amalgamation* (Cmd 468), pp. 22–5.

13 Burrough (D.O., Aba) to R.O.P., 27 November 1922, Rivprof 8/10/718, file OW 850/22; Aba Div. Rep., April–June 1923, Abadist 1/15/32, file 41/1923; Ass. Rep., Bende Div., 1927, Abadist 1/5/16, file OW 342/27, p. 8.

14 Similar trends are noted by M. Chanock, *Law, Custom and Social Order: the Colonial Experience in Malawi and Zambia* (Cambridge, 1985), chs. 4–6.

15 For the development of colonial research into local laws of land tenure, see: Lugard to Harcourt, 19 February 1913, C.O. 520/122 (returns to the West African Lands Committee); J. G. C. Allen, 'Supplementary Intelligence Reports on the Ngwa Clan, Aba Division, Owerri Province', 1933, CSO 26/29033, vols. i and ii; C. K. Meek, *Law and Authority in a Nigerian Tribe: a Study in Indirect Rule* (1950; 1st edn, 1937); L. T. Chubb, *Ibo Land Tenure* (Ibadan, 1961; 1st edn, 1947); S. N. Chinwuba Obi, *The Ibo Law of Property* (1963); Elias, *Nigerian Land Law and Custom*; and, for an illustration of how colonial precedents and anthropological findings continue to form the basis of Nigerian legal practice, A. O. Obilade, *The Nigerian Legal System* (1979). For an eloquent argument against acceptance of the 'customary' basis of post-colonial law, see M. Chanock, 'Making Customary Law: Men, Women and Courts in Colonial Northern Rhodesia', in M. J. Hay and M. Wright, eds., *African Women and the Law: Historical Perspectives* (Boston, 1982), pp. 53–67.

16 Bende Dist. Rep., April–June 1913, Rivprof 3/7/237, file E 1776/13; Aba Div. Rep., January–March 1923, Abadist 1/15/32, file 41/1923; *Nduke* v. *Obonna Awo*, Prov. Court Suit no. 12 of 1931, Abadist 1/7/16, file OW 807; *Weke Elebe* v. *Okere and Uhuka*, Prov. Court Suit no. 3 of 1933, Abadist 1/7/276, file OW 1730.

17 Aba Div. Rep., January–March 1923, Abadist 1/15/32, file 41/1923; A.R., Aba Div., 1924, Abadist 1/28/14, p. 7; *Chukwueke* v. *Chief Obonna* (N.C. Case): memorandum, D.O. Aba to R.O.P., 11 September 1923, Abadist 1/15/56, file 69/23.

18 A.R., Aba Div., 1925, Abadist 1/11/34, file 40/19; A.R. Aba Div., 1927, Abadist 1/28/20.

19 On population, see Statistical appendix, Table 11; the absence of 'affrays' within the Ngwa region has been deduced from the absence of reports of these in the district records consulted for this study.

20 Petition by Enweremadu, 30 September 1935, Abadist 1/7/674, file OW 2813.

21 Ahiaba N.C. Civil Cause Books, 1932 and 1932–3, Ahiaba N.C. 5/1/1 and 5/1/2.

22 This impression is gained from a survey of the cases in the Civil Judgement Book, 1930, Ahiaba N.C. 3/1/1; and the file 'Petitions in Connection with N.C. Cases, Ngwa-Uku Group Court, Aba Division, 1935', Abadist 1/7/674, file OW 2813. Cases of this kind involving Ubanis tended to be heard in the Provincial Court, and appear in the file 'Resident's Court Cases, 1918–27', Abadist 1/10/15, file 15/18.

23 Gardner (D.O., Aba) to R.O.P., 29 May 1929, Abadist 1/1/2, file C 4/1929.

24 M. M. Green, *Igbo Village Affairs* (1964; 1st edn, 1947), ch. IX.

25 M. M. Green, *Land Tenure in an Ibo Village in South-Eastern Nigeria* (1941), pp. 17–18; Green, *Igbo Village Affairs*, pp. 211–12; see also Sally Engle Merry, 'The Articulation of Legal Spheres', in Hay and Wright, eds., *African Women and the Law*, pp. 68–89.

26 Kelly to R.O.P., 30 May 1932, and Allen, 'First Report on the Ngwa', pp. 25–6 and 33–4, CSO 26/29033, vol. I.

27 Allen to Deputy R.O.P., 16 September 1933, Abadist 1/26/292, file 570.

28 *Ibid.*

29 Interviews nos. 1, 3, 10 and 18; no. 8 for a recollection of the narrow definition of *Nkwo Okpulo*; and, on the 1960s, T. C. Mbagwu, 'The Oil Palm Economy in Ngwaland (Eastern Nigeria)' (unpublished Ph.D. thesis, University of Ibadan, 1970), pp. 88–90.

30 Chanock, *Law, Custom and Social Order*, chs. 6, 8 and 10.

31 *Ibid.*, pp. 172–82.

32 A. E. Afigbo, *The Warrant Chiefs: Indirect Rule in South-Eastern Nigeria, 1891–1929* (1972), pp. 264–70; Adewoye, *Judicial System*, pp. 203–9. See also Chanock, *Law, Custom and Social Order*, ch. 5.

33 J. Jackson, 'Intelligence Report upon the Ngwa Clan, Aba Division, Owerri Province', 1931, CSO 26/29033, vol. I, p. 69; Allen, 'First Report on the Ngwa', *ibid.*, pp. 74–5.

34 Civil Cause Books, 1932 and 1932–3, Ahiaba N.C. 5/1/1 and 5/1/2.

35 'Resident's Court Cases, 1918–27', Abadist 1/10/15, file 15/18; Aba Supreme Court Civil Judgement Books, 1925–6 and 1928, Abamag 6/1/1 and Abamag 6/2/2; Report on the Trust System by E. J. G. Kelly, 17 January 1931, CSO 26/26209.

36 Civil Cause Books, 1932 and 1932–3, Ahiaba N.C. 5/1/1 and 5/1/2; *J. K. Taribo* v. *O. M. Uranta*, Case 119/30; *Jonathan* v. *Ukegbu*, Case 230/30; *Matthew* v. *Nwoguala*, Case 298/30; *Stephen* v. *Nnakwu*, Case 256/30; and *Matthew* v. *I. Ugunmuo*, Case 297/30, in Civil Judgement Book, 1930, Ahiaba N.C. 3/1/1.

37 *J. Akaparanta* v. *N. Nzere*, Case 78/30; *Akparanta* v. *N. Obuokiri*, Case 80/30; *J. K. Taribo* v. *O. M. Uranta*, Case 119/30; *Ochulor* v. *Wogu*, Case 127/30; and *G. Alozie* v. *J. Nwachukwu*, Case 197/30, in Civil Judgement Book, 1930, Ahiaba N.C. 3/1/1.

38 Jones to R.O.P., 22 April 1938, Umprof 5/1/36, file OW 3898; *Gabriel* v. *Wachuku*, Case 272/30, Civil Judgement Book, Ahiaba N.C. 3/1/1; Petition by Agumo, 1 June 1933, Abadist 1/26/141, file 180.

39 A.R., Ow. Prov., 1921, CSO 26/03928, p. 10; Circular by J. Watt, R.O.P., 8 August 1921, CSO 15/15/1, file B 262/1924.

40 *Wabeke* v. *Wanjuku*, Case 140/30, Civil Judgement Book, 1930, Ahiaba N.C. 3/1/1.

41 Civil Cause Books, 1932 and 1932–3, Ahiaba N.C. 5/1/1 and 5/1/2.

42 Forty-two summonses for unlawful detention, and forty-two for refund of dowry, were

issued by Ahiaba Native Court in 1931–2: Civil Cause Books, 1932 and 1932–3, Ahiaba N.C. 5/1/1 and 5/1/2. The cases were often contentious: see Petitions by Njoku, 6 November 1929, and Wankpa, 21 November 1929, Abadist 1/21/4, file 5/1929; *Wahanwuo* v. *Ujoakuonu and Nwakwa*, Cases 302/30 and 303/30, Civil Judgement Book, 1930, Ahiaba N.C. 3/1/1; Petition by I. N. Adighku, 18 May 1932, and Ahuchama *et al.*, 6 December 1932, Abadist 1/26/141, file 180.

43 Report on a case of unlawful detention, by Pleass, 4 March 1935, Abadist 1/7/351, file OW 2538.

44 Petition by Ihiedacho Njoku Adighku, 18 May 1932, Abadist 1/26/141, file 180.

45 On pre-colonial practice, see Allen, 'First Report on the Ngwa', CSO 26/29033, vol. I, p. 74.

46 E. M. Falk, 'Notes on the Customs and Superstitions etc. of the Population of the Aba Division' (unpublished Mss., 1920), R.H. Mss. Afr. s. 1000 (1), p. 15; Evidence of Olenga, Ejiatu and Mbakwu, *Aba Commission of Inquiry: Notes of Evidence Taken by the Commission of Inquiry appointed to Inquire into the Disturbances in the Calabar and Owerri Provinces, December, 1929* (Nigeria: Sessional Paper no. 9 of 1931), C.O. 657/31, pp. 665, 803, and 842; Adewoye, *Judicial System*, pp. 205–6.

47 Falk, 'Customs and Superstitions', p. 15; although C. J. Pleass, 'Report', 4 March 1935, Abadist 1/7/351, file OW 2538, clearly views the woman's responsibility to repay her bridewealth as onerous.

48 *Wahanwuo* v. *Ujoakuonu and Nwakwa*, Cases 302/30 and 303/30, Civil Judgement Book, 1930, Ahiaba N.C. 3/1/1; Petition by Onyema, 13 November 1933, Abadist 1/26/141, file 180.

49 J. S. Harris, 'Some Aspects of the Economics of Sixteen Ibo Individuals', pp. 305–19.

50 *Ibid.*, pp. 306, 309–10 and 313.

51 Civil Cause Books, 1932 and 1932–3, Ahiaba N.C. 5/1/1 and 5/1/2.

52 Report by Capt. J. N. Hill, 9 December 1929, and letter, R.O.P. to S.S.P., 31 December 1929, Umprof 1/5/1, file C 53/1929, vol. I, part I; Evidence of Olenga, Ikonnia, Nwanyeruwa, Nwannedie and Nwugo Enyidie, *Aba Commission: Notes of Evidence*, C.O. 657/31, pp. 665, 20–1, 28–9, 31 and 59–60.

53 *Ibid.*, and interview no. 6.

54 I attended meetings of the Omurunwa Women's Meeting, a club whose members all belong to Umuigwe section of Ahiaba-Okpuala, on 18 December 1980 and 3 January 1981.

55 Evidence of Nwanyeruwa, *Aba Commission: Notes of Evidence*, C.O. 657/31, pp. 28–9; interview no. 6.

56 Interviews nos. 6 and 18.

57 *Uzoaro* v. *Nwankpa*, Case 25/30, Civil Judgement Book, 1930, Ahiaba N.C. 3/1/1.

58 Report by J. G. Allen, 17 July 1933, Abadist 1/26/278, file 529.

59 See, for example the story of Wogu (Nwatu) as told by Mr Samuel Ochulo Nwaogwugwu, aged about eighty, of Ahiaba-Okpuala, on 24 January 1981, and recounted in Chapter 3.

60 The administrative reorganisation followed the recommendations made by Allen in his three 'Supplementary Intelligence Reports on the Ngwa Clan', CSO 26/29033, vols. I and II; see also M. Perham, *Native Administration in Nigeria* (1937), ch. XVI; and J. E. N. Nwaguru, *Aba and British Rule: the Evolution and Administrative Developments of the Old Aba Division of Igboland, 1896–1960* (Enugu, 1973), ch. VII.

61 A.R., Abak Dist., 1923, Calprof 5/14/50, file C56/24.

62 Interviews, Samuel Ochulo Nwaogwugwu, aged about eighty, of Ahiaba-Okpuala, 24 January 1981; J. W. Nwogu, aged about eighty, of Amiri, 4 February 1981; A. A. Nwogu, his brother and son of Warrant Chief Nwogu, aged about seventy-five, of Amiri, 6 February 1981; Edward Uche Uche, aged about sixty-five, grandson of Warrant Chief Awom, of Umuode-Nsulu, 10 February 1981; Chief I. W. Ebere, aged about eighty of Nbawsi, 10 February 1981.

63 Interviews nos. 18 and 19; see also Nwaguru, *Aba and British Rule*, appendix III, section 4, where Nwogu is mentioned.
64 S. S. Berry, 'The Food Crisis and Agrarian Change in Africa: a Review Essay', *African Studies Review*, 27, 2 (1984), pp. 89–97.
65 *Ibid.*, p. 92.
66 Sara S. Berry, *Fathers Work for Their Sons: Accumulation, Mobility and Class Formation in an Extended Yoruba Community* (Berkeley and London, 1985), p. 30.
67 *Ibid.*, pp. 31–7.

8. Trade, credit and mobility

1 See Statistical appendix, Table 6.
2 R. K. Udo, *Migrant Tenant Farmers of Nigeria: a Geographical Study of Rural Migrations in Nigeria* (Lagos, 1975), pp. 20 and 25–8.
3 B. N. Ukegbu, 'Production in the Nigerian Oil Palm Industry, 1900–1954' (unpublished Ph.D. thesis, University of London (external), 1974), pp. 90–2.
4 Sources for Map 7: *ibid.*, pp. 90–118; Udo, *Migrant Tenant Farmers*, pp. 20–37; A.R., Ow. Prov., 1921, CSO 26/03928, para. 24; D.O., Ahoada to R.O.P., 2 March 1921, Rivprof 8/9/209, file OW 245/21 A; and, on yams, D. Northrup, *Trade Without Rulers* (Oxford, 1978), pp. 218–19; A. J. H. Latham, *Old Calabar, 1600–1891* (Oxford, 1973), pp. 5–6; J. W. Wallace, 'Agriculture in Abakaliki and Afikpo', *Farm and Forest*, 2 (1941), pp. 89–93; on population densities: A. F. B. Bridges, 'Report on Oil Palm Survey, Ibo, Ibibio and Cross River Areas', June 1938, R.H. Mss. Afr. s. 697 (1), Map 1.
5 See Chapter 2, note 75.
6 See Statistical appendix, Tables 12 and 13.
7 Aba Div. Rep., April–June 1916, Rivprof 8/4/343, file OW 382/16.
8 A.R., Cal. Prov., 1918, Calprof 5/9/80, file C 100/19, para. 31.
9 See Statistical appendix, Tables 7 and 8.
10 Cookey to C.S.G., 29 May and 1 June 1916, CSO 19/3, file N 3531/1915; F. D. Hammond, *Report on the Railway System of Nigeria* (Crown Agents, 1924), p. 114.
11 Ow. Div. Rep., July–December 1919, Rivprof 16/1/45 A; A.R., Ow. Prov., 1920–1, Rivprof 8/9/551, file OW 655/21, para. 27; 1930s debt cases cited in Chapter 7, notes 33–7; interviews nos. 1, 7, and 23.
12 Bende Dist. Rep., January–June 1916, Rivprof 8/4/343, file OW 382/16; A.R., Ow. Prov., 1916, CSE 12/1/344, file EP 1308/4.
13 Bende Dist. Rep., January–June 1918, Rivprof 8/6/377, file OW 388/18.
14 *N.R.A.R.*, 1917, C.O. 657/4, p. 111.
15 *Nigeria Handbook*, 1919, appendix IV (volume consulted in Ibadan Archives).
16 P. A. Talbot, *The Peoples of Southern Nigeria*, vol. IV, *Linguistics and Statistics* (1926), p. 22.
17 Interview no. 8.
18 *Report of the Commission of Inquiry Appointed to Inquire into the Disturbances in the Calabar and Owerri Provinces, December, 1929* (Lagos, 1930), C.O. 583/176/1002/1930, para. 173.
19 *N.R.A.R.*, 1919–30, appendix IV: in C.O. 657 series, file references as in note to Tables 5 and 6, Statistical appendix.
20 F. Pedler, *The Lion and the Unicorn in Africa: a History of the Origins of the United Africa Company, 1787–1931* (1974), pp. 150, 194–5 and 226.
21 *Ibid.*, p. 226.
22 *Nigeria Handbook*, 1919, appendix IV (on open shelves in N.N.A., Ibadan); A.R., Aba Div., 1924, Abadist 1/28/14, pp. 23–5.
23 See note 11; and A. I. Nwabughuogu, 'From Wealthy Entrepreneurs to Petty Traders: the Decline of African Middlemen in Eastern Nigeria, 1900–1950', *J.A.H.*, 23, 3 (1982), esp. p. 371.

24 A.R., Cal. Prov., 1918, Calprof 5/9/80, file C 100/19, paras. 26 and 29; see also Statistical appendix, Tables 7 and 8.
25 See Map 1 for the location of the railway in relation to the main rivers of south-eastern Nigeria; on the trade of Umuahia, see D.C., Bende, to P.S.E.P., 8 November 1908, Calprof 14/3/807, file E 2760/8; A.D.O., Bende to Maxwell (via Maclaren), 6 November 1915, Rivprof 8/3/420, file OW 590/15; Bende Dist. Rep., January–June 1911, Rivprof 3/5/104, file E 3031/11; Bende Dist. Rep., January–March 1916, Rivprof 8/4/185, file OW 236/16 E; Bende Dist. Rep., January–June 1918, Rivprof 8/6/377, file OW 388/18; Ow. Div. Rep., July–December 1919, Rivprof 16/1/45A, p. 8; *A.R.M.D.*, 1924, C.O. 657/12, p. 23.
26 Bende Dist. Rep., January–June 1916, Rivprof 8/4/343, file OW 382/16; interviews nos. 3, 8, 9 and 18; on European firms, see also H. L. van der Laan, 'Modern Inland Transport and the European Trading Firms in Colonial West Africa', *Cahiers d'Etudes africaines*, 21, 4 (1981), pp. 547–75; and C. W. Newbury, 'Trade and Technology in West Africa: the Case of the Niger Company, 1900–1920', *J.A.H.*, 19, 4 (1978), pp. 551–75.
27 A.R., Bende Div., 1927, Rivprof 8/15/390, file OW 482/27; Ass. Rep., Bende Div., 1927, CSO 26/20646, p. 8; *N.R.A.R.*, 1927, C.O. 657/20, appendix IV.
28 Interviews nos. 3, 8, 9, 14 and 19.
29 O. N. Njoku, 'Development of Roads and Road Transport in Southeastern Nigeria, 1903–1939', *Journal of African Studies*, 5, 4 (1978), pp. 471–97.
30 A.R., Cal. Prov., January 1920–March 1921, CSO 26/50324, p. 36; A.R., Abak Dist., 1921, Calprof 5/12/121, file C 133/1922.
31 A.R., Ow. Prov., 1923, CSO 26/11930, vol. I, p. 19; A.R., Ow. Prov., 1924, CSO 26/11930, vol. II, p. 42; Buchanan Smith (S.S.P.) to R.C.P., 31 July 1925, Calprof 5/6/204, file C 455/16.
32 Sources for Map 8: Stanford's Library Map of the Central and Eastern Provinces of Southern Nigeria, 1910 (S.O.A.S. Library reference F/map E 20:8 (1)); 1925: S.S.P. to R.C.P., 31 July 1925, Calprof 5/6/204, file C 455/16; 1930s: Stanford's Library Map of Africa, Sheet North B32/N III (Aba), 1935 (S.O.A.S. Library reference E 20 (44)), and maps supplied with Intelligence Reports, as listed in the Bibliography.
33 A.R., Abak Dist., 1921, Calprof 5/12/121, file C 133/1922; Report by Biffen, 17 April 1916, in Cookey to C.S.G., 29 May 1916, CSO 19/3, file N 3531/1915; Ass. Rep., Ikot Ekpene Dist., 1927, CSO 26/20687, vol. I, p. 51.
34 Ass. Rep., Ikot Ekpene Dist., 1927, CSO 26/20687, vol. I, p. 51; A.R., Ow. Prov., 1924, CSO 26/11930, vol. II, p. 32; A.R., Aba Div., 1924, Abadist 1/28/14, pp. 23–5; A.R., Aba Div., 1925, Abadist 1/11/34, file 40/19, p. 8; A.R., Ow. Prov., 1930, Abadist 1/28/25, p. 68.
35 Helleiner, *Peasant Agriculture*, table IV-A-10, p. 515.
36 Helleiner, *Peasant Agriculture*, table IV-A-10, p. 515; and Osborne (Ag. Dir., P.W.D.) to S.S.P., 19 August 1918, CSO 19/6, file N 2423/1918.
37 On the bicycle and court members: Int. Rep., Okun and Afaha Clans, Ikot Ekpene Div., 1931, CSO 26/26506, p. 2; Int. Rep., Ediene and Itak Clans, Ikot Ekpene Div., 1932, CSO 26/27615, pp. 3–4.
38 On young men, bicycles and trade: *ibid.*, and Ass. Rep., Abak Dist., 1927, CSO 26/20678, p. 27; A.R., Aba Div., 1931, Abadist 1/26/148, file 195, pp. 5 and 16; Kelly to R.O.P., 30 May 1932 and Allen, 'First Report, Ngwa Clan', p. 8, CSO 26/29033, vol. I.
39 Ass. Rep., Aba N.C. Area, 1927, CSO 26/20610, p. 10; Ass. Rep., Abak Dist., 1927, CSO 26/20678, p. 27; Int. Rep., Ediene and Itak Clans, Ikot Ekpene Div., 1932, CSO 26/27615, pp. 3–4.
40 Harris, 'Economics of Sixteen Ibo Individuals', *passim*; interviews nos. 6, 11, 15 and 20; Nwannedie Chigbundu, of Ahiaba, appears to have been the exception to this rule: see Chapter 7.
41 Int. Rep., Ediene and Itak Clans, Ikot Ekpene Div., 1932, CSO 26/27615, pp. 3–4; Ass. Rep., Ikot Ekpene Dist., 1927, CSO 26/20687, vol. I, p. 51; A.R., Aba Div., 1931, Abadist 1/26/148, file 195, p. 16.

42 Ingles (R.O.P.) to S.S.P., 23 December 1929, CSO 26/15184, vol. I.
43 Henderson (Chairman of Agents, Port Harcourt) to R.O.P., 10 November 1917, Rivprof 8/5/584, file OW 577/17.
44 R.C.P. to S.S.P., 10 July 1925, CSO 26/15184, vol. I.
45 R.C.P. to S.S.P., 10 July 1925, and R.O.P. to S.S.P., 13 August 1925, CSO 26/15184, vol. I.
46 R. Fry, *Bankers in West Africa: the Story of the Bank of British West Africa Limited* (1976), pp. 106–10.
47 Birtwistle, 'Report on Cross River Trade', 24 May 1905, in Egerton to Lyttelton, 6 June 1905, C.O. 520/31.
48 A.R., Aba Div., 1924, Abadist 1/28/14, p. 26; A.R., Aba Div., 1926, Abadist 1/28/18, p. 9; and A.R., Aba Div., 1930, Abadist 1/22/71, file 97/30, vol. I, p. 29.
49 Report by Birtwistle, 17 February 1913, in Lugard to Harcourt, 23 June 1913, C.O. 520/125.
50 Kelly (D.O., Aba) to R.O.P., 17 January 1931, CSO 26/26209.
51 See Statistical appendix, Tables 14 and 15.
52 *Joseph Akparanta of Akwete* v. *Nwachuku Nzere of Ihie*, Case 78/30; *Akparanta* v. *Nwaogu Obuokiri of Ayaba*, Case 80/30; *James K. Taribo of Nbawsi* v. *Okorie Mark Uranta of Nbawsi*, Case 119/30; *Joseph of Akwete* v. *Ohuoba of Ayaba*, Case 139/30; *Matthew of Ohambele* v. *Nwoguala of Ihie*, Case 298/30; *Matthew of Ohambele* v. *Isaac Ugunmuo of Ihie*, Case 297/30; *Stephen of Opobo* v. *Nnakwu of Ihie*, Case 256/30; all in Civil Judgement Book, 1930, Ahiaba N.C. 3/1/1.
53 Hill (D.O. Bende), 'Diary of Events', 13 December 1929–1 January 1930, Umprof 1/5/1, file C 53/1929, vol. I, part 1, ff. 92–139 and 219–30; A.R., Aba Div., 1931, Abadist 1/26/148, file 195, p. 45.
54 *Ochulor* v. *Chibundu*, and *Chibundu* v. *Ochulor*, Cases 51/30 and 55/30; *Chibundu* v. *Ihekoronye*, Case 32/30, Civil Judgement Book, 1930, Ahiaba N.C. 3/1/1.
55 *Gabriel* v. *Wachuka*, Case 272/30, Civil Judgement Book, 1930, Ahiaba N.C. 3/1/1; Petition by Agumuo, 1 June 1933, Abadist 1/26/141, file 180.
56 Petition by Njoku, 6 November 1929, Abadist 1/21/4, file 5/1929; *Wahanwuo* v. *Ujoakuonu and Nwakwa*, Cases 302/30 and 303/30, Civil Judgement Book, 1930, Ahiaba N.C. 3/1/1; Petitions by Ihiedacho Njoku Adighku, 18 May 1932; Ahuchama *et al.*, 6 December 1932; and H. I. Jumbo, 5 July 1933; in Abadist 1/26/141, file 180.
57 Interviews nos. 13, 14 and 18.
58 Harris, 'Economics of Sixteen Ibo Individuals', pp. 305–15, esp. account VIII.
59 *Ibid.*, account IV, p. 308.
60 Harris, 'Some Aspects of the Economics of Sixteen Ibo Individuals', pp. 305–15; interviews nos. 1, 14 and 17.
61 Interviews nos. 3, 10 and 17.
62 Lawrence to Watt, 22 June 1921, Rivprof 8/9/545, file OW 645/21.
63 Monthly returns of trade in oleaginous produce, CSO 26/02130, vol. II.
64 A.R., Aba Div., 1925, Rivprof 8/13/310, file OW 444/1925; J. H. J. Farquhar, *The Oil Palm and its Variéties* (1913), pp. 28–9; see also Map 9, derived from Bridges, 'Oil Palm Survey', R.H. Mss. Afr. s. 697 (1) appendices II and VII.
65 Farquhar, *The Oil Palm*, pp. 25–6; O. T. Faulkner and C. J. Lewis, 'Native Methods of Preparing Palm Oil – II', *Second Annual Bulletin of the Agricultural Department, Nigeria* (Lagos, 1923), pp. 6–10.
66 See Chapter 7, notes 26–9.
67 Interviews nos. 1, 8, 9, 10, 14, 17, 18, 19 and 22.
68 Interview, Thomas Nwadike, aged about seventy, of Ngwama-Ovungwu, 2 February 1981.
69 Interview, Augustine Amaeze Nwogu, aged about seventy-five, of Amiri, 6 February 1981.
70 Interview, Edward Uche Uche, aged about sixty-five, of Umuode-Nsulu, 10 February 1981.

71 Interview, Rufus Erondu, aged about sixty-five, of Umuakwu-Nsulu, 27 January 1981.
72 Interview, Mr J. W. Nwogu, aged about eighty, of Amiri, 4 February 1981.
73 Interview, Samuel Ochulo Nwaogwugwu, aged about eighty, of Ahiaba-Okpuala, 24 January 1981.
74 Of those cited in note 67, Mr Uche and Mr Erondu are involved with S.H.O.P.P..
75 Interview, Chief I. W. Ebere, aged about eighty, of Nbawsi, 10 February 1981.

9. Production and protest: the Women Riot, 1929

1 Contemporary views of the revolt and of women's roles are provided by M. M. Green, *Igbo Village Affairs* (1964; 1st edn, 1947); S. Leith-Ross, *African Women: a Study of the Ibo of Nigeria* (1965; 1st edn, 1939); and M. Perham, *Native Administration in Nigeria* (1937), ch. xiv. Notable recent interpretations of the revolt include A. E. Afigbo, 'Revolution and Reaction in Eastern Nigeria, 1900–1929', *J.H.S.N.*, 3, 3 (1966), pp. 539–57; H. A. Gailey, *The Road to Aba* (1971); C. Ifeka-Moller, 'Female Militancy and Colonial Revolt: the Women's War of 1929, Eastern Nigeria', in S. Ardener, ed., *Perceiving Women* (1975), pp. 135–45; J. van Allen, '"Aba Riots" or Igbo "Women's War"? Ideology, Stratification and the Invisibility of Women', in N. J. Hafkin and E. G. Bay, eds., *Women in Africa* (Stanford, 1976); and N. E. Mba, *Nigerian Women Mobilized: Women's Political Activity in Southern Nigeria, 1900–1965* (Berkeley, 1982), ch. iii.
2 A general literature survey and commentary on rival interpretations is provided in S. M. Martin, 'The History of the Oil Palm Industry in South-Eastern Nigeria: the Case of the Ngwa Region, 1891–1929' (unpublished Ph.D. thesis, University of Birmingham, 1984), ch. 7.
3 *Report of the Commission of Inquiry Appointed to Inquire into the Disturbances in the Calabar and Owerri Provinces, December, 1929* (Lagos, 1930), C.O. 583/176/1002/1930, pp. 9–92.
4 See Statistical appendix, Tables 3, 4, 12 and 13; indices are for Lagos prices, which followed similar trends to Opobo prices throughout the period for which Opobo price data are available.
5 See Statistical appendix, Tables 4, 7 and 8.
6 *Ibid.*, Tables 7 and 8.
7 *N.R.A.R.*, 1919–30, appendix iv: in C.O. 657 series, file references as in note to Table 6, Statistical appendix.
8 A.R., Bende Div., 1927, Rivprof 8/15/390, file OW 482/27, p. 10; Ass. Rep., Bende Div., 1927, CSO 26/20646, p. 11.
9 A. F. B. Bridges, 'Report of Oil Palm Survey, Ibo, Ibibio and Cross River Areas' (unpublished Mss., 1938), R.H. Mss. Afr. s. 697 (1), appendix ii.
10 R.O.P. to Comptroller of Customs, Lagos, 30 November 1917, Rivprof 8/5/661, file OW 630/17; Wright (Chairman, Umuahia Agents) to Hill, 2 January 1930, Umprof 1/5/1, file C 53/1929, vol. i, part 1; interviews nos. 11, 15 and 20.
11 Interviews nos. 11, 15 and 20.
12 R. Gore Clough, *Oil Rivers Trader: Memories of Iboland* (1972), pp. 36–7 and 41–5; Leith-Ross, *African Women*, pp. 240 and 343.
13 In a sense this is working backwards since I began by studying the views expressed by the women at the time of the Riot, and my subsequent research into and interpretation of Ngwa economic history has been informed by these views. However, in the interests of a clearer narrative I have decided to deal with the emergence of intervention and other grievances first, and outline the women's reaction later.
14 Burrough (D.O., Aba) to R.O.P., 21 February 1923, Rivprof 8/11/108, file OW 128/23, vol. i.

185

15 William Oko Jaja *et al.* to Opobo Agents, 8 June 1918, enclosed in Pollen to R.C.P., 15 June 1918, Calprof 5/8/430, file C497/18.

16 Port Harcourt Chamber of Commerce to R.O.P., 14 September 1926; Oguta Agents to D.O. Owerri, 29 September 1926; and D.O. Owerri to R.O.P., 27 September 1927, Rivprof 8/14/273, file OW 343/1926; court cases reported in A.R., Aba Div., 1927, Abadist 1/28/20, p. 8; A.R., Ow. Prov., 1927, Rivprof 8/15/390, file OW 482/27, p. 28.

17 Henderson (U.A.C., Aba) to R.O.P., 7 January 1930, Umprof 1/5/2, file C53/1929, vol. I, part 2.

18 *Report of a Committee upon the System of Produce Inspection in Nigeria, 1931* (Nigeria: Sessional Paper no. 1 of 1932), C.O. 657/35, pp. 4–5; David (Opobo Agents) to R.C.P., 19 October 1926, Calprof 5/8/430, file C 497/18; R.O.P. to S.S.P., 21 October 1926, Rivprof 8/14/273, file OW 343/1926.

19 *A.R.S.P.*, 1928, C.O. 657/22, p. 54.

20 See Statistical appendix, Tables 7 and 8.

21 R. Waley Cohen (Chairman, U.A.C.) to Amery, 6 March 1929, and minute by J. E. W. Flood on a meeting with Sir Roy Wilson, 30 November 1929, C.O. 554/81/4174/29; Cohen to Passfield, 3 January 1930, C.O. 554/83/4236/30.

22 Wright to Hill, 2 January 1930, Umprof 1/5/1, file C 53/1929, vol. I, part 1.

23 See Statistical appendix, Tables 1–4, 14 and 15.

24 G. K. Helleiner, *Peasant Agriculture, Government, and Economic Growth in Nigeria* (Homewood, Illinois, 1966), tables IV-A-1 and V-E-3/4; E. J. Usoro, *The Nigerian Oil Palm Industry* (Ibadan, 1974), pp. 2 and 5.

25 For other examples, see J. Guyer, 'The Depression and the Administration in South-Central Cameroun', *African Economic History*, 10 (1981), pp. 67–79; O. Ikime, 'The Anti-Tax Riots in Warri Province, 1927–1928', *J.H.S.N.*, 3, 3 (1966), pp. 559–73; S. Shaloff, 'Income Tax, Indirect Rule, and the Depression: the Gold Coast Riots of 1931', *Cahiers d'Etudes Africaines*, 15 (1974), pp. 359–75.

26 Gailey, *Road to Aba*, ch. IV; Ikime, 'Anti-Tax Riots', pp. 559–65.

27 A.R., Bende Div. and A.R., Owerri Div., 1927, Rivprof 8/15/390, file OW 482/27.

28 *Ibid.*, and *Aba Commission Report*, C.O. 583/176/1002/30, p. 93.

29 Ass. Rep., Aba N.C. Area, 1927, CSO 26/20610, p. 9.

30 Ass. Rep., Aba Div., 1927, CSO 26/20610, p. 2; Ag.S.S.P. to C.S.G., 24 January 1928, CSO 26/20646; R.C.P. to S.S.P., 1 September 1927, CSO 26/20687, vol. I; see also Statistical appendix, Tables 14 and 15.

31 R.O.P. to D.O., Aba, 13 August 1928, and Jackson to R.O.P., 8 December 1929, Abadist 1/1/3, file Conf 6/1929.

32 *Aba Commission Report*, C.O. 583/176/1002/30, pp. 11–18 and 23–37.

33 *Ibid.*, pp. 18, 35–59 and 73–85; interviews nos. 11, 15 and 20; see also Mba, *Nigerian Women Mobilized*, ch. III, which is based partly on oral evidence from Ngwa and neighbouring women.

34 Evidence of Olenga, *Aba Commission of Inquiry: Notes of Evidence Taken by the Commission of Inquiry Appointed to Inquire into the Disturbances in the Calabar and Owerri Provinces, December, 1929* (Nigeria: Sessional Paper no. 9 of 1931), C.O. 657/31, p. 665.

35 *Aba Commission Report*, C.O. 583/176/1002/30, ch. III; Map 10 is drawn from p. 159 of this Report.

36 *Ibid.*, pp. 37, 57–8, 61, 72 and 91; D.O., Bende to R.O.P., 2 January 1930, Umprof 1/5/2, file C 53/1929, vol. I, part 2; confirmed in interviews nos. 11, 15 and 20.

37 *Aba Commission Report*, C.O. 583/176/1002/30, pp. 44–6 and annexures IV and V (casualty lists).

38 Wauton, 'Diary of Pacification Tour, Owerri Province', 28 February 1930, and other documents in Umprof 1/5/2, file C 53/1929, vol. I.

39 Evidence of Akpamgbo, Enyeremaka, Nwanyima, Olenga, and Nwoto, *Aba Commission: Notes of Evidence*, C.O. 657/31, pp. 83, 109, 659, 665–6, and 805; quote from evidence of Ejiohu, *ibid.*, p. 515.
40 Evidence of Ikonnia, Nwanyeruwa, Nwugo Enyidie and Enyidia, *Aba Commission: Notes of Evidence*, C.O. 657/31, pp. 22, 25, 60 and 80.
41 The contradictions between ideology and practice have been well explored by Ifeka-Moller, 'Female Militancy and Colonial Revolt', in S. Ardener, ed., *Perceiving Women* (1975), *passim*.
42 Evidence of Nwanyeruwa, Uloigbo, Nwudaro, Olenga and Nwayo, *Aba Commission: Notes of Evidence*, C.O. 657/31, pp. 25–6, 74–5, 588, 665, and 762.
43 Evidence of Igbeaku, Ubala, and Nwanyezi, *ibid.*, pp. 139, 147 and 148.
44 Evidence of Akpamgbo, Ahudi, and Ubala, *ibid.*, pp. 83, 115 and 147.
45 Evidence of Nwoto, *ibid.*, p. 805.
46 *Aba Commission Report*, C.O. 583/176/1002/30, p. 93.
47 Assessment Schedules, Owerri Province, 1929–30 and 1930–1, Abadist 1/1/7, file C 10/1929; A.R., Aba Dist., 1930, Abadist 1/22/71, file 97/30, vol. I.
48 *Aba Commission Report*, C.O. 583/176/1002/30, p. 102.
49 Evidence of Nwanyima of Obikabia, *Aba Commission: Notes of Evidence*, C.O. 657/31, p. 659; correspondence in CSO 26/26247, vol. I, esp. ff. 118–42.
50 *Report on Produce Inspection*, C.O. 657/35, pp. 28–9; Capt. J. R. Mackie, 'Papers on Nigerian Agriculture etc., 1939–45' (unpublished Mss.), R.H. Mss. Afr. s. 823 (1), pp. 88–92.
51 Compare J. Guyer, 'Food, Cocoa and the Division of Labour by Sex in Two West African Societies', *Comparative Studies in Society and History*, 22 (1980), pp. 355–73.

10. Cash cropping and economic change, 1930–80

1 See Statistical appendix, Table 4.
2 See Statistical appendix, Tables 5 and 9.
3 See Statistical appendix, Tables 6 and 10.
4 *T.R.*, 1935, C.O. 657/40, p. 81.
5 H. A. Gailey, *The Road to Aba* (1971), pp. 150–5; *A.R.S.P.*, 1937, C.O. 657/45, p. 61.
6 *A.R.S.P.*, 1938, C.O. 657/46, pp. 3–4.
7 C. Coquery-Vidrovitch, 'L'Afrique coloniale française et la crise de 1930: crise structurelle et genese du sous-developpement. Rapport d'ensemble', *Revue Française d'Histoire d'Outre-Mer*, 63, 232–3 (1976), pp. 401–22.
8 This also happened in the long run in neighbouring Cameroon: see J. I. Guyer, 'Head Tax, Social Structure and Rural Incomes in Cameroun, 1922–1937', *Cahiers d'Etudes Africaines*, 20, 3 (1980), pp. 305–29.
9 Gailey, *Road to Aba*, pp. 145–55.
10 J. G. C. Allen, 'First Supplementary Intelligence Report on the Ngwa', CSO 26/29033, vol. I, pp. 77–8 and 88–92.
11 C.S.G. to S.S.P., 27 December 1933, CSO 26/29033, vol. I; J. E. N. Nwaguru, *Aba and British Rule: the Evolution and Administrative Developments of the Old Aba Division of Igboland, 1896–1960* (Enugu, 1973), pp. 113–18 and 126.
12 Nwaguru, *Aba and British Rule*, pp. 124–8 and 136–49.
13 See Chapter 7, above.
14 Nwaguru, *Aba and British Rule*, pp. 124–5.
15 *Ibid.*, p. 127.
16 *Ibid.*, pp. 136–7.
17 See Statistical appendix, Table 4.
18 *Ibid.*, Table 6; Nwaguru, *Aba and British Rule*, pp. 133–4; A. I. Nwabughuogu, 'Political Change, Social Response and Economic Development: the Dynamics of Change in Eastern

Nigeria, 1930–1950' (unpublished Ph.D. thesis, Dalhousie University, 1981), ch. VI; *A.R.E.P.*, 1943, C.O. 657/55, p. 1.

19 J. R. Mackie, 'Papers on Nigerian Agriculture, Etc.,' 1939–45, R.H. Mss. Afr. s. 823 (4), p. 4.

20 Colonial No. 211: *Report of the Mission Appointed to Inquire into the Production and Transport of Vegetable Oils and Seeds Produced in the West African Colonies* (H.M.S.O., 1947), appendix XII.

21 *Ibid.*, appendix XIV; *A.R.E.P.*, 1940, C.O. 657/54, p. 25.

22 Nwabughuogu, 'Political Change', pp. 214–17 and 258–9; *A.R.E.P.*, 1944, C.O. 657/56, p. 27.

23 *A.R.A.D.*, 1950–1, C.O. 657/73, p. 89.

24 W. B. Morgan, 'Farming Practice, Settlement Pattern and Population Density in South-Eastern Nigeria', *Geographical Journal*, 121, 3 (1955), p. 331.

25 *Census of Nigeria, 1931*: vol. III, *Southern Provinces*, by H. B. Cox (Crown Agents, 1932), p. 24; *Nigeria: Department of Statistics, Population Census of Nigeria, 1952–53*, summary tables (Lagos, n.d.), p. 10; *East-Central State of Nigeria, Statistical Digest, 1970* (Enugu, 1972), p. 2; J. de St Jorre, *The Nigerian Civil War* (1972), p. 260.

26 Interviews nos. 2 and 19; Morgan, 'Farming Practice', pp. 328 and 331; de St. Jorre, *Nigerian Civil War*, p. 260; E. Isichei, *A History of the Igbo People* (1976), p. 206.

27 Morgan, 'Farming Practice', p. 330; interviews nos. 6 and 20, confirmed by informal conversations at Ahiaba-Okpuala, 1980; Anne Martin, *The Oil Palm Economy of the Ibibio Farmer* (Ibadan, 1956), p. 48.

28 Morgan, 'Farming Practice', pp. 326–8 and 331; see also Statistical appendix, Table 11.

29 L. C. Uzozie, 'Patterns of Crop Combination in the Three Eastern States of Nigeria', *Journal of Tropical Geography*, 33 (December 1971), pp. 62–72.

30 T. C. Mbagwu, 'The Oil Palm Economy in Ngwaland (Eastern Nigeria)' (unpublished Ph.D. thesis, University of Ibadan, 1970).

31 *Population Census of Nigeria, 1952–53*, p. 10; *East-Central State, Statistical Digest, 1970*, p. 2; Mbagwu, 'Oil Palm Economy', p. 42.

32 Mbagwu, 'Oil Palm Economy', pp. 34–5, 56–62, 77–8 and 229–45.

33 *Ibid.*, pp. 211–13, 234–5 and 243.

34 *Ibid.*, pp. 27–8 and 56.

35 *Ibid.*, pp. 215–17 and 242.

36 A. Martin, *Oil Palm Economy*, pp. 7 and 33–7.

37 G. K. Helleiner, *Peasant Agriculture, Government, and Economic Growth in Nigeria* (Homewood, Illinois, 1966), table II-B-2, on import prices.

38 A. Martin, *Oil Palm Economy*, p. 30; 'adult' here means older than fifteen.

39 Helleiner, *Peasant Agriculture*, tables II-B-2 and II-B-3.

40 *Ibid.*, tables II-B-2, II-B-3 and IV-A-8.

41 *Ibid.*, table II-B-4; S. S. Berry, *Cocoa, Custom and Socio-Economic Change in Rural Western Nigeria* (Oxford, 1975), p. 224.

42 P. T. Bauer, *West African Trade* (1954) and original articles in the *Economic Journal*, 1952–4; R. Bates, *Markets and States in Tropical Africa* (Berkeley, 1981), ch. 1.

43 Colonial No. 211, *Report of the Vegetable Oils and Seeds Mission*, p. 24.

44 See Chapter 5, note 11.

45 E. J. Usoro, *The Nigerian Oil Palm Industry: Government Policy and Export Production, 1906–1965* (Ibadan, 1974), p. 75.

46 Helleiner, *Peasant Agriculture*, p. 161.

47 *Ibid.*, pp. 160–2.

48 *Ibid.*, pp. 161–2.

49 Colonial no. 211, *Report of the Vegetable Oils and Seeds Mission*, pp. 7 and 10.

50 *Ibid.*, pp. 15–16.

51 Usoro, *Nigerian Oil Palm Industry*, p. 83.

52 *Ibid.*, pp. 90 and 100; P. Kilby, 'The Nigerian Palm Oil Industry', *Food Research Institute Studies*, 7, 2 (1967), p. 184.

53 Kilby, 'Nigerian Palm Oil Industry', p. 190; R. Scott, 'Production for Trade', in D. Forde and R. Scott, *The Native Economies of Nigeria*: vol. I, *The Economics of a Tropical Dependency*, ed. M. Perham (1946), p. 237.

54 W. Miller, 'An Economic Analysis of Oil Palm Fruit Processing in Eastern Nigeria' (unpublished Ph.D. thesis, Michigan State University, 1965), pp. 38 and 51.

55 'Palm Oil Production in Nigeria: the Pioneer Oil Mill', *U.A.C. Statistical and Economical Review*, 7 (1951), pp. 1–11; Kilby, 'Nigerian Palm Oil Industry', pp. 184–5.

56 Kilby, 'Nigerian Palm Oil Industry', pp. 184–5; Usoro, *Nigerian Oil Palm Industry*, pp. 88–92.

57 A. Martin, *Oil Palm Economy*, p. 13; on the Ngwa, N. E. Mba, *Nigerian Women Mobilized* (Berkeley, 1982), pp. 108–9.

58 Interview with Mr Owuala, 21 December 1980.

59 Martin, *Oil Palm Economy*, p. 16.

60 *Ibid.*, p. 13; Miller, 'Oil Palm Fruit Processing', p. 104; Usoro, *Nigerian Oil Palm Industry*, pp. 88–92 and 104–10; Kilby, 'Nigerian Palm Oil Industry', pp. 189–94.

61 Helleiner, *Peasant Agriculture*, pp. 163–4 and table v-E-3.

62 Berry, *Cocoa, Custom and Change*, pp. 183–6.

63 R. Galletti, K. D. S. Baldwin and I. O. Dina, *Nigerian Cocoa Farmers* (1956), p. 573.

64 J. D. Y. Peel, *Ijeshas and Nigerians: the Incorporation of a Yoruba Kingdom, 1890s–1970s* (Cambridge, 1983), pp. 147–52.

65 *Census of Nigeria, 1931*, vol. III, pp. 20 and 29; *Eastern Nigeria: Statistical Digest, 1966* (4th edn, Enugu, 1967), pp. 1 and 7; see also Isichei, *History of the Igbo People*, pp. 186–9 and 234.

66 Isichei, *History of the Igbo People*, pp. 209–15; de St Jorre, *Nigerian Civil War*, pp. 98–9; J. S. Coleman, *Nigeria: Background to Nationalism* (Berkeley, 1958), pp. 332–3.

67 Personal observation, 1980–1; see also Buchi Emecheta, *The Joys of Motherhood* (1979); and for similar and very detailed observations of contemporary Yoruba society, Sara Berry, *Fathers Work for their Sons: Accumulation, Mobility and Class Formation in an Extended Yoruba Community* (London and Berkeley, 1985), chs. 5–7.

68 Nwaguru, *Aba and British Rule*, pp. 136–40.

69 *Ibid.*, p. 138; conversation with Mrs Jaja Wachukwu, Nbawsi, 27 January 1981.

70 Nwaguru, *Aba and British Rule*, pp. 144–8.

71 *Eastern Region, Nigeria: Policy for Local Government* (Sessional Paper no. 2 of 1956, Eastern House of Assembly).

72 *Eastern Region, Nigeria: Report of the Committee on Bride Price* (Enugu, 1955), pp. 24 and 46–7.

73 G. I. Jones, *Report of an Inquiry into the Position, Status and Influence of Chiefs and Natural Rulers in the Eastern Region of Nigeria* (Enugu, 1958).

74 *Ibid.*, pp. 8–15 and 58–9.

75 Nwaguru, *Aba and British Rule*, pp. 173–4, 187–96 and 245–6.

76 *Ibid.*, pp. 159–73.

77 de St Jorre, *Nigerian Civil War*, p. 408.

78 *Ibid.*, pp. 87–8, 148–50, 207, 255–60, 292 and 379.

79 *Ibid.*, pp. 225 and 237–8.

80 Interviews nos. 4, 6, 18, 19, 20; and general conversation with the women of Umuigwe compound, Ahiaba-Okpuala, 14 December 1980.

81 J. Lagemann, *Traditional African Farming Systems in Eastern Nigeria: an Analysis of Reaction to Increasing Population Pressure* (Munich, 1977), pp. 2–3.

82 *Ibid.*, pp. 44 and 98.

83 Mbagwu, 'Oil Palm Economy', pp. 108–9.

189

84 Lagemann, *Traditional Farming Systems*, pp. 23–7, 33–42 and 55.

85 *Ibid.*, pp. 50–62.

86 *Ibid.*, pp. 25, 101 and 109–15.

87 M. Watts, *Silent Violence: Food, Famine and Peasantry in Northern Nigeria* (Berkeley, 1983), pp. 489–506; A. Kirk-Greene and D. Rimmer, *Nigeria Since 1970: a Political and Economic Outline* (1981), pp. 72–80; G. Williams, 'The World Bank and the Peasant Problem', and T. Forrest, 'Agricultural Policies in Nigeria, 1900–1978', in J. Heyer, P. Roberts and G. Williams, eds., *Rural Development in Tropical Africa* (New York, 1981).

88 M. J. Purvis, 'New Sources of Growth in a Stagnant Smallholder Economy in Eastern Nigeria: the Oil Palm Rehabilitation Scheme', in C. K. Eicher and C. Liedholm, eds., *Growth and Development of the Nigerian Economy* (Michigan, 1970), pp. 267–81.

89 Interviews nos. 3, 16 and 18; Mbagwu, 'Oil Palm Economy', pp. 90–1 and ch. 8.

90 Oral information; see also Kirk-Greene and Rimmer, *Nigeria Since 1970*, p. 76.

11. Conclusion

1 K. Hart, *The Political Economy of West African Agriculture* (Cambridge, 1982), pp. 117 and 140; J. D. Y. Peel, *Ijeshas and Nigerians: the Incorporation of a Yoruba Kingdom, 1890s–1970s* (Cambridge, 1983), pp. 120 and 128.

2 M. Watts, *Silent Violence: Food, Famine and Peasantry in Northern Nigeria* (Berkeley, 1983), ch. 1.

3 F. Teal, 'The Supply of Agricultural Output in Nigeria, 1950–1974', *Journal of Development Studies*, 19, 2 (1983), pp. 191–206.

Interviews conducted in the Ngwa region, 1980–1

INFORMANTS

1. Oji Akpuka, aged about seventy-five, of Ahiaba-Ubi, 28 December 1980
2. Virginia Nwannedie Akwarandu, aged about sixty-five, of Umuakpara, 20 December 1980
3. Bob Anyanwu, aged about sixty-five, of Mububu-Nsulu, 27 January 1981
4. A. A. Chigbundu, schoolteacher, aged about sixty, of Ahiaba-Okpuala, 19 December 1980
5. Nwakocha Chigbundu, aged about seventy, of Ahiaba-Okpuala, 17 December 1980
6. Nwannedie Chigbundu, aged about sixty-five, of Ahiaba-Okpuala, 15, 16 and 17 December 1980
7. Stephen C. Chigbundu, schoolteacher, aged about fifty-five, of Ahiaba-Okpuala, 6 December 1980
8. Chief I. W. Ebere, aged about eighty, of Umuomainta, Nbawsi, 10 February 1981
9. Rufus Erondu, aged about sixty-five, of Umuakwu-Nsulu, 27 January 1981
10. Josiah Onuoha Ihediacho, aged about eighty, of Abayi, 4 January 1981
11. Onyema Sabina Kanu, aged about a hundred, of Umuala, 24 and 28 December 1980
12. Patrick Ikonne Ndubisi, aged about fifty-five, of Ikputu-Nsulu, 27 January 1981
13. Achonna Njoku, aged about eighty, of Umuacha, 13 February 1981
14. Thomas Nwadike, aged about seventy, of Ngwama-Ovungwu, 2 February 1981
15. Jemima Nwakwa Nwannunu, aged about seventy-five, of Umuacha, 21 December 1980
16. Samuel Nwannunu, aged about forty-five, of Umuacha, 21 December 1980
17. Samuel Ochulo Nwaogwugwu, aged about eighty, of Ahiaba-Okpuala, 24 January 1981
18. Augustine Amaeze Nwogu, aged about seventy-five, of Amiri, 6 and 8 February 1981
19. J. W. Nwogu, aged about eighty, of Amiri, 4 February 1981
20. Selina Danne Nwosu, aged about sixty-five, of Ahiaba-Okpuala, 15 December 1980 and 21 February 1981
21. Paul Abakwo Onyenweaku, aged about seventy-five, of Amiri, 8 February 1981
22. Edward Uche Uche, aged about sixty-five, of Umuode-Nsulu, 10 February 1981
23. Chief J. Isaac Wabara, local historian, of Ohambele, 18 January 1981

INTERPRETERS

Beatrice Ebere Chigbundu, of Ahiaba-Okpuala (informant no. 6)
Catherine Obioma Chigbundu, of Ahiaba-Okpuala (6, 10, 15, 20)
Chris U. Emelogu, of Ahiaba-Okpuala (17)
Dr A. Epelle, of Ohambele (23)

Interviews conducted in the Ngwa region

Lawrence Anya Njoku, of Mbaise (extension worker, Smallholder Oil Palm Project) (3, 9, 12, 22)
Sylvester Ihemmadu Nwogu, of Amiri (14, 18, 21)
Florence Nwosu, of Ahiaba-Okpuala (11, 13)
Monday Chinatu Nwosu, of Ahiaba-Okpuala (1)
Regina Nwaoma Osuji, of Omoba (2, 6, 11)

Bibliography

DOCUMENTS CONSULTED AT THE NIGERIAN NATIONAL ARCHIVES, IBADAN

The following series were used:

Calprof: Files 9/1, 9/2 and 10/3, which contain correspondence and Annual Reports from the Secretariat of the High Commissioner for Southern Nigeria, 1900–6

CSO 26: The files of the Central Secretary's Office, Nigeria, 1906–40. This series contains some illuminating correspondence between the Secretary, Southern Provinces and the Central Secretary's Office, including summaries of the results of village-level economic surveys. It also contains the Assessment and Intelligence Reports which are listed below

CSO 14, CSO 15, CSO 16, CSO 17: These fragmentary series contain files which deal directly with the oil palm industry and with Forestry Department investigations, 1910–16

CSO 19, CSO 20: Despatches from the Nigerian administration to the Secretary of State for the Colonies, 1913–21

Assessment reports (made in 1927)
Aba Division, Owerri Province, CSO 26/20610
Abak District, Calabar Province, CSO 26/20678
Aro District, Calabar Province, CSO 26/20690
Bende Division, Owerri Province, CSO 26/20646
Eket Division, Calabar Province, CSO 26/20679
Ikot Ekpene District, Calabar Province, CSO 26/20678
Itu District, Calabar Province, CSO 26/20688
Opobo Division, Calabar Province, CSO 26/20677
Uyo District, Calabar Province, CSO 26/20682

Intelligence reports
Abam Clan, Bende Division, Owerri Province, n.d., CSO 26/28939
Ediene and Itak Clans, Ikot Ekpene Division, Calabar Province, 1932, CSO 26/27615
Ibeku Clan, Bende Division, Owerri Province, 1935, CSO 26/30291
Ibere Clan, Bende Division, Owerri Province, 1933, CSO 26/28869
Ibiono Clan, Itu District, Calabar Province, CSO 26/28881
Ikono Clan, Ikot Ekpene Division, Calabar Province, 1932, CSO 26/29949
Ndoki Clan, Aba Division, Calabar Province, 1933, CSO 26/29281
Ngwa Clan, Aba Division, Owerri Province, by Jackson, 1931, with Supplementary Reports by Allen, 1933 and 1934, CSO 26/29033, 2 vols.

Bibliography

Nkalu Clan, Ikot Ekpene Division, Calabar Province, 1934, CSO 26/30865
Oboro Clan, Bende Division, Owerri Province, 1934, CSO 26/29741
Okun and Afaha Clans, Ikot Ekpene District, Calabar Province, 1931, CSO 26/26506
Olokoro Clan, Bende Division, Owerri Province, 1935, CSO 26/30829
Otoro or Northern Anang Group, Ikot Ekpene Division, Calabar Province, 1933, CSO 26/28780
Ubakala Clan, Bende Division, Owerri Province, 1934, CSO 26/29828
Ukana Group, Ikot Ekpene Division, Calabar Province, 1931, CSO 26/27604

DOCUMENTS CONSULTED AT THE NIGERIAN NATIONAL ARCHIVES, ENUGU

The following series were used:
CSE: The counterpart of Ibadan's CSO series, but damaged during the Civil War
Calprof and *Rivprof*: The files of the Resident's offices, Provinces of Calabar (now Cross River State) and Owerri (now Imo and Rivers States) respectively. These records cover the period after 1906, and include despatches from District and Divisional Officers to the Residents, Annual and Quarterly Reports on each District, and District Officers' Handing-Over Notes
Abadist and *Umprof*: These series contain documents relating to Aba and Bende Divisions. The files are similar to those in the Calprof and Rivprof series, with some additional files relating to court cases under appeal and to the Collective Punishment Inquiries held after the Women's War in 1929–30
Ahiaba N.C.: Court records, available only after 1930

DOCUMENTS CONSULTED AT THE PUBLIC RECORD OFFICE, LONDON

The following series were used:
F.O. 2, F.O. 84: Despatches concerning the administration of the Niger Coast Protectorate in the 1890s
F.O. 403, F.O. 881, C.O. 879, C.O. 885: Confidential Prints
C.O. 444, C.O. 520: Correspondence between the Colonial Office and the High Commissioner, Protectorate of Southern Nigeria, 1899–1913
C.O. 583: Correspondence between the Colonial Office and the Governor of Nigeria, 1914–30
C.O. 554: Colonial Office correspondence concerning West Africa, including files on the oil palm industry, 1914–30
C.O. 464: Blue Books, Niger Coast Protectorate, 1896–1900
C.O. 473: Blue Books, Protectorate of Southern Nigeria, 1900–6
C.O. 592: Annual Reports and Sessional Papers, Southern Nigeria, 1906–13. This series includes annual Trade Reports, Reports on the Eastern Province and Departmental Reports
C.O. 657: Sessional Papers, Nigeria, 1912–32. This series is similar to C.O. 592, but includes some additional reports on economic matters and on specific events, for example the Women's War

DOCUMENTS CONSULTED AT RHODES HOUSE, OXFORD

Colonel G. Adams, 'Five Nigerian Tales', Mss. Afr. s. 375
A. F. B. Bridges, 'Report of Oil Palm Survey, Ibo, Ibibio and Cross River Areas' (1938), Mss. Afr. s. 697 (1)
E. M. Falk, 'Nigeria Papers' (1910–33), Mss. Afr. s. 1000 (1–6)
S. M. Grier, Letters and Reports, 1897–1922, Mss. Afr. s. 1379
E. Harmer, 'The Versatile Palm' (1945), Mss. Afr. s. 424
J. S. Harris, 'Ibo Papers' (1938–9), Mss. Afr. s. 1505 (8)

John Holt Papers, Mss. Afr. s. 1525, boxes 1 and 19
Captain J. R. Mackie, 'Papers on Nigerian Agriculture, Etc.' (1939–45), Mss. Afr. s. 823 (1–5)
Major L. R. C. Sumner, 'A Short Account of My Tours in Nigeria, 1921–1939', Mss. Afr. s. 538

OTHER ARCHIVAL SOURCES

John Holt Papers, Liverpool Record Office: Trade Diaries (series 380 HOL 1:6); Photographs (series 380 HOL 1:10–11); and Ledgers (series 380 HOL II)
Methodist Missionary Society Papers, S.O.A.S. Library, London: M.M.S. boxes 567 and 585; and Journals, *The Herald* (1916–18, 1919–20 and 1921–2) and *Advance* (1923–32)
Church Missionary Society Papers, Heslop Room, University of Birmingham, Library, files G3 A3/0, G3 A3/P5/1906–16, and G3 A3/P6/1916–34
C.M.S. Annual Reports, 1922–31, C.M.S. Library, 157 Waterloo Road, London

OFFICIAL PUBLICATIONS

Administrative reports
The early *Reports on the Administration of the Niger Coast Protectorate*, 1891–9, were published annually as Parliamentary Papers from 1895 to 1900. Later, the *Annual Reports, Southern Nigeria*, 1899–1913, were published as Parliamentary Papers in the special series Colonial Reports: Annual. The *Annual Reports: Nigeria*, 1914–19, also have both a Command Paper and a Colonial Reports: Annual (C.R.A.) reference number. From 1920, these reports ceased to appear as Parliamentary Papers and so have only a C.R.A. reference number. In the notes, the C.R.A. reference has been given wherever the report concerned was consulted as a separate publication, outside the Parliamentary Papers (P.P.) series. These detailed references will not be repeated here.

Other Parliamentary Papers
Economic Agriculture on the Gold Coast, 1889 (P.P. 1890, xlviii, C 5897–40)
Translations of Protocols and General Act of the Slave Trade Conference Held at Brussels, 1889–1890; with Annexed Declaration (P.P. 1890, l, C 6049–1)
Royal Commission on Shipping Rings: Minutes of Evidence, Days 1–19 (P.P. 1909, xlvii, Cd 4670)
Southern Nigeria: Report and Minutes of Evidence of the Committee of Inquiry into the Liquor Trade in Southern Nigeria (P.P. 1909, lx, Cd 4906 and Cd 4907)
West Africa: Departmental Committee Appointed to Inquire into Matters Affecting the Currency of the British West African Colonies and Protectorates: Report and Minutes of Evidence (P.P. 1912–13, xlviii, Cd 6426 and Cd 6427)
West Africa: Correspondence Respecting the Grant of Exclusive Rights for the Extraction of Oil from Palm Fruits (P.P. 1912–13, lix, Cd 6561)
Colonial Reports, Miscellaneous, no. 88: Imperial Institute: Selected Reports from the Scientific and Technical Department, V: *Oil-Seeds, Oils, Fats, and Waxes* (P.P. 1914, lix, Cd 7260)
West Africa: Committee on Edible and Oil-Producing Nuts and Seeds: Report and Minutes of Evidence (P.P. 1916, iv, Cd 8247 and Cd 8248)
Nigeria: Report by Sir F. D. Lugard on the Amalgamation of Northern and Southern Nigeria, and Administration, 1912–1919 (P.P. 1919, xxxvi, Cmd 468)
Report of a Committee on Trade and Taxation for British West Africa (P.P. 1922, xvi, Cmd 1600)
Report by the Hon. W. G. A. Ormsby-Gore, M.P., On his Visit to West Africa during the Year 1926 (P.P. 1926, ix, Cmd 2744)

Other official publications (available in the British Library)

Colonial no. 10: *West Africa: Palm Oil and Palm Kernels, Report of a Committee Appointed by the Secretary of State for the Colonies, Sept. 1923, to Consider the Best Means of Securing Improved and Increased Production* (H.M.S.O., 1925)

Colonial no. 211: *Report of the Mission Appointed to Inquire into the Production and Transport of Vegetable Oils and Seeds Produced in the West African Colonies* (H.M.S.O., 1947)

F. M. Dyke, *Report on the Oil Palm Industry in British West Africa* (Lagos, 1927)

Empire Marketing Board, no. 54: *Survey of Vegetable Oilseeds and Oils*, vol. I: *Oil Palm Products* (H.M.S.O., 1932)

Empire Marketing Board, E.M.B./C/4, *Oilseeds and Vegetable Oils: a Summary of Figures of Production and Trade* (H.M.S.O., 1932)

J. H. J. Farquhar, *The Oil Palm and its Varieties*, edited and revised by H. N. Thompson (Crown Agents, 1913)

F. D. Hammond, *Report on the Railway System of Nigeria* (Crown Agents, 1924)

Proceedings of the First West African Agricultural Conference, held at Ibadan, Nigeria, March, 1927 (Lagos, 1927)

Third West African Agricultural Conference: Papers (Lagos, 1938)

United Nations, Food and Agricultural Organisation, Commodity Series Bulletin no. 13, *Fats and Oils* (August 1949)

No. 27, *Cacao* (November 1955)

West Africa: Minutes of Evidence Taken Before the Committee on Trade and Taxation for British West Africa (Crown Agents, 1921)

RARE JOURNALS

Bulletin of the Imperial Institute, 7–24 (1909–26); consulted in the British Library

Farm and Forest, 2–6 (1941–5); consulted in the library of the Royal Commonwealth Society, London

Journal of the West African Institute for Oil Palm Research, 1–2 (1954–9); consulted in the library of Ibadan University.

Nigeria: Annual Bulletins of the Agricultural Department, 1922–9; consulted in the library of the Royal Commonwealth Society, London

Royal Gardens, Kew: Bulletin of Miscellaneous Information (Kew Bulletin), 1889–94; consulted in the library of Birmingham University.

The United Africa Company Ltd., Statistical and Economic Review, 1–7 (1948–51); consulted in S.O.A.S. library.

BOOKS

This is a select list of works cited in the footnotes. It excludes empirical studies of other regions of West Africa, except where these are of special theoretical relevance.

General

Amin, S. (ed.) *Modern Migrations in Western Africa* (1974)

Accumulation on a World Scale: a Critique of the Theory of Underdevelopment (1974; 1st edn, Paris, 1970)

Unequal Development: an Essay on the Social Formations of Peripheral Capitalism (1976; 1st edn, Paris, 1973)

Anthony, K., Jones, W. O., Johnston, B. F., and Uchendu, V. C. *Agricultural Change in Tropical Africa* (Ithaca and London, 1978)

Baran, P. A. *The Political Economy of Growth* (1973; first edn, 1957)

Bloch, Maurice (ed.) *Marxist Analyses and Social Anthropology* (1975)

Bohannan, P., and Dalton, G. (eds.) *Markets in Africa* (Evanston, 1962)

Boserup, E. *The Conditions of Agricultural Growth: the Economics of Agrarian Change under Population Pressure* (1965)
Population and Technology (Oxford, 1981)
Woman's Role in Economic Development (1970)

Braudel, F. *Capitalism and Material Life, 1400–1800* (Fontana edn, 1974; first edn, Paris, 1967)

Chayanov, A. V. *The Theory of Peasant Economy*, edited by D. Thorner, B. Kerblay and R. E. F. Smith (Homewood, Illinois, 1966; 1st edn, Moscow, 1925)

Emmanuel, A. *Unequal Exchange: a Study of the Imperialism of Trade* (1972; 1st edn, Paris, 1969)

Frank, A. G. *Capitalism and Underdevelopment in Latin America: Historical Studies of Chile and Brazil* (1971; 1st edn, New York, 1967)
Dependent Accumulation and Underdevelopment (1978)
Latin America: Underdevelopment or Revolution (1969)

Gann, L. H., and Duignan, P. (eds.) *Colonialism in Africa, 1870–1960*, vol. 4, *The Economics of Colonialism* (Cambridge, 1975)

Goody, J. (ed) *Literacy in Traditional Societies* (1968)
Cooking, Cuisine and Class: a Study in Comparative Sociology (Cambridge, 1982)
Production and Reproduction: a Comparative Study of the Domestic Domain (Cambridge, 1976)
Technology, Tradition and the State in Africa (1971)

Grigg, David, *The Dynamics of Agricultural Change: the Historical Experience* (1982)

Hafkin, N. J., and Bay, E. G. (eds.) *Women in Africa: Studies in Social and Economic Change* (Stanford, 1976)

Hancock, W. K. *A Survey of British Commonwealth Affairs*, vol. ii, part 2 (1942)

Hargreaves, J. D. *West Africa Partitioned*, vol. i, *The Loaded Pause, 1885–1889* (1974)

Hart, K. *The Political Economy of West African Agriculture* (Cambridge, 1982)

Hay, M. J., and Wright, M. (eds.) *African Women and the Law: Historical Perspectives* (Boston, 1982)

Henige, D. P. *The Chronology of Oral Tradition: Quest for a Chimera* (Oxford, 1974)

Hopkins, A. G. *An Economic History of West Africa* (1973)

Kay, G. *Development and Underdevelopment: a Marxist Analysis* (1975)

Klein, M. A. (ed.) *Peasants in Africa* (1980)

Kula, W. *An Economic Theory of the Feudal System: Towards a Model of the Polish Economy, 1500–1800* (1976; 1st edn, 1962)

le Roy Ladurie, E., *The Territory of the Historian* (1979; 1st edn, Paris, 1973)
Times of Feast, Times of Famine: a History of Climate Since the Year 1000 (New York, 1971; 1st edn, Paris, 1967)

Levi, John, and Havinden, Michael. *Economics of African Agriculture* (1982)

McPhee, Allan. *The Economic Revolution in British West Africa* (1926)

Marx, K. *Capital*, vol. i (1974; 1st edn, 1887)
Pre-Capitalist Economic Formations, edited by E. J. Hobsbawm (1964; translated from *Grundrisse der Kritik der Politischen Ökonomie*, Moscow, 1939–41)

Meillassoux, Claude (ed.) *The Development of Indigenous Trade and Markets in West Africa* (Oxford, 1971)
Maidens, Meal and Money: Capitalism and the Domestic Community (Cambridge, 1981; 1st edn, Paris, 1975)

Miller, J. C. (ed.) *The African Past Speaks: Essays on Oral Tradition and History* (Archon, Folkestone, and Hamden, Connecticut, 1980)

Morgan, W. B., and Pugh, J. C. *West Africa* (1969)

Myint, H. *The Economics of the Developing Countries* (1973; 1st edn, 1964)

Rey, P. P. *Les Alliances de classes* (Paris, 1973)

197

Rodney, W. *How Europe Underdeveloped Africa* (1973)

Ruthenberg, H. *Farming Systems in the Tropics* (Oxford, 1980; 1st edn, 1971)

Sahlins, Marshall. *Stone Age Economics* (1974; 1st edn, Chicago, 1972)

Schultz, T. W. *Transforming Traditional Agriculture* (New Haven, 1964)

Scott, James C. *The Moral Economy of the Peasant: Rebellion and Subsistence in South-East Asia* (Yale and London, 1976)

Seddon, D. (ed.) *Relations of Production: Marxist Approaches to Economic Anthropology* (1978).

Shanin, T. (ed.) *Peasants and Peasant Societies* (1971)

Smith, A. *An Inquiry into the Nature and Causes of the Wealth of Nations* (Cannan edn, New York, 1937; 1st edn, 1776)

Terray, E. *Marxism and 'Primitive' Societies* (1972; 1st edn, Paris, 1969)

Vansina, J. *Oral Tradition: a Study in Historical Methodology* (1965; 1st edn, Paris, 1961)

Warren, B. *Imperialism: Pioneer of Capitalism* (1980)

On Nigeria, palm production and trade

Adewoye, O. *The Judicial System in Southern Nigeria, 1854–1954: Law and Justice in a Dependency* (1977)

Afigbo, A. E. *The Warrant Chiefs: Indirect Rule in South-Eastern Nigeria, 1891–1929* (1972)

Alagoa, E. J. *A History of the Niger Delta* (Ibadan, 1972)

Andreski, I. *Old Wives' Tales: Life-Stories from Ibibioland* (1970)

Anene, J. C. *Southern Nigeria in Transition, 1885–1906: Theory and Practice in a Colonial Protectorate* (Cambridge, 1966)

Ayandele, E. A. *The Missionary Impact on Modern Nigeria, 1842–1914* (1966)

Basden, G. T. *Among the Ibos of Nigeria: an Account of the Curious and Interesting Habits, Customs and Beliefs of a Little Known African People by One who has for Many Years Lived Amongst them on Close and Intimate Terms* (1966; 1st edn, 1921)

Niger Ibos: a Description of the Primitive Life, Customs and Animistic Beliefs, etc., of the Ibo People of Nigeria by One who, for Thirty-Five Years, Enjoyed the Privilege of their Intimate Confidence and Friendship (1966; 1st edn, 1938)

Berry, S. S. *Cocoa, Custom and Socio-Economic Charge in Rural Western Nigeria* (Oxford, 1975)

Billows, H. C., and Beckwith, H. *Palm Oil and Kernels: 'The Consols of the West Coast'* (Liverpool, 1913)

Bunting, B., Georgi, C. D. V., and Milsum, J. N. *The Oil Palm in Malaya* (Kuala Lumpur, 1934)

Chubb, L. T. *Ibo Land Tenure* (Ibadan, 1961; 1st edn, 1947)

Clough, R. Gore. *Oil Rivers Trader: Memories of Iboland* (1972)

Coursey, D. G. *Yams* (1967)

Creutzberg, P. (ed.) *Changing Economy in Indonesia* (Amsterdam, 1975)

Davies, P. N. *The Trade Makers: Elder Dempster in West Africa, 1852–1972* (1973)

(ed.) *Trading in West Africa, 1840–1920* (1976)

Dike, K. O. *Trade and Politics in the Niger Delta, 1830–1885: an Introduction to the Economic and Political History of Nigeria* (Oxford, 1956)

Ekechi, F. K. *Missionary Enterprise and Rivalry in Igboland, 1857–1914* (1971)

Ekundare, R. O. *An Economic History of Nigeria, 1860–1960* (1973)

Elias, T. O. *Nigerian Land Law and Custom* (1951)

Fieldhouse, D. K. *Unilever Overseas: the Anatomy of a Multinational, 1895–1965* (London and Stanford, 1978)

Forde, D., and Jones, G. I. *The Ibo and Ibibio-Speaking Peoples of South-Eastern Nigeria* (1950)

Forde, D., and Scott, R. *The Native Economies of Nigeria*: vol. I, *The Economics of a Tropical Dependency*, edited by M. Perham (1946)

Fry, Richard. *Bankers in West Africa: the Story of the Bank of British West Africa Limited* (1976)

Gailey, Harry A. *The Road to Aba: a Study of British Administrative Policy in Eastern Nigeria* (1971)

Green, M. M. *Igbo Village Affairs: Chiefly with Reference to the Village of Umueke-Agbaja* (1964; 1st edn, 1947)
    Land Tenure in an Ibo Village in South-Eastern Nigeria (LSE Monographs on Social Anthropology, no. 6, 1941)

Harlan, J. R., de Wet, J. M. J., and Stemler, A. B. L. (eds.) *Origins of African Plant Domestication* (The Hague and Paris, 1976)

Harris, R. L. *The Political Organization of the Mbembe, Nigeria* (1965)

Hartley, C. W. S. *The Oil Palm (Elaeis Guineensis Jacq.)* (1977; 1st edn, 1967)

Hedges, E. S. *Tin in Social and Economic History* (1964)

Helleiner, G. K. *Peasant Agriculture, Government, and Economic Growth in Nigeria* (Homewood, Illinois, 1966)

Hives, F., and Lumley, G. *Ju-Ju and Justice in Nigeria* (1930)

Hodder, B. W., and Ukwu, U. I. *Markets in West Africa: Studies of Markets and Trade Among the Yoruba and Ibo* (Ibadan, 1969)

Ilogu, Canon E. *Christianity and Ibo Culture* (Leiden, 1974)

Isichei, Elizabeth. *A History of the Igbo People* (1976)
    Igbo Worlds: an Anthology of Oral Histories and Historical Descriptions (1978)

Jones, G. I. *The Trading States of the Oil Rivers: a Study of Political Development in Eastern Nigeria* (1963)

Jones, W. O. *Manioc in Africa* (Stanford, 1959)

Kirk-Greene, A., and Rimmer, D. *Nigeria Since 1970: a Political and Economic Outline* (1981)

Lagemann, J. *Traditional African Farming Systems in Eastern Nigeria: an Analysis of Reaction to Increasing Population Pressure* (Munich, 1977)

Latham, A. J. H. *Old Calabar, 1600–1891: the Impact of the International Economy Upon a Traditional Society* (Oxford, 1973)

Leith-Ross, Sylvia. *African Women: a Study of the Ibo of Nigeria* (1965; 1st edn, 1939)
    Stepping-Stones: Memoirs of Colonial Nigeria, 1907–1960 (1983)

Leonard, A. G. *The Lower Niger and its Tribes* (1906)

Leplae, E. *Le Palmier à huile en Afrique: son exploitation au Congo Belge et en Extrême-Orient* (Brussels, 1939)

Leubuscher, C. *The West African Shipping Trade, 1909–1959* (Leiden, 1963)

Lieber, J. W. *Ibo Village Communities* (Occasional Publication no. 12, Institute of Education, University of Ibadan, Nigeria: Ibadan, 1971)

Macmillan, A. *The Red Book of West Africa* (1968; 1st impression, 1920)

Martin, A. *The Oil Palm Economy of the Ibibio Farmer* (Ibadan, 1956)

Mba, N. E. *Nigerian Women Mobilized: Women's Political Activity in Southern Nigeria, 1900–1965* (Berkeley, 1982)

Meek, C. K. *Law and Authority in a Nigerian Tribe: a Study in Indirect Rule* (1950; 1st edn, 1937)

Minchinton, W. E. *The British Tinplate Industry: a History* (Oxford, 1957)

Northrup, D. *Trade Without Rulers: Pre-Colonial Economic Development in South-Eastern Nigeria* (Oxford, 1978).

Nwaguru, J. E. N. *Aba and British Rule: the Evolution and Administrative Developments of the Old Aba Division of Igboland, 1896–1960* (Enugu, 1973)

Obi, S. N. Chinwuba. *The Ibo Law of Property* (1963)

Obichere, B. I. (ed.) *Studies in Southern Nigerian History* (1982)

Obilade, A. O. *The Nigerian Legal System* (1979)

Ofomata, G. E. K. (ed.) *Nigeria in Maps; Eastern States* (Benin City, 1975)

Bibliography

Ofonagoro, W. I. *Trade and Imperialism in Southern Nigeria, 1881–1929* (New York, London and Lagos, 1979)

Osuntokun, A. *Nigeria in the First World War* (1979)

Partridge, C. *Cross River Natives: Obubara Hill District* (1905)

Pedler, F. *The Lion and the Unicorn in Africa: a History of the Origins of the United Africa Company, 1787–1931* (1974)

Perham, M. *Native Administration in Nigeria* (1937)

van Stuyvenberg, J. H. (ed.) *Margarine: an Economic, Social, and Scientific History, 1869–1969* (Liverpool, 1969)

Talbot, P. A. *The Peoples of Southern Nigeria: a Sketch of their History, Ethnology and Languages*, 4 vols. (1926)

Tamuno, T. N. *The Evolution of the Nigerian State: the Southern Phase, 1898–1914* (1972)

Tasie, G. O. M. *Christian Missionary Enterprise in the Niger Delta, 1864–1918* (Leiden, 1978)

Uchendu, V. C. *The Igbo of Southeastern Nigeria* (New York, 1965)

Udo, R. K. *Geographical Regions of Nigeria* (1970)

Migrant Tenant Farmers of Nigeria: a Geographical Study of Rural Migrations in Nigeria (Lagos, 1975)

Usoro, Eno J. *The Nigerian Oil Palm Industry: Government Policy and Export Production, 1906–1965* (Ibadan, 1974)

Wilson, Charles *The History of Unilever: a Study in Economic Growth and Social Change*, 2 vols. (1954)

ARTICLES: A SELECT LIST

General

Amin, S. 'Underdevelopment and Dependence in Black Africa – Origins and Contemporary Forms', *Journal of Modern African Studies*, 10, 4 (1972), pp. 503–24

Baumann, H. 'The Division of Work According to Sex in African Hoe Culture', *Africa*, 1, 3 (1928), pp. 289–319

Bradby, B. 'The Destruction of Natural Economy', in H. Wolpe, ed., *The Articulation of Modes of Production* (1980), pp. 93–127

'Male Rationality in Economics – a Critique of Godelier on Salt Money', *Critique of Anthropology*, 3, 9–10 (1977), pp. 131–8

Brenner, R. 'Agrarian Class Structure and Economic Development in Pre-Industrial Europe', *Past and Present*, 70 (1976), pp. 30–75

'The Agrarian Roots of European Capitalism', *Past and Present*, 97 (1982), pp. 16–113

Brown, Judith K. 'A Note on the Division of Labour by Sex', *American Anthropologist*, 72 (1970), pp. 1073–8

Cain, P. J., and Hopkins, A. G. 'The Political Economy of British Expansion Overseas, 1750–1914', *Economic History Review*, 2nd ser. 33, 4 (1980), pp. 463–90

Croot, P., and Parker, D. 'Agrarian Class Structure and Economic Development', *Past and Present*, 78 (1978), pp. 37–47

Freund, W. M., and Shenton, R. W. '"Vent-for-Surplus" Theory and the Economic History of West Africa', *Savanna*, 6, 2 (1977), pp. 191–6

Guyer, J. 'Anthropological Models of African Production: the Naturalization Problem', *Boston University African Studies Center Working Papers*, 78 (1983)

'The Depression and the Administration in South-Central Cameroun', *African Economic History*, 10 (1981), pp. 67–79

'Food, Cocoa, and the Division of Labour by Sex in Two West African Societies', *Comparative Studies in Society and History*, 22 (1980), pp. 355–73

Hogendorn, J. S. 'The "Vent-for-Surplus" Model and African Cash Agriculture to 1914', *Savanna*, 5, 1 (1976), pp. 15–28; and Rejoinder, *Savanna*, 6, 2 (1977), pp. 196–9 van der Laan, H. L. 'Modern Inland Transport and the European Trading Firms in Colonial West Africa', *Cahiers d'Etudes Africaines*, 21, 4 (1981), pp. 547–75

Meredith, David. 'The British Government and Colonial Economic Policy, 1919–1939', *Economic History Review*, 2nd ser. 28 (1975), pp. 484–99

Molyneux, M. 'Androcentrism in Marxist Anthropology', *Critique of Anthropology*, 3, 9–10 (1977), pp. 55–81

Myint, H. 'The "Classical Theory" of International Trade and the Underdeveloped Countries', *Economic Journal*, 68, 2 (1958), pp. 317–37

Post, Ken. '"Peasantization" and Rural Political Movements in Western Africa', *Archives Européennes de Sociologie*, 13 (1972), pp. 223–54

Rathbone, R. J. A. R. 'World War I and Africa: Introduction', *J.A.H.*, 19, 1 (1978), pp. 1–9

Rey, P.-P. 'The Lineage Mode of Production', *Critique of Anthropology*, no. 3 (1975), pp. 27–79

'Class Contradiction in Lineage Societies', *Critique of Anthropology*, 4, 13–14 (1979), pp. 41–60

Shanin, T. 'The Nature and Logic of the Peasant Economy: I: A Generalisation; II: Diversity and Change; and III: Policy and Intervention', *Journal of Peasant Studies*, 1, 1 (1973), pp. 63–80, and 1, 2 (1974), pp. 186–206

Tosh, J. 'The Cash-Crop Revolution in Tropical Africa: an Agricultural Reappraisal', *African Affairs*, 79 (1980), pp. 79–94

Whitehead, A. '"I'm Hungry, Mum": the Politics of Domestic Budgeting', in K. Young, C. Wolkowitz and R. McCullagh, eds., *Of Marriage and the Market: Women's Subordination in International Perspective* (1981), pp. 88–111

On Nigeria, Palm Production and Trade

Afigbo, A. E. 'Revolution and Reaction in Eastern Nigeria, 1900–1929: the Background to the Women's Riot of 1929', *J.H.S.N.*, 3, 3 (1966), pp. 539–57

Bull, R. A. 'A Preliminary List of the Oil Palm Diseases Encountered in West Africa', *Journal of the West African Institute for Oil Palm Research*, 2 (Sept. 1954), pp. 53–93

Ekechi, F. K. 'Aspects of Palm Oil Trade at Oguta (Eastern Nigeria), 1900–1950', *African Economic History*, 10 (1981), pp. 35–65

Ekejiuba, Felicia Ifeoma. 'The Aro System of Trade in the Nineteenth Century', part 1, *Ikenga* 1, 1 (1972); part 2, *Ikenga* 1, 2 (1972), pp. 10–21

Forde, C. D. 'Land and Labour in a Cross River Village, Southern Nigeria', *Geographical Journal* 5, 90 (1937), pp. 24–51

Harris, J. S. 'Papers on the Economic Aspect of Life Among the Ozuitem Ibo', *Africa*, 14, 1 (1943–44), pp. 12–23

'Some Aspects of the Economics of Sixteen Ibo Individuals', *Africa*, 24, 6 (1944), pp. 302–35

Horton, W. R. G. 'The Ohu System of Slavery in a Northern Ibo Village-Group', *Africa*, 24, 4 (1954), pp. 311–36

Ifeka-Moller, C. 'Female Militancy and Colonial Revolt: the Women's War of 1929, Eastern Nigeria' in S. Ardener, ed., *Perceiving Women* (1975), pp. 127–57

Ikime, Obaro. 'The Anti-Tax Riots in Warri Province, 1927–1928', *J.H.S.N.*, 3, 3 (1966), pp. 559–73

Johnston, G. D. 'A Project in Local Church Histories', *West African Religion*, 4 (1965), pp. 8–13

Jones, G. I. 'Ibo Age Organization, with Special Reference to the Cross River and North-Eastern Ibo', *Journal of the Royal Anthropological Institute of Great Britain and Ireland*, 92, 2 (1962), pp. 191–211

'Ibo Land Tenure', *Africa*, 19, 4 (1949), pp. 309–23

'Native and Trade Currencies in Southern Nigeria During the Eighteenth and Nineteenth Centuries', *Africa*, 28, 1 (1958), pp. 43–54

201

Bibliography

Kalu, O. U. 'Missionaries, Colonial Government and Secret Societies in South-Eastern Igboland, 1920–1950', *J.H.S.N.*, 9, 1 (1977), pp. 75–90

'Waves from the Rivers: the Spread of the Garrick Braide Movement in Igboland, 1914–1934', *J.H.S.N.*, 8, 4 (1977), pp. 95–110

Kilby, P. 'The Nigerian Palm Oil Industry', *Food Research Institute Studies*, 7, 2 (1967), pp. 177–203 (reprinted in Kilby, *Industrialization in an Open Economy: Nigeria, 1945–1966* (Cambridge, 1969), pp. 139–68)

Latham, A. J. H. 'Price Fluctuations in the Early Palm Oil Trade', *J.A.H.*, 19, 2 (1978), pp. 213–18

Leonard, A. G. 'Notes of a Journey to Bende', *Journal of the Manchester Geographical Society*, 14 (1898), pp. 190–207

Morgan, W. B. 'Farming Practice, Settlement Pattern and Population Density in South-Eastern Nigeria', *Geographical Journal*, 121, 3 (1955), p. 320–33

'The Influence of European Contacts on the Landscape of Southern Nigeria', *Geographical Journal*, 125, 1 (1959), pp. 48–64 (reprinted in R. Mansell Prothero, ed., *People and Land in Africa South of the Sahara* (Oxford, 1972), pp. 193–207)

Newbury, C. W. 'Prices and Profitability in Early Nineteenth-Century West African Trade', in C. Meillassoux, ed., *The Development of Indigenous Trade and Markets in West Africa* (Oxford, 1971), pp. 91–106

'Trade and Technology in West Africa: the Case of the Niger Company, 1900–1920', *J.A.H.*, 19, 4 (1978), pp. 551–75

Njoku, O. N. 'Development of Roads and Road Transport in Southeastern Nigeria, 1903–1939', *Journal of African Studies*, 5, 4 (1978), pp. 471–97

'Oil Palm Syndrome in Nigeria: Government Policies and Indigenous Response, 1918–1939', *Calabar Historical Journal*, 2, 1 (1978), pp. 78–97

Northrup, D. 'The Compatibility of the Slave and Palm Oil Trades in the Bight of Biafra', *J.A.H.*, 17, 3 (1976), pp. 353–64

'Nineteenth-Century Patterns of Slavery and Economic Growth in South-Eastern Nigeria', *International Journal of African Historical Studies*, 12, 1 (1979), pp. 1–16

Nwabughuogu, A. I. 'From Wealthy Entrepreneurs to Petty Traders: the Decline of African Middlemen in Eastern Nigeria, 1900–1950', *J.A.H.*, 23, 3 (1982), pp. 365–79

Ohadike, D. C. 'The Influenza Pandemic of 1918–1919 and the Spread of Cassava Cultivation on the Lower Niger: a Study in Historical Linkages', *J.A.H.*, 22, 3 (1981), pp. 379–91

Onwuejeogwu, M. A. 'The Dawn of Igbo Civilization in the Igbo Culture Area', *Ọdinani* (the Journal of the Ọdinani Museum, Nri, Anambra State, Nigeria) 1, 1 (March 1972), pp. 15–56

Onwuteaka, V. C. 'The Aba Riot of 1929 and its Relation to the System of "Indirect Rule"', *Nigerian Journal of Economic and Social Studies*, 7, 3 (1965), pp. 273–82

Oriji, J. N. 'A Re-Assessment of the Organisation and Benefits of the Slave and Palm Produce Trade Among the Ngwa-Igbo', *Canadian Journal of African Studies*, 16, 3 (1982), pp. 523–48

Ottenberg, P. V. 'The Changing Economic Position of Women among the Afikpo Ibo', in W. R. Bascom and M. J. Herskovits, eds., *Continuity and Change in African Cultures* (Chicago, 1959), pp. 205–23

Tasie, G. O. M. 'Christian Awakening in West Africa, 1914–1918: a Study in the Significance of Native Agency', *West African Religion*, 16 (1975), pp. 45–60

Udo, R. K. 'Disintegration of Nucleated Settlement in Eastern Nigeria', *Geographical Review*, 55 (1965), pp. 53–67

'The Migrant Tenant Farmer of Eastern Nigeria', *Africa*, 34, 4 (1964), pp. 326–39

Ukwu, Ukwu I. 'The Development of Trade and Marketing in Iboland', *J.H.S.N.*, 3, 4 (1967), pp. 647–62.

Uzozie, L. C. 'Patterns of Crop Combination in the Three Eastern States of Nigeria', *Journal of Tropical Geography*, 33 (December 1971), pp. 62–72

UNPUBLISHED THESES AND DISSERTATIONS

Agboola, S. A. 'Yam and Cassava in Western Nigeria: a Study of Change in an African Food Crop Economy' (Ph.D. thesis, University of London, 1967)

Bowden, J. H. 'Colonial Policy Towards the Liquor Trade in Southern Nigeria, 1905–1912' (M.A. dissertation, University of Birmingham, 1975)

Constantine, S. 'The Formulation of British Policy on Colonial Development, 1914–1929' (Ph.D. thesis, University of Oxford, 1974)

Egboh, E. O. 'British Forestry Policy in Nigeria: a Study in Colonial Exploitation of Forest Produce, 1897–1940' (Ph.D. thesis, University of Birmingham, 1975)

Essang, S. M. 'The Marketing of Palm Oil in a Rural Community' (M.Sc. dissertation, University of Ibadan, 1967)

Huth, W. P. 'Traditional Institutions and Land Tenure as Related to Agricultural Development Among the Ibo of Eastern Nigeria' (Ph.D. thesis, University of Wisconsin, 1969)

Iroegbu, C. C. 'Community Oil Palm Plantations in the East Central State' (M.Sc. dissertation, University of Ibadan, 1971)

Johnson, I. W. (now I. W. Jimonu). 'A Study of Local Community of Ngwauku-Ofoasato' (B.A. dissertation, Institute of Education, University of Ibadan, April 1965)

Manning, P. 'Palm Oil and Kernel Exports from Nigeria, 1880–1905: a Study in Econometric History' (M.Sc. dissertation, University of Wisconsin, 1966)

Martin, S. M. 'The Igbo Women's War of 1929' (M.Soc.Sc. dissertation, University of Birmingham, 1979)

Mbagwu, T. C. 'The Oil Palm Economy in Ngwaland (Eastern Nigeria)' (Ph.D. thesis, University of Ibadan, 1970)

Meredith, D. G. 'The British Government and Colonial Economic Development, with Particular Reference to British West Africa, 1919–1939' (Ph.D. thesis, University of Exeter, 1976)

Miller, W. 'An Economic Analysis of Oil Palm Fruit Processing in Eastern Nigeria' (Ph.D. thesis, Michigan State University, 1965)

Nwabughuogu, A. I. 'Political Change, Social Response, and Economic Development: the Dynamics of Change in Eastern Nigeria, 1930–1950' (Ph.D. thesis, Dalhousie University, Halifax, Canada, 1981)

Okeke, D. C. 'Policy and Practice of the Church Missionary Society in Igboland, 1857–1929' (Ph.D. thesis, Aberdeen University, 1977)

Oriji, J. N. 'A History of the Ngwa People: Social and Economic Developments in an Igbo Clan, from the Thirteenth to the Twentieth Centuries' (Ph.D. thesis, Rutgers University, The State University of New Jersey, New Brunswick, 1977)

Ottenberg, P. V. 'Marriage Relationships in the Double Descent System of the Afikpo Ibo of South-Eastern Nigeria' (Ph.D. thesis, Northwestern University, 1958)

Oyewumi, J. A. O. 'The Development and Organisation of Palm Oil and Palm Kernel Production in Nigeria, 1807–1960' (M.Soc.Sc. dissertation, University of Birmingham, 1972)

Ozigboh, R. A. 'A Christian Mission in the Era of Colonialism: a Study of the Catholic Missionary Enterprise in South-Eastern Nigeria, 1885–1939' (Ph.D. thesis, University of Birmingham, 1980)

Stilliard, N. H. 'The Rise and Development of Legitimate Trade in Palm Oil with West Africa' (M.A. dissertation, University of Birmingham, 1938)

Udom, D. S. 'Demand and Supply Analyses for Nigerian Oil Palm Products with Policy Implications' (Ph.D. thesis, University of Reading, 1980)

Ukegbu, B. N. 'Production in the Nigerian Oil Palm Industry, 1900–1954' (Ph.D. thesis, University of London (external), 1974)

Wogugu, M. O. 'Evolution and Analysis of Roads and Road Transport, Aba Division' (B.A. dissertation, University of Ibadan, 1967)

Index

Index

Harris, J. S., writer, on Ozuitem Igbo, 22, 73, 76, 85, 100
Harris, Prophet, 70
Helleiner, G. K., writer, on Marketing Boards, 126–9
Hill, P., writer, on rural inequality, 163 n. 39
Holt, John, trading firm, 92–4, 103, 111
Hopkins, A. G., writer, on West African history, 31, 37
hunting, 14

Ibagwa mill, 61–2
Ibibio, 2, 22, 25, 28, 31, 33, 37, 45, 52–4, 75, 80, 90, 92, 107–8, 110, 113, 123–6, 128–9, 139, 141–2, Map 7
Ibo, *see* Igbo
Ifeka-Moller, C., writer, on Igbo culture, 68–9, 71, 187 n. 41
Igbo: Northern (Nri), 17–18, 129, 132–3, Map 3; Southern (Owerri), 17–18, 22–3, 25–9, 45, 75, 90, 129, 132–3, Map 3; week-days, 29
Igbo Women's War, *see* Women Riot
Ihie, 5, 44, 48, Map 2
Ikot-Ekpene, 52, 62, 71, 95–6, 113–15, 123, Map 5
Imo River, 18, 29, 33, 43–4, 48, 52–3, 71, 92–5, 108, Map 1; railway station, 93, 111, 113–14, Map 10
influenza, 70–1
Intelligence Reports, 121, 164 n. 9
International Institute of Tropical Agriculture, 134
iron, 23, 29, 43, 45, 50, 133, 136, 141
Itu, 95–6, 111, 114, Map 10

Jackson, J., colonial official, 17, 113
Jones, G. I., writer and former official, 15, 131

Klein, M., writer, on women and slavery, 25
kola, 48
Kula, W., writer, on feudal economies, 10
Kwa (Ibibio), 38, 42, 53, 110. *See also* Anang
Kwa Ibo River, 44, 95, Map 1

Lagemann, J., writer, on Igbo agriculture, 133
Lagos, 32, 46, 72, 103, 136; palm produce prices, 14, 57, 59–60, 78
Lands Committee, British West Africa, 60, 79
Latham, A. J. H., writer, on eastern Nigerian trade, 17
Leonard, A. G., journey to Bende, 35, 38

le Roy Ladurie, E., writer, on climate history, 13
Lever, William, industrialist, 60–1, 128
lineage mode of production, 9–10
liquor trade, 42, 58. *See also* gin
Liverpool prices for palm produce, 14, 29, 45, 48, 51, 57
lorries, 71, 88, 94–5, 102, 114
Lugard, F. D., 58

MacIver, W. B., trading firm, 92
maize, 14, 23, 47, 124, 134
Malaya, 59, 61–4
manillas, 29, 43, 49–50, 92, 97–8, 103, 109–110, 138
Marketing Boards, 1917 proposal, 57, 126; post-1930 implementation, 117, 119, 126–9, 134, 139–40
Martin, A., writer, on Ibibio economy, 125
Marx, K., theory of capitalism and technical progress, 6; views on pre-capitalist society, 8
Mba, N., writer, on Women Riot, 107
Mbagwu, T. C., writer, on Ngwa agriculture, 124–6, 134
mechanisation, 6–7, 60–6, 79, 86–8, 125, 127–9, 134, 139–40
Meek, C. K., writer, on Igbo culture, 25
Meillassoux, C., writer, on lineage mode of production, 9–10
melons, 22
Methodists, 70, 75–6
mgbede (fattening), 75
middlemen, *see* Ubani
Miller Brothers, trading firm, 64, 92–4
mills, *see* mechanisation
Miller, W., writer, on palm oil, 127, 129
Morgan, W. B., writer, on Ngwa agriculture, 124
Myint, H., vent-for-surplus theorist, 6–8

Native Authorities, 121–2, 131. *See also* courts, warrant chiefs
Native Councils, 86, 121–2, 131–2
Nbawsi, 86, 93–4, 100, 103–4, 114, 132, Map 8
Ndoki, 23, 29, 48–9, 52–3, 70, 123, Map 5
neo-Marxist anthropologists, 8–10
New Calabar, 48, Map 1
New World crops, 23
Newbury, C. W., writer, on nineteenth-century trade, 29, 45–6
Ngwa (Igbo): age-grades, 27; agriculture, 13–14, 22, 31, 34, 67, 72, 81, 99, 104, 124, 134–7, 142–3; bridewealth (dowry), 84, 99–100, 131; Christian conversion, 68–70, 74–7, 140; clan council, 121, 131; and

206

208